# Excel

## Get the Results You Want!

# Year 7 NAPLAN*-style Tests

**Associate Professor James Athanasou with Angella Deftereos**

PASCAL PRESS

T0358059

* This is not an officially endorsed publication of the NAPLAN program and is produced by Pascal Press independently of Australian governments.

© 2010 James Athanasou, Angella Defteros and Pascal Press
Revised for NAPLAN test changes 2011
New NAPLAN test question formats added 2012
New NAPLAN test question formats added 2013
Reprinted 2014
Conventions of Language questions updated 2016
Reprinted 2017, 2018

**Revised in 2020 for the NAPLAN Online tests**

Reprinted 2020, 2021, 2022, 2023, 2024 (twice), 2025

ISBN 978 1 74125 193 7

Pascal Press Pty Ltd
PO Box 250
Glebe NSW 2037
www.pascalpress.com.au

Publisher: Vivienne Joannou
Project Editor: Mark Dixon
Edited by Christine Eslick and Rosemary Peers
Proofread and answers checked by Peter Little and Dale Little
Cover and page design by DiZign Pty Ltd
Typeset by DiZign Pty Ltd and Grizzly Graphics (Leanne Richters)
Printed by Vivar Printing/Green Giant Press

While care has been taken in the preparation of this study guide, students should check with their teachers about the exact requirements or content of the tests for which they are sitting.

NAPLAN is a trademark of Australian Curriculum, Assessment and Reporting Authority (ACARA).

The publisher thanks the Royal Australian Mint for granting permission to use Australian currency coin designs in this book.

**Notice of liability**

The information contained in this book is distributed without warranty. While precautions have been taken in the preparation of this material, neither the authors nor Pascal Press shall have any liability to any person or entity with respect to any liability, loss or damage caused or alleged to be caused directly or indirectly by the instructions and content contained in the book.

All efforts have been made to obtain permission for the copyright material reproduced in this book. In the event of any oversight, the publisher welcomes any information that will enable rectification of any reference or credit in subsequent editions.

# CONTENTS

Welcome to the *Excel Year 7 NAPLAN\*-style Tests*. This book has been specially written to help parents and teachers of Year 7 students in their preparation for the Year 7 NAPLAN tests. It is also helpful as a general revision for Year 7.

This book was first published in 2010 and has been revised for NAPLAN changes several times. It has been widely used and many thousands of copies have been published throughout the years. In this edition the content has been reorganised for the new online version of the NAPLAN tests.

The aim of this brief introduction is to provide parents, guardians and teachers with some background to NAPLAN.

The book is a collaboration by a specialist in educational testing and an experienced NAPLAN marker. Both are trained teachers.

It is designed for use by parents who want to help their child and by teachers who wish to prepare their class for the NAPLAN tests. Some parents also use these books for general revision or when tutoring their child.

We hope you find this guide easy to use. In the following sections we will try to answer some frequently asked questions about the tests.

**Associate Professor James Athanasou, LittB, MA, PhD, DipEd, MAPS**
**Angella Deftereos, BA, MTeach**

## What is different about this edition?

This is the latest and most thorough revision of the Year 7 book. It has been designed to accommodate the new online tests in an easy-to-use book format. The tests in this book contain excellent practice questions from very easy to very hard.

## What is NAPLAN?

NAPLAN stands for *National Assessment Program—Literacy and Numeracy*. It is the largest educational testing program in Australia. It is conducted every year in March and the tests are taken by students in Year 3, Year 5, Year 7 and Year 9. All students in these year levels are expected to participate in the tests.

The tests cover Reading, Writing, Conventions of Language (spelling, grammar and punctuation) and Numeracy. In other words, they cover what are known to many people as the basic skills of reading, writing and arithmetic.

## What is the purpose of NAPLAN?

Although NAPLAN has been designed mainly to provide administrators and politicians with information about Australian schools and educational systems, it is also relevant for each pupil. It provides a public record of their educational achievement.

Increasingly it is among the most valuable series of tests students will undertake in their primary schooling and probably their first formal and public examination.

## What is being assessed?

The content of NAPLAN is based on what is generally taught across Australia. So do not be surprised if NAPLAN does not match exactly what each child is learning in their class. Most schools should be teaching more than the basic levels.

NAPLAN covers only a specific range of skills. This is because literacy and numeracy are considered to be the basis of future learning in school. Of course we know that there are many other personal or social skills that are important in life.

We also realise that each child has their own special talents and aptitudes but at the same time governments also want to be able to assess their educational achievement in the fundamental skills. It is important to emphasise that there are many different kinds of literacy and numeracy, and that these tests cover only some aspects.

## What is NAPLAN Online?

Until 2017 NAPLAN tests were all paper-and-pencil tests. From 2022 all students have taken the NAPLAN tests on a computer or on a tablet. With NAPLAN paper-and-pencil tests, all students in each year level took exactly the same tests. In the NAPLAN Online tests this isn't the case; instead, every student takes a tailor-made test based on their ability.

In the NAPLAN Online tests a student is given specially selected questions that try to match their ability. This means that in theory a very bright student should not have to waste time answering very easy questions. Similarly, in theory, a student who is not so capable should not be given difficult questions that are far too hard for them.

Please visit the official ACARA site for a detailed explanation of the tailored test process used in NAPLAN Online and also for general information about the tests: https://nap.edu.au/online-assessment.

These tailor-made tests will mean broadly, therefore, that a student who is at a standard level of achievement will take a test mostly comprised of questions of a standard level; a student who is at an intermediate level of achievement will take a test mostly comprised of questions of an intermediate level; and a student who is at an advanced level of achievement will take a test mostly comprised of questions of an advanced level.

## Do the tests in this book match those in NAPLAN Online?

The practice tests in this book are the same length as in NAPLAN Online. This book provides items across a wide range of difficulty.

Of course there is no way of predicting what actual questions will be asked but practice using these questions will help to familiarise a student with the content of the tests.

Naturally there will be some questions that can be presented on a computer that are harder to present in a book, but the content and skills will be similar.

Like in the NAPLAN Online tests, there are multiple-choice questions in this book but there are some differences. The spelling test is a good example. In the computer version the words are dictated by the computer. We cannot do this in a book but we have prepared a list of words for parents, guardians or teachers to dictate.

## Are the questions in this book similar to those in NAPLAN Online?

Parents can have confidence that the questions in this book reflect the online NAPLAN. We believe that we have covered all the types of questions in a convenient book format.

On the whole it is our impression that some of the questions in this book will be much harder than those in NAPLAN. We have deliberately included some more challenging questions.

We have also made a special effort to cover as many different question formats as possible. For instance, spelling questions have been altered to be given orally to the student.

Naturally it is not possible to use the same processes as the online test, such as click and drag, but it is possible to use the same thinking processes.

The Check your skills pages after each test suggest the approximate level of difficulty of questions so you can see what levels of difficulty of questions a student is able to answer.

On the Check your skills pages, questions are divided into standard, intermediate or advanced. This will help you prepare for the standard, intermediate or advanced test that your child will sit. Please refer to page 33 to see an example of a checklist page from the book.

Please refer to the next page to see some examples of question types that are found in NAPLAN Online and how they compare to questions in this book. As you will see, the content tested is exactly the same but the questions are presented differently.

# NAPLAN ONLINE QUESTION TYPES

| NAPLAN Online question types | Equivalent questions in Numeracy Tests in this book |
|---|---|
| **Click**<br>Here is a series of numbers.<br><br>(23) (34) (27) (38) (31) (?)<br><br>Which is the next number?<br>Click on the correct number.<br><br>(40) (41) (42) (43) | To answer these questions colour in the circle with the correct answer.<br>Here is a series of numbers.<br><br>(23) (34) (27) (38) (31) (?)<br><br>What would be the next number?<br><br>40    41    42    43<br>O    O    O    O |

| NAPLAN Online question types | Equivalent questions in Reading Tests in this book |
|---|---|
| **Drag and drop**<br>Read *Pan in Wall Street* and answer the question.<br>Drag pairs of words to fill the spaces below:<br><br><table><tr><td>Greece</td><td>Sicily</td></tr><tr><td>marble front</td><td>Wall Street</td></tr><tr><td>Broadway</td><td>Brooklyn Ferry</td></tr></table><br>Doric pillars are to ▮▮▮▮ as Trinacrian hills are to ▮▮▮. | Read *Pan in Wall Street* and answer the question.<br><br>Doric pillars are to ▮▮▮▮ as Trinacrian hills are to ▮▮▮.<br><br>O  Greece, Sicily<br>O  marble front, Wall Street<br>O  Broadway, Brooklyn Ferry |
| **Dropdown**<br>Read the table with the details of the airline's fleet. Use the tab to give your answer.<br><br>Which word completes the meaning?<br><br>Maximum is to minimum as utmost is to:<br><br>small. ↓<br>slight.<br>furthest.<br>least.<br>most. | Read the table with the details of the airline's fleet.<br><br>Which word completes the meaning?<br>Maximum is to minimum as utmost is to<br>_____ .<br><br>O  small<br>O  slight<br>O  furthest<br>O  least<br>O  most |

# NAPLAN ONLINE QUESTION TYPES

| NAPLAN Online question types | Equivalent questions in Conventions of Language Tests in this book |
|---|---|
| **Drag and drop**<br><br>Drag the correct word to fill in the space.<br><br>| was | | were | | we're |<br><br>The man and woman ▓▓▓▓<br>seated on my right. | Read the sentence. The sentence has a gap. Choose the correct word to complete the sentence.<br><br>The man and woman ▓▓▓▓ seated on my right.<br><br>○ was<br>○ were<br>○ we're |
| **Click**<br><br>Which two circles should be replaced by speech marks? Click on the circles.<br><br>"Josephine, get inside right now, said Granny.<br><br>You need to start your homework immediately." | Shade **two** circles to show where the missing speech marks (" and ") should go.<br><br>"Josephine, get inside right now, said Granny.<br><br>You need to start your homework immediately." |
| **Text entry**<br><br>It is _____ goal for our team.<br><br>Click on the play button to listen to the missing word.<br><br>‖ ◀))  ●━━━  0.08 / 0.09<br><br>Type the correct spelling of the word in the box. | Ask your teacher or parent to read the spelling words for you. The words are listed on page 200. Write the spelling words on the lines below.<br><br>✏ **Test 3 spelling words**<br><br>26. _____<br><br>**Spelling words for Conventions of Language Test 3**<br><br>| Word | Example |<br>|---|---|<br>| **26.** another | It is another goal for our team. | |

As you can see there are differences between the processes involved in answering the questions in NAPLAN Online and this book but we think they are minimal.

Nevertheless we strongly advise that students should practise clicking and dragging until they are familiar with using a computer or tablet to answer questions.

## What are the advantages of revising for the NAPLAN Online tests in book form?

There are many benefits to a child revising for the online test using books.

- One of the most important benefits is that writing on paper will help your child retain information. It can be a very effective way to memorise. High quality educational research shows that using a keyboard is not as good as note-taking for learning.

- Students will be able to prepare thoroughly for topic revision using books and then practise computer skills easily. They will only succeed with sound knowledge of topics; this requires study and focus. Students will not succeed in tests simply because they know how to answer questions digitally.

- Also, some students find it easier to concentrate when reading a page in a book than when reading on a screen.

- Furthermore it can be more convenient to use a book, especially when a child doesn't have ready access to a digital device.

- You can be confident that *Excel* books will help students acquire the topic knowledge they need, as we have over 35 years experience in helping students prepare for tests. All our writers are experienced educators.

## How *Excel Test Zone* can help you practise online

We recommend you go to www.exceltestzone.com.au and register for practice in NAPLAN Online–style tests once you have completed this book. The reasons include:

- for optimal performance in the NAPLAN Online tests we strongly recommend students gain practice at completing online tests as well as completing revision in book form

- students should practise answering questions on a digital device to become confident in this process

- students will be able to practise tailored tests like those in NAPLAN Online as well as other types of tests

- students will also be able to gain valuable practice in onscreen skills such as dragging and dropping answers, using an online ruler to measure figures and using an online protractor to measure angles.

Remember that *Excel Test Zone* has been helping students prepare for NAPLAN since 2009; in fact we had NAPLAN online questions even before NAPLAN tests went online!

We also have updated our website along with our book range to ensure your preparation for NAPLAN Online is 100% up to date.

## What do the tests indicate?

They are designed to be tests of educational achievement; they show what a person has learnt or can do.

They are not IQ tests. Probably boys and girls who do extremely well on these tests will be quite bright. It is possible, however, for some intelligent children to perform poorly because of disadvantage, language, illness or other factors.

## Are there time limits?

Yes, there are time limits for each test. These are usually set so that 95% of pupils can complete the tests in the time allowed.

If more than one test is scheduled on a day then there should be a reasonable rest break of at least 20 minutes between tests. In some special cases pupils may be given some extra time and allowed to complete a response.

## Who takes the NAPLAN tests?

The NAPLAN testing program is designed for all pupils. Some schools may exempt pupils from the tests. These can include children in special English classes and those who have recently arrived from non–English speaking backgrounds or children with special needs.

Our advice to parents and guardians is that children should only undertake the tests if it is likely to be of benefit to them. It would be a pity if a pupil was not personally or emotionally ready to perform at their best and the results underestimated their ability. The results on this occasion might label them inaccurately and it would be recorded on their pupil record card. Some parents have insisted successfully that their child be exempt from testing.

## Who developed these tests?

The tests were developed by ACARA. These are large-scale educational tests in which the questions are trialled extensively. Any unsuitable questions will be eliminated in these trials. They should produce results with high validity and reliability.

## How can the results be used?

The results of the NAPLAN tests offer an opportunity to help pupils at an early stage. The findings can be used as early indicators of any problem areas.

It would be a pity to miss this chance to help students at this stage in their schooling when it is relatively easy to address any issues. The findings can also be used as encouragement for students who are performing above the minimum standard.

It is important for parents and teachers to look closely at the student report. This indicates areas of strength and weakness. The report can be a little complex to read at first but it contains quite a helpful summary of the skills assessed in Reading, Writing, Conventions of Language and Numeracy. Use this as a guide for any revision.

If NAPLAN indicates that there are problems, then repeated testing with other measures of educational achievement is strongly recommended. It is also relevant to compare the results of NAPLAN with general classroom performance.

Remember that all educational test results have limitations. Do not place too much faith in the results of a single assessment.

## Does practice help?

There is no benefit in trying to teach to the test because the questions will vary from year to year. Nevertheless a general preparation for the content of NAPLAN tests should be quite helpful. Some people say that practising such tests is not helpful but we do not agree.

Firstly practice will help to overcome unfamiliarity with test procedures. Secondly it will help pupils deal with specific types of questions. Test practice should help students perform to the best of their ability.

Use the tests in this book to practise test skills and also to diagnose some aspects of learning in Year 7. Parents should make sure their child is interested in taking these practice tests. There is no benefit in compelling children to practise.

Sometimes it is easy to forget that they are still young children. We recommend that you sit with them or at least stay nearby while they are completing each test. Give them plenty of praise and encouragement for their efforts.

## How are students graded?

One of the big advantages of NAPLAN is that there is a clear scale of achievement. It is consistent from Year 3 right through to Year 9, which shows how much progress is being made.

There are now four levels of achievement:

• Exceeding

• Strong

• Developing

• Needs additional support.

This new grading system is simpler than the previous structure that had ten levels and was not always easy to interpret.

**Exceeding** describes students who are very proficient/advanced and have achieved at a level well beyond the limits expected at this stage of their schooling.

**Strong** indicates students who are of average to high-average competency. Their performance is solid and at the expected level of their school year.

**Developing** encompasses those students who are not yet proficient. These students are moving towards competency. They are progressing and their performance is towards the low-average level.

**Needs additional support** gives a firm indication that help is needed.

It is important to track each student's development from Year 3 through Year 5, Year 7 and Year 9 to see whether they are exceeding, strong, developing or need additional support in each area of NAPLAN.

NAPLAN shows how a student compares with the national average and provides other useful information for students, parents/guardians and teachers.

## What results are provided?

Parents receive comprehensive test results, as do teachers and schools. The results are first reported against the four levels of achievement (Exceeding, Strong, Developing, Needs additional support). For students to be proficient they need to be at the Exceeding or Strong levels.

It is easy to look only at the level reached on these tests but it is more important to see what the student knows or can do. The levels are not a percentage score or the number of questions answered correctly.

Instead they describe the level of achievement. Descriptors are included that make clear each pupil's literacy and numeracy skills. The national average is also provided; this is a useful comparison.

A band covering the middle 60% of students is shown. Despite the considerable difference in ability between the pupils at the top and bottom of this band, it still indicates whether a student is performing above, below or within the typical range of performance.

So check to see what students know or can do to identify the areas in which they need extra help. Also look at their strengths in the areas of literacy and numeracy. It is important to use the results for the benefit of the students.

## Are the tests in Year 7 and Year 9 the same?

The tests increase in difficulty but the general content is much the same. Some questions might be repeated. This is to allow the test developers to standardise the results across Years 7 and 9. The similar questions act like anchors for all the other questions.

## When are the tests held?

The tests are held in March on an agreed date. The actual timetable is listed on the official website at www.nap.edu.au. They may be spread over several days. Ideally the tests should be given in the mornings.

## How is NAPLAN related to *My School*?

The My School website reports the NAPLAN results for around 10 000 Australian schools. *My School* is available at www.myschool.edu.au.

## Will children be shown what to do?

The testing program is normally very well organised with clear instructions for schools and teachers. Teachers receive special instructions for administering the tests.

Teachers will probably give children practice tests in the weeks before the NAPLAN tests.

## How our book's grading system works

### Step 1

In this book you will notice that we have provided Check your skills pages. These pages provide you with information about the content of each question.

### Step 2

Once you have completed the checklists you will be able to see the content that was easy for the student or the questions that were difficult.

• • • • • • • •

Please note that it is not possible to accurately predict the content of the NAPLAN tests. NAPLAN focuses on the 'essential elements that should be taught at the appropriate year levels'.

Thank you for your patience in working through this introduction. We hope you find this guide helpful. It is designed to be easy to use and to help pupils prepare. We wish every pupil well in the NAPLAN tests and in their future studies.

**Associate Professor James A Athanasou, LittB, MA, PhD, DipEd, MAPS**
**Angella Deftereos, BA, MTeach**

# INSTRUCTIONS FOR PARENTS AND TEACHERS USING THIS BOOK

## How is this book organised?

It is divided into sample questions and practice tests. We start with samples of the numeracy and literacy (reading and conventions of language) questions. Work through these examples so that every student knows what needs to be done. At the very least please ensure that your child is familiar with the sample questions.

This is followed by four practice tests for numeracy, four practice tests for reading and four practice tests for conventions of language. There is also a sample writing task and four practice tests for writing. At the very least try to revise the samples if you do not have enough time to do the practice tests.

## Numeracy tests

The Numeracy tests in this book have 48 questions and should take up to 65 minutes. Some children will finish quickly while others will need all the time available.

Try not to explain terms during the testing. This can be done after the test session. If a question is still too hard, it is better to leave it at this stage. Some students may not be ready for the task.

## Literacy tests

Literacy is divided into three tests: Reading, Conventions of Language and Writing.

The Writing test offers help with aspects of writing using prompts and stimulus materials.

Allow up to 65 minutes for Reading tests, 45 minutes for Conventions of Language tests and 42 minutes for Writing tests, with a break in between.

- In the Reading test students will read stories, letters and non-fiction writing. There will be supporting pictures and charts. Students will be asked to find information, make conclusions, find the meaning and look at different ideas.

- The Conventions of Language test is divided into two parts: grammar and punctuation, and spelling. Students must be able to use verbs and punctuation, such as speech marks and commas, correctly. Also they will be asked to spell words.

- In the Writing test students will write a specific type of text. They will be judged on the structure of their writing, as well as their grammar, punctuation and spelling.

## Test materials

All test materials are contained in this book. There are answers for scoring the responses.

## Equipment

Students will not need white-out, pens or calculators. It is best to use a pencil. Children should be provided with a pencil, an eraser and a blank sheet of paper for working out.

## Time limits

Try to keep roughly to the time limits for the tests. You may give some students extra time if they are tired. Even a short break every 20 minutes is appropriate.

## Instructions to students

Explain patiently what needs to be done. Students should only attempt these tests if they wish to and do no more than one test in a session.

## Recording answers

Show students the way to mark the answers. They have to colour in circles, shapes or numbers, or write the answers in the boxes or on the lines provided.

In the new NAPLAN Online there are eight non-calculator questions and 40 questions where a calculator may be used if needed. The sample questions in this book are also divided into non-calculator and calculator.

Here are some sample Numeracy: Calculator Allowed questions. Make sure you read each question carefully so that you know exactly:

• what information is given to you in the question
• what the question is asking you to find.

Then make sure you read each answer option carefully in order to choose the correct answer. You can use a calculator to help you answer these questions. There is no time limit for the sample questions.

If you are already familiar with these type of questions, go straight to the Numeracy Tests on page 24.

To answer these questions, write the answer in the box or colour in the circle with the right answer. Colour in only one circle for each answer.

1. There is a pattern in these numbers. Write the number that is missing.

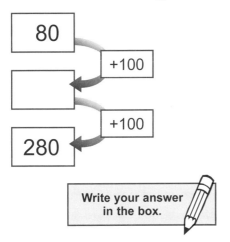

Write your answer in the box.

2. This table shows some weights for cooking.

| Imperial weights | Metric weights |
|---|---|
| $\frac{1}{4}$ ounce | 10 grams |
| $\frac{1}{2}$ ounce | 15 grams |
| $\frac{3}{4}$ ounce | 20 grams |
| 1 ounce | 25 grams |
| $1\frac{1}{4}$ ounce | 35 grams |
| $1\frac{1}{2}$ ounce | 40 grams |

How many grams do $\frac{1}{4}$ ounce and $1\frac{1}{2}$ ounces make together?

Write your answer in the box.

3. A chicken snack pack costs $4. A boy buys three packs for his family.

Fill in the number sentence below. Show how much he spent.

$\boxed{\phantom{xx}} \times 3 = \$ \boxed{\phantom{xx}}$

4. Here are some presents. They are a telescope, a helmet and a ball. Their prices in the shop are also shown.

$186          $117          $41

Here are four sums. They show a quick way to guess or estimate the price of the three presents. Which is the best way?

○ $180 + $120 + $40
○ $180 + $130 + $50
○ $190 + $120 + $40
○ $190 + $130 + $50

5. 763 − 289 = $\boxed{\phantom{xxx}}$

**6.** $2.9 + 3.6 =$ ☐

**7.** $1631 \div 7 =$ ☐

**8.** Write one number in each space to complete this sum.

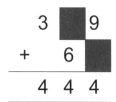

```
  3 ■ 9
+   6 ■
  4 4 4
```

**9.** Here is a piece of wood. There is a tape under the wood.

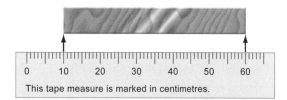

This tape measure is marked in centimetres.

How long is this piece of wood?

30 cm    40 cm    50 cm    60 cm

○      ○      ○      ○

**10.** To find the distance travelled multiply the speed by the time taken.

For example, if the speed was 60 kilometres per hour and the time taken was 6 hours, the distance travelled must be 360 kilometres.

Here is a problem for you: If the time taken was 5 hours and the speed was 110 kilometres per hour, what distance was travelled?

☐ km    **Write your answer in the box.**

**11.** Which of the numbers below is closest to 1.7?

1.5      1.8      1.2      1.4

○      ○      ○      ○

**12.** In many countries wood is burned for fuel. Often the main use of this wood is for cooking.

The chart below shows some countries that are the major users of wood for fuel.

They burn about 600 million cubic metres of wood altogether.

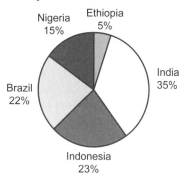

**Major users of wood for fuel**

Nigeria 15%    Ethiopia 5%    India 35%    Indonesia 23%    Brazil 22%

About how many million cubic metres does Nigeria burn? (Remember that all these countries together burn about 600 million cubic metres.)

15    30    60    90    120

○    ○    ○    ○    ○

**13.** What is the perimeter (the distance around the outside edges) of this figure?

The perimeter is shown by the dark line. Note that some of the lengths are not shown in the figure.

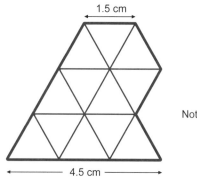

1.5 cm

Not to scale

4.5 cm

9 cm    12 cm    15 cm    18 cm    21 cm

○    ○    ○    ○    ○

**14.** Here is a map. It shows three cities. The map is divided into sections.

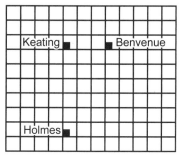

Not to scale

The distance from Keating to Holmes is 1800 km.

How far is it from Keating to Benvenue?

○ 300 km       ○ 600 km

○ 900 km       ○ 1200 km

○ 1500 km

**15.** The length of this car from the front to the back is 3.0 m.

The size of the wheel is half a metre (0.5 m).

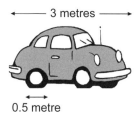

3 metres

0.5 metre

How long is the car compared to its wheel?

○ 3 times as long       ○ 4 times as long

○ 5 times as long       ○ 6 times as long

**16.** In a group of 80 people 40% are doctors. How many people are doctors?

○ 30       ○ 32

○ 34       ○ 36

○ 38       ○ 40

**17.** A plane leaves Perth at 6:40 and arrives at its destination overseas at 18:20 (Perth time). How long was that journey?

11:40       6:40       24:60       12:20
○           ○           ○           ○

**18.** Solve:

$$(0.6 \times 5) \div \frac{3}{4} - (0.5 \times 3) = ?$$

1.5       1.75       2.25       2.5
○         ○          ○          ○

**19.** This graph shows employment in Australia from 1978 to 2007. It starts at around 6 million and reaches just over 10 million.

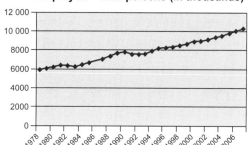

**Employed – total persons (in thousands)**

By which period had employment in Australia increased by 50% from 1978?

○ 2000–2001       ○ 1998–1999

○ 1990–1991       ○ 2004–2005

**20.** Here is a table that shows today's currency values. The currencies are the euro and the Australian dollar.

| Euro | Australian Dollar |
|------|-------------------|
| €1   | A$1.83            |
| €50  | ?                 |

What is the value in Australian dollars of €50?

A$89.50   A$95.50   A$91.50   A$97.50
○          ○          ○          ○

Here are some sample Numeracy: Non-calculator questions. Make sure you read each question carefully so that you know exactly:
- what information is given to you in the question
- what the question is asking you to find.

Then make sure you read each answer option carefully in order to choose the correct answer. Calculators are not allowed in this test. There is no time limit for the sample questions.

To answer these questions, write the answer in the box or colour in the circle with the right answer. Colour in only one circle for each answer.

**21.** Part of this grid is shaded. The grid is made up of squares.

☐ = 1 square

How many square units are shaded? (Hint: Add the half squares.)

| 4 | 6 | 8 | 10 |
|---|---|---|---|
| ○ | ○ | ○ | ○ |

**22.** How many blocks make up this shape? (Note that the pattern in the front is continued.)

| 8 | 12 | 16 | 20 |
|---|---|---|---|
| ○ | ○ | ○ | ○ |

**23.** Here is a pattern of some blocks.

Which one of the four block patterns below is the same as the one above? Is it A, B, C or D?

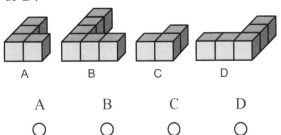

| A | B | C | D |
|---|---|---|---|
| ○ | ○ | ○ | ○ |

**24.** There are different types of galaxies. Some, such as our Milky Way, are spiral. Others are irregular spiral, irregular or elliptical. This chart shows the numbers of galaxies in the Local Group (the group that includes the Milky Way).

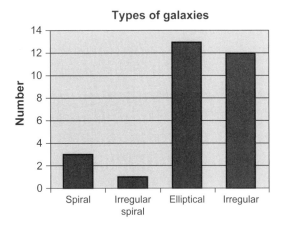

Types of galaxies

Which answer is correct?

○ There are more spiral than irregular spiral galaxies.

○ There are more spiral than elliptical galaxies.

○ There are fewer elliptical than irregular galaxies.

○ There are fewer spiral than irregular spiral galaxies.

**25.** There are some objects in a box.

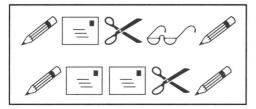

One object is chosen without looking.
What is the chance of choosing a pencil?

○ certain

○ more than half

○ less than half

○ impossible

**26.** Two triangular prisms have been joined together.

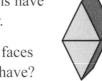

How many separate faces does the new shape have?

   3        4        6        9

○       ○       ○       ○

Did you colour in one of the circles?

**27.** I folded this pattern in half.

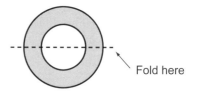

Fold here

Which shape could I see?

○       ○       ○       ○

**28.**

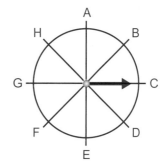

To which letter would the arrow be pointing if it moved two spaces clockwise?

   A        B        D        E

○       ○       ○       ○

# END OF TEST

Well done! You have completed the sample questions for Numeracy. Even if you don't practise any others, at least you will have some familiarity with the method used in the NAPLAN Tests.

How did you go with these sample questions? Check to see where you did well and where you had problems. Try to revise the questions that were hard for you.

There are now four more Numeracy Tests to practise, each containing 48 questions. They include many of the same types of questions, plus a few other types.

## Numeracy: Calculator Allowed

1.  **180.** The numbers increase by 100. We start with 80 and then add 100 to make 180. Then we add 100 to 180 to make 280. Did you write your answer in the box?

2.  **50 grams.** The $\frac{1}{4}$ ounce is 10 grams and the $1\frac{1}{2}$ ounce is 40 grams. Add these together to make 50 grams. We used imperial weights in Australia before changing to the metric system.

3.  **$4 × 3 = $12.** The snack packs cost $4. The boy buys three snack packs, so the sum is $4 × 3 = $12. Did you write your answer in the box?

4.  **$190 + $120 + $40.** You need to round the numbers up or down before adding them to estimate the answer quickly. So $186 becomes roughly $190 (it is closest to 190), $117 becomes $120 (it is closest to 120), and $41 becomes $40 (it is closest to 40). If the number ends in five or more, round it up; otherwise, round it down.

5.  **474.** $763 - 289 = 474$. Make sure that you know how to do these types of sums.

6.  **6.5.** $2.9 + 3.6 = 6.5$

7.  **233.** $1631 \div 7 = 233$

8.  **The missing numbers are 7 and 5.** The sum is $379 + 65 = 444$.

9.  **50 cm.** The wood starts at 10 cm and finishes at 60 cm, and this makes it 50 cm long.

10. **550.** If the speed is 110 and the time is 5, then the distance must be 550 because $110 × 5 = 550$. This is actually an easy question but the wording of the problem might have been unclear to you.

11. **1.8.** This number is closest to 1.7.

12. **90.** There are 600 million cubic metres altogether, so 15% for Nigeria is 90. A quick way of working this out is to take 10%, which is 60, and so 5% would be 30. 60 + 30 gives you 90.

13. **15 cm.** The perimeter is 4.5 cm along the bottom, 4.5 cm along the left-hand side, 1.5 cm across the top and 4.5 cm on the right-hand side.

14. **900 km.** You need to count the squares. The six squares from Keating to Holmes equal 1800 km, so each square is 300 km. There are three squares from Keating to Benvenue, and so this distance is 900 km.

15. **6 times**

16. **32.** 40% of 80 = 32. 10% would be 8 people and so 40% would be 4 times 8, equals 32.

17. **11:40.** It takes 11 hours and 40 minutes. You subtract 6:40 from 18:20.

18. **2.5.** This has to be broken down into steps. $(0.6 × 5) = 3$, and then divide this by $\frac{3}{4}$ to give you 4. Then from this subtract the $(0.5 × 3)$, which is equal to 1.5. 4 minus 1.5 equals 2.5.

19. **2000–2001.** In the year 2000 it increased by exactly 50% from 1978. Here is the actual table from which the chart was drawn and the third column shows the percentage increase.

| Month & Year | Persons | % increase |
|---|---|---|
| Aug. 1978 | 5942.1 | 100% |
| Aug. 1979 | 6032.8 | 102% |
| Aug. 1980 | 6220.6 | 105% |
| Aug. 1981 | 6350.0 | 107% |
| Aug. 1982 | 6336.1 | 107% |
| Aug. 1983 | 6220.7 | 105% |
| Aug. 1984 | 6445.9 | 108% |
| Aug. 1985 | 6649.6 | 112% |
| Aug. 1987 | 7073.5 | 119% |
| Aug. 1988 | 7337.3 | 123% |
| Aug. 1989 | 7689.2 | 129% |
| Aug. 1990 | 7795.2 | 131% |
| Aug. 1991 | 7562.7 | 127% |
| Aug. 1992 | 7565.3 | 127% |
| Aug. 1993 | 7607.3 | 128% |
| Aug. 1994 | 7870.2 | 132% |
| Aug. 1995 | 8170.4 | 138% |
| Aug. 1996 | 8254.0 | 139% |
| Aug. 1997 | 8300.6 | 140% |
| Aug. 1998 | 8517.3 | 143% |
| Aug. 1999 | 8640.0 | 145% |
| Aug. 2000 | 8905.9 | 150% |
| Aug. 2001 | 8951.8 | 151% |
| Aug. 2002 | 9120.5 | 153% |
| Aug. 2003 | 9318.0 | 157% |
| Aug. 2004 | 9510.9 | 160% |
| Aug. 2005 | 9815.6 | 165% |
| Aug. 2006 | 10021.6 | 169% |
| Aug. 2007 | 10258.5 | 173% |

20. **A$91.50.** One euro is A$1.83 and so €50 would be 50 times $1.83.

## Numeracy: Non-calculator

**21.** **6.** There are four whole squares and four half squares. When you add the four whole plus the four half squares, you get six squares altogether.

**22.** **16.** There are four blocks in each section and there are four sections. It may not be easy for you to see because of how it is drawn and you need to visualise or imagine some parts of the diagram.

**23.** **D.** This pattern is L-shaped with five blocks. The others are quite different. Sometimes you will find these patterns easy to see and sometimes it is a little hard. It may help if you try to draw the shape and then rotate it.

**24.** **There are more spiral than irregular spiral galaxies.**

**25.** **Less than half.** There are 10 objects and there are 4 pencils. The chance of choosing a pencil is 4 out of 10. This is less than half.

**26.** **6.** Each prism has five faces but when they are joined there are only six faces.

**27.** **The first answer is correct.** We have tried to show this in the diagram (it is not drawn to scale). When you put both halves together then you get a circle.

**28.** **E.** After one space the arrow points to D and after another space it points to E.

# SAMPLE QUESTIONS—READING

Here are some sample Reading questions. You will need to look at or read a text. Make sure you read each question carefully so that you know exactly what the question is asking. Then find the relevant section in the text. Finally make sure you read each answer option carefully in order to choose the correct answer. There is no time limit for the sample questions.

To answer these questions, write the answer in the box or colour in the circle with the right answer. Colour in only one circle for each answer.

These questions are meant to be much easier than the questions in the practice tests. If you are already familiar with these type of questions, go straight to the Reading Tests on page 66.

Read *Digital library quick start guide* and answer questions 1 to 5.

## Digital library quick start guide

**Download audio-books and e-books anytime, anywhere.**

The digital library is a new service from our local council library. It is available only to registered borrowers. The digital library download service allows you to browse through a collection of audio-books and e-books.

An audio-book is a digitised version of a recorded reading of a book. The software to download an audio-book is free and easy to use.

The term *e-book* is short for 'electronic book'. It is any publication that can be viewed on a computer monitor. You can browse through the library's collection for e-books online and then download them and read them offline.

A collection of titles is now available to you anytime and anywhere, provided you have computer access. To use this service you will need a computer that is connected to the internet. You will need your library card. The software is available free from the library's own website.

1.  What is the main purpose of this text?
    ○ to sell a new service to borrowers
    ○ to attract new borrowers to the library
    ○ to provide new computer software for borrowers
    ○ to offer a new service to borrowers

2.  What is the name of the service described in the text?
    ○ internet download package
    ○ digital library download service
    ○ audio-book digital service
    ○ e-book library service

3.  What is a requirement for the service that is advertised in the text?
    ○ The service is available to new borrowers.
    ○ The service is available to anyone with an internet connection.
    ○ The service is available to registered borrowers.

4.  Which product can be read offline?
    ○ the e-book
    ○ the audio-book
    ○ the voice recording
    ○ the library's collection

**5.** Colour in the circles for the two words that are likely to be the newest words in our language.

○ audio-book

○ e-book

○ download

○ software

○ internet

○ computer

○ digital

Read *Celebrate Family History Week* and answer questions 6 to 10.

# Celebrate Family History Week

**Join Peter Tatham from the National Archives for a presentation of how the immigration records in the National Archives can be useful in your family history research.**

**Thursday, 3 August 2012**
**Wellington Library and Community Centre**
**153–155 Featherston Street, Wellington**
**2.00 pm – 4.00 pm**

Free, but bookings are required on 0496 1880.

**Afternoon tea will be served.**

**6.** What is the theme of the notice?

○ the National Archives

○ Wellington Library and Community Centre

○ family history

○ a presentation

**7.** Who might have a special interest in the topic?

○ some children of immigrants

○ all historians

○ the library

**8.** Find the word that completes the comparison:

Archive is to record as history is to __?__

○ store

○ library

○ book

○ event

**9.** What must be done before attending?

○ A booking must be made.

○ A family history must be prepared.

○ Afternoon tea must be made.

**10.** Which word in the notice means the same as a *talk*?

○ record

○ presentation

○ research

○ history

○ booking

Did you colour in one of the circles?

**Read *Deposit card* and answer questions 11 to 15.**

## Deposit card

A St James Deposit Only Card gives you true peace of mind. It allows other people to deposit money safely into your account. It is convenient and secure. Money can be deposited through any ATM or branch of St James Bank.

A St James Deposit Only Card is useful for a variety of customers. For example, it is ideal for any company that wants its customers to deposit money into an account, and it is safe for any retailer who wants employees to deposit funds into an account. It may be useful for landlords. They can ask for rent payments to be deposited directly by their tenants. More than one Deposit Only Card can be issued for an account.

All other transactions are barred. This includes withdrawing funds or checking the balance in an account.

**11.** What can we say about a Deposit Only Card?

- ○ A Deposit Only Card allows people to withdraw funds.
- ○ A Deposit Only Card allows people to deposit funds.
- ○ A Deposit Only Card allows people to check account balances.

**12.** Why is a Deposit Only Card useful?

- ○ It can be used for payments.
- ○ It can be used only at a branch.
- ○ It allows someone to make purchases.

**13.** What are *funds*?

- ○ Funds are good times.
- ○ Funds are cheques.
- ○ Funds are deposit slips.
- ○ Funds are money.

**14.** Look at the statement below and decide whether it is correct, partly correct or incorrect.

A Deposit Only Card has limited functions.

- ○ This statement is correct.
- ○ This statement is partly correct.
- ○ This statement is incorrect.

**15.** What is a tenant?

- ○ someone who buys a property
- ○ a landlord
- ○ someone who rents a property
- ○ a real estate agent

**Read *Victor Harbour* and answer questions 16 to 19.**

## Victor Harbour

Source: Ian W Fieggen, www.wikimedia.org
File: 20040610

If you are visiting South Australia, Victor Harbour is a popular holiday and tourist destination on the Fleurieu Peninsula.

It is a little over an hour's drive south from Adelaide and you can also visit the McLaren Vale wine region along the way.

There are many activities to occupy the traveller and much to see. A unique experience when you get to Victor Harbour is to catch the horse-drawn tram across the causeway to Granite Island. This is unforgettable. Hang around until dusk, when you can catch glimpses of the fairy penguins returning to the island.

Its location on the peninsula means that the area is becoming well known as a site for whale watching from mid-winter to the middle of spring. Why not visit the South Australian Whale Centre in Railway Terrace, Victor Harbour? Here you will see interactive displays and you can even undertake a virtual shark dive.

There are many cafes and craft shops for the visitor. These attractions include the Alexandrina Cheese Company in Sneyd Road, Mount Jagged. Here you can sample handmade cheese products. On Saturday mornings Grosvenor Gardens hosts a farmers' market, with fresh fruit and vegetables from the region.

The coastal scenery is beautiful and there are seaside walks, trails and bike paths along the cliffs and shores. Among the nearby seaside villages is Port Elliot. Try some fish and chips at the Flying Fish Cafe, 1 The Foreshore, at Horseshoe Bay, Port Elliot.

You will enjoy Victor Harbour and the surrounding regions.

Adapted from Jane Peach, 'V for Victor', *Qantas Magazine*, November 2009, pp. 65–6

**16.** What would you find in Grosvenor Gardens?
- ○ Alexandrina Cheese Company
- ○ Flying Fish Cafe
- ○ South Australian Whale Centre
- ○ the farmers' market

**17.** In what direction is Victor Harbour from Adelaide?
- ○ north
- ○ south
- ○ east
- ○ west

**18.** Where does the horse-drawn tram take the visitor?
- ○ Port Elliot
- ○ McLaren Vale
- ○ Granite Island
- ○ Fleurieu Peninsula

**19.** What is *the virtual shark dive* mentioned in the text?
- ○ a real shark dive
- ○ a real shark dive with experts to help you
- ○ a real shark dive with the protection of a cage
- ○ a simulated shark dive
- ○ an imaginary shark dive
- ○ a video of a real shark dive

**You are about halfway through the sample questions—well done!**

Read *Down the rabbit-hole* and answer questions 20 to 27.

## Down the rabbit-hole

Alice was beginning to get very tired of sitting by her sister on the bank, and of having nothing to do: once or twice she had peeped into the book her sister was reading, but it had no pictures or conversations in it, 'and what is the use of a book,' thought Alice 'without pictures or conversation?'

So she was considering in her own mind (as well as she could, for the hot day made her feel very sleepy and stupid), whether the pleasure of making a daisy-chain would be worth the trouble of getting up and picking the daisies, when suddenly a White Rabbit with pink eyes ran close by her.

There was nothing so VERY remarkable in that; nor did Alice think it so VERY much out of the way to hear the Rabbit say to itself, 'Oh dear! Oh dear! I shall be late!' (when she thought it over afterwards, it occurred to her that she ought to have wondered at this, but at the time it all seemed quite natural); but when the Rabbit actually TOOK A WATCH OUT OF ITS WAISTCOAT-POCKET, and looked at it, and then hurried on, Alice started to her feet, for it flashed across her mind that she had never before seen a rabbit with either a waistcoat-pocket, or a watch to take out of it, and burning with curiosity, she ran across the field after it, and fortunately was just in time to see it pop down a large rabbit-hole under the hedge.

In another moment down went Alice after it, never once considering how in the world she was to get out again.

The rabbit-hole went straight on like a tunnel for some way, and then dipped suddenly down, so suddenly that Alice had not a moment to think about stopping herself before she found herself falling down a very deep well.

From *Alice's Adventures in Wonderland*, by Lewis Carroll, Sam'l Gabriel Sons & Company, New York, 1916

**20.** Who is the main character in this story?

○ Alice

○ the Rabbit

○ Alice's sister

**21.** What type of text is this?

○ fiction

○ non-fiction

○ historical fiction

○ science fiction

**22.** How would you describe Alice at the start of this story?

○ interested

○ excited

○ bored

○ tired

**23.** What seemed quite natural to Alice at the time?

○ that the rabbit-hole went straight on like a tunnel for some way

○ that the book had no pictures or conversations in it

○ to hear the Rabbit say to itself, 'Oh dear!'

○ that the pleasure of making a daisy-chain would be worth the trouble of getting up and picking the daisies

**24.** When did Alice become curious in the first place?

- ○ when she was sitting by her sister on the bank
- ○ when she had peeped into the book her sister was reading
- ○ when she was thinking of whether making a daisy-chain would be worth the trouble of getting up and picking the daisies
- ○ when the Rabbit actually took a watch out of its pocket
- ○ when she heard the Rabbit say to itself, 'Oh dear!'

**25.** Why does the word *Rabbit* have a capital letter?

- ○ It is a proper animal.
- ○ It is a name.
- ○ It comes at the start of a sentence.
- ○ It is a common animal.

**26.** Which word in the text means the same as *opportunely*?

- ○ fortunately
- ○ sleepy
- ○ actually
- ○ suddenly

**27.** How do we know that Alice was impetuous?

- ○ Alice was beginning to get very tired of sitting by her sister on the bank.
- ○ Alice was considering whether the pleasure of making a daisy-chain was worth getting up and picking the daisies.
- ○ Alice never once considered how she was to get out of the hole again.
- ○ Alice was burning with curiosity.

**Read *Uranus and Gaea* and answer questions 28 to 35.**

## Uranus and Gaea

The ancient Greeks had several different theories with regard to the origin of the world, but the generally

accepted notion was that before this world came into existence, there was in its place a confused mass of shapeless elements called Chaos. These elements, becoming at length consolidated (by what means does not appear), resolved themselves into two widely different substances, the lighter portion of which, soaring on high, formed the sky or firmament, and constituted itself into a vast, overarching vault, which protected the firm and solid mass beneath.

Thus came into being the two first great primeval deities of the Greeks, Uranus and Ge or Gaea.

Uranus, the more refined deity, represented the light and air of heaven, possessing the distinguishing qualities of light, heat, purity, and omnipresence, whilst Gaea, the firm, flat, life-sustaining earth, was worshipped as the great all-nourishing mother. Her many titles refer to her more or less in this character, and she appears to have been universally revered among the Greeks, there being scarcely a city in Greece which did not contain a temple erected in her honour; indeed Gaea was held in such veneration that her name was always invoked whenever the gods took a solemn oath, made an emphatic declaration, or implored assistance.

Uranus, the heaven, was believed to have united himself in marriage with Gaea, the earth; and a moment's reflection will show what a truly poetical, and also what a logical idea this was; for, taken in a figurative sense, this union actually does exist. The smiles of heaven produce the flowers of earth, whereas his long-continued frowns exercise so depressing an influence upon his loving partner, that she no longer decks herself in bright and festive robes, but responds with ready sympathy to his melancholy mood.

The first-born child of Uranus and Gaea was Oceanus, the ocean stream, that vast expanse of ever-flowing water which encircled the earth. Here we meet with another logical though fanciful conclusion, which a very slight knowledge of the workings of nature proves to have been just and true. The ocean is formed from the rains which descend from heaven and the streams which flow from earth. By making Oceanus therefore the offspring of Uranus and Gaea, the ancients, if we take this notion in its literal sense, merely assert that the ocean is produced by the combined influence of heaven and earth, whilst at the same time their fervid and poetical imagination led them to see in this, as in all manifestations of the powers of nature, an actual, tangible divinity.

From *Myths and Legends of Ancient Greece and Rome*, by EM Berens, Maynard, Merrill & Co., 1886

**28.** What was the idea of the ancient Greeks about the creation of the world?

○ They had a theory that there was Chaos.

○ They had a theory that there was Uranus.

○ They had a theory that there was Gaea.

○ They had a theory that there was Oceanus.

**29.** What did Uranus represent?

○ a mass of shapeless elements

○ the sky, or firmament

○ the firm and solid mass beneath

○ the origin of the world

**30.** Which of these is an example of a deity?

○ Chaos

○ an ancient Greek

○ Gaea

**31.** Where would you expect to find a text like this?

○ in a book about science

○ in a book about history

○ in a book about geography

○ in a book about myths or legends

**32.** Which word in the third paragraph means nearly the same as *regard*?

○ refined

○ represented

○ omnipresence

○ declaration

○ veneration

**33.** Which marriage is said actually to exist?

○ the marriage of Uranus and Gaea

○ the marriage of Uranus and Oceanus

○ the marriage of heaven and earth

○ the marriage of heaven and the oceans

**34.** Why was the conclusion in the final paragraph described as *logical though fanciful*?

○ The idea that Uranus and Gaea formed Oceanus was imaginary but made sense.

○ The imaginary idea that the union of the gods produced the oceans is reflected in reality.

○ The idea that the union of the gods produced the oceans is imaginary.

○ The idea that the union of heaven and earth produced the oceans is imaginary.

**35.** What does the author state about the ancient Greeks?

○ They saw reality in nature.

○ They related their religious ideas to nature.

○ They had a poetical view of religion.

○ They related their religious ideas to imagination.

# END OF TEST

Well done! You have completed the sample questions for Reading. Even if you don't practise any other Reading Tests, at least you will have some familiarity with the method used in the NAPLAN Tests.

How did you go with these sample questions? Check to see where you did well and where you had problems. Try to revise the questions that were hard for you.

There are four more Reading Tests, each containing 50 questions. They are longer and the questions are a little more difficult. We have sorted the questions into levels of difficulty for you.

The spelling, grammar and punctuation questions are in the Conventions of Language sample test. You can do this test now or you can leave it until later. Now take a break before you start any more tests.

1. **to offer a new service to borrowers.** Be careful to read all the text before you start. If you aren't sure of an answer, just guess and come back to it later when you have some time.

2. **digital library download service**

3. **The service is available to registered borrowers.**

4. **the e-book**

5. **audio-book, e-book.** These were the two words that we selected as the newest words in our language. Some other words, such as *download*, *software* and even *internet*, may not appear in some older dictionaries.

6. **family history**

7. **some children of immigrants.** Note that some, but not all, historians may have an interest in the topic.

8. **event.** This is an analogy, which shows the relationship between two words. The analogy is repeated. In the same way that a record makes up an archive, so an event makes up a history.

9. **A booking must be made before attending.**

10. **presentation**

11. **A Deposit Only Card allows people to deposit funds.**

12. **It can be used for payments.**

13. **Funds are money.**

14. **This statement is correct.** It allows deposits but not withdrawals.

15. **someone who rents a property.** The tenant rents the property from a landlord.

16. **farmers' market.** Remember to read the text carefully—the answer is there somewhere.

17. **south**

18. **Granite Island**

19. **a simulated shark dive.** This was a harder question because you need to know the meanings of *simulated* and *virtual*. The answer is not really in the text.

20. **Alice.** This was an easy question.

21. **fiction**

22. **bored.** Later we are told that she was sleepy.

23. **to hear the Rabbit say to itself, 'Oh dear!'**

24. **when the Rabbit actually took a watch out of its pocket**

25. **It is a name.**

26. **fortunately**

27. **Alice never once considered how she was to get out of the hole again.**

28. **They had a theory that there was Chaos.**

29. **the sky, or firmament**

30. **Gaea**

31. **in a book about myths or legends**

32. **veneration**

33. **The marriage of heaven and earth.**

34. **The imaginary idea that the union of the gods produced the oceans is reflected in reality.**

35. **They related their religious ideas to nature.** We thought this was a difficult question. Don't worry if you found it too hard.

# SAMPLE QUESTIONS—CONVENTIONS OF LANGUAGE

This section tests whether you can find spelling, grammar and punctuation errors in a text and whether you can write correctly. Most of the questions are multiple choice. Sometimes you will have to write an answer.

Make sure you read each question carefully and study each answer option in order to choose the correct answer. There is no time limit for the sample questions.

If you are already familiar with these type of questions, go straight to the Conventions of Language Tests on page 118.

---

Read the following sentence. Correct the punctuation and write the correct sentence on the lines provided. Be careful: There may be more than one mistake.

**1.** in december andrew had an operation to replace a torn knee ligament using screws designed by dr pinkle at the knee research institute of australia

_____

_____

---

Colour in the circle with the correct answer.

**2.** Which sentence has the correct punctuation?

○ We can get to Brisbane quicker can't we? If we take the freeway.

○ We can get to Brisbane quicker can't we if we take the freeway?

○ We can get to Brisbane quicker, can't we? if we take the freeway.

○ We can get to Brisbane quicker, can't we, if we take the freeway?

**3.** Colour in the circle to show where the question mark ( **?** ) should go.

"It's nearly the school holidays I hope you will be able to visit us soon When will you

next be in Perth"

**4.** Which word correctly completes the sentence?

I ▮▮▮▮▮ the envelope containing money that I had hidden.

found       finded       founded       find

○          ○          ○          ○

---

**5.** Which sentence is correct?

○ Neither Nick nor Jim likes brussels sprouts.

○ Either Nick nor Jim likes brussels sprouts.

○ Neither Nick and Jim likes brussels sprouts.

○ Neither Nick or Jim likes brussels sprouts.

**6.** Which sentence has the correct punctuation?

○ Chrissy said to meet Amy this afternoon, so we went.

○ Chrissy said "to meet Amy this afternoon, so we went."

○ Chrissy said to "meet Amy this afternoon, so we went."

○ Chrissy said "To meet Amy this afternoon, so we went."

**7.** Which sentence has the correct punctuation?

○ Many companies, make sugar-free soft drinks which contain less sugar but they do not taste quite the same.

○ Many companies, make sugar-free soft drinks, which contain less sugar but they do not taste quite the same.

○ Many companies make sugar-free soft drinks, which contain less sugar, but they do not taste quite the same.

○ Many companies, make sugar-free soft drinks, which contain less sugar, but they do not taste quite the same.

**8.** Read the sentence. Which of the following correctly completes the sentence?

Pedro is the ▮▮▮▮▮ person I have ever met.

| clumsiest | clumsier | most clumsiest | most clumsier |
|:---:|:---:|:---:|:---:|
| ○ | ○ | ○ | ○ |

**9.** Which sentence has the correct punctuation?

○ Yvette said Time for our piano lesson.

○ "Yvette said time for our piano lesson."

○ Yvette said, "time for our piano lesson."

○ Yvette said, "Time for our piano lesson."

**10.** Where should the missing apostrophe ( ' ) go?

The womens handbags were stolen and their credit cards were never found.

**11.** Colour in **two** circles to show where the missing speech marks ( " and " ) should go.

"Hey, Theo, what do you think? said Christian. Do we have time for another game?"

---

**Read the text *Delta Electrical*. The spelling mistakes and missing words have been highlighted. Choose the correct spelling or missing word to complete the sentence.**

---

## Delta Electrical

Tired of waiting all day for _____ **12**

Delta Electrical can service all your electrical problems 24 hrs a day, 7 days a week.

Customer service is an important part of our buisiness **13**.

Don't wait days for a return call, or for a repair you _____ **14** today.

Call Delta Electrical NOW on 1800 494 567 for immediate service, or visit our website www.deltaelectrical.com and leave your details.

_____ **15** offer fixed prices and no hourly rates so you get an upfront price before we comense **16** work with no obligation to go ahead with our services.

"I have known Matthew of Delta Electrical for a number of years, and have used Delta every time I needed electrical work done. I have always found Matthews **17** work to be of a high standard and feel as though I can recommend him to any of my clients."          *Rick, RJ's Roofing*

"Previously, I had to wait days before we had electricity back _____ **18** the house _____ **19** it would take ages to get someone to come out and fix the problem. Now I get immediate service."          *TW, Cronulla*

**12.**  ○ service!   ○ service.   ○ service?   ○ service;

**13.**  ○ business   ○ buisness   ○ biusiness   ○ biusness

**14.**  ○ require   ○ required   ○ requiring

**15.**  ○ Us   ○ We   ○ He   ○ She

**16.**  ○ commense   ○ comence   ○ commence

**17.**  ○ Matthew's   ○ Matthews'   ○ Matthew

**18.**  ○ in   ○ at   ○ on   ○ through

**19.**  ○ but   ○ although   ○ if   ○ because

**Read the sentences and choose the correct word or words to complete the sentence. Colour in only one circle for each answer.**

**20.** Nick and Leo ▓▓▓▓ fish for lunch.

   ○ is eating   ○ are eating   ○ will eating

**21.** Jim is ▓▓▓▓ father.

   ○ Anthonys   ○ Anthony's   ○ Anthonys'

**22.** Max, who is a teacher ▓▓▓▓ used to live in Maroubra.

   ○ ,   ○ .   ○ ?   ○ !

**23.** John said that his sore leg is ▓▓▓▓.

   ○ better   ○ gooder   ○ bestest

**24.** Peter is the ▓▓▓▓ in the family.

   ○ tallest   ○ most tallest   ○ more tallest

**25.** My mother and ▓▓▓▓ went to the doctor.

   ○ me   ○ I   ○ we

# SAMPLE QUESTIONS—CONVENTIONS OF LANGUAGE

**To the student**

Ask your teacher or parent to read the spelling words for you. The words are listed on page 199. Write the spelling words on the lines below.

**Sample spelling words**

26. _____     34. _____

27. _____     35. _____

28. _____     36. _____

29. _____     37. _____

30. _____     38. _____

31. _____     39. _____

32. _____     40. _____

33. _____

---

**Read *Boy caught in bath drain*. The spelling mistakes have been underlined. Write the correct spelling for each underlined word in the box.**

## Boy caught in bath drain

A <u>todler</u>[41] was

<u>injared</u>[42] when he had his fingers trapped down

a bath drain on <u>Saterday</u>[43] night. The Glebe boy,

aged 3, was having a bath when two of his <u>finges</u>[44]

became <u>traped</u>.[45]

41. ☐

42. ☐

43. ☐

44. ☐

45. ☐

---

Keep on reading the rest of *Boy caught in bath drain*. This time there is now one spelling mistake in each sentence. Write the correct spelling of the word in the box.

**46.** The Police Resque unit was called.

**47.** They could not free the boy, so the bathtub had to be remooved.

**48.** He was taken to hospittal by ambulance.

**49.** He was still attatched to the drain.

**50.** Fourtunatley the boy was not seriously hurt.

Write your answers in the boxes.

# END OF TEST

Well done! You have completed the sample questions for Conventions of Language. Even if you don't practise any other Conventions of Language Tests, at least you will have some familiarity with the method used in the NAPLAN Tests.

How did you go with these sample questions? They were examples to help you get used to the types of questions. Most were taken from our earlier Year 5 book.

There are four more Conventions of Language Tests to practise, each containing around 50 questions. These contain completely new questions. They include many of the same types of questions, plus a few other types.

1. **In December Andrew had an operation to replace a torn knee ligament using screws designed by Dr Pinkle at the Knee Research Institute of Australia.** We have underlined the changes that have been made to make it easier for you. In cases like this, look for capital letters, punctuation marks, spelling or grammar. Get someone to explain what is meant if it isn't clear to you.

2. **We can get to Brisbane quicker, can't we, if we take the freeway?** This is a question and so requires a question mark. It also requires the commas. We can test this by removing the phrase surrounded by the commas and seeing if the sentence still makes sense, as it does: *We can get to Brisbane quicker, (can't we), if we take the freeway?*

3. **"It's nearly the school holidays. I hope you will be able to visit us soon. When will you next be in Perth?"** The third circle should be coloured in. Remember that punctuation marks, such as full stops, question marks and commas, always go inside the quotation marks.

4. **found**

5. **Neither Nick nor Jim likes brussels sprouts.** *Neither* can be paired with *nor* but is never paired with *or*. *Either* is used to show two possibilities. It can be paired with *or* but never *nor*.

6. **Chrissy said to meet Amy this afternoon, so we went.** This is an example of indirect speech and so does not need speech marks. Be careful not to put speech marks around an indirect question. If the exact words spoken were included within the statement, then we do need speech marks, e.g. *Chrissy said, "Let's meet Amy this afternoon", so we went.*

7. **Many companies make sugar-free soft drinks, which contain less sugar, but they do not taste quite the same.** We can test where the commas should go by removing the phrase surrounded by the commas and seeing if the sentence still makes sense, as it does: *Many companies make sugar-free soft drinks (which contain less sugar) but they do not taste quite the same.*

8. **clumsiest**

9. **Yvette said, "Time for our piano lesson."** Remember that the first word of the spoken phrase takes a capital letter. Also note that the speech marks go around the spoken words and any punctuation marks.

10. **The women's handbags were stolen and their credit cards were never found.** Plural nouns such as *handbags* and *credit cards* do not take an apostrophe.

11. **"Hey, Theo, what do you think?" said Christian. "Do we have time for another game?"**

12. **service?**　　13. **business**

14. **require**　　15. **We**

16. **commence**　　17. **Matthew's**

18. **in**　　19. **because**

20. **are eating** (*Nick and Leo are eating fish for lunch.*)

21. **Anthony's** (*Jim is Anthony's father.*)

22. **,** Place a comma after teacher, that is: *Max, who is a teacher, used to live in Maroubra.*

23. **better** (*John said that his sore leg is better.*)

24. **tallest** (*Peter is the tallest in the family.*)

25. **I** (*My mother and I went to the doctor.*)

26. **journey**　　27. **recognise**

28. **operation**　　29. **city**

30. **Wednesday**　　31. **accident**

32. **excellent**　　33. **better**

34. **anyone**　　35. **jasmine**

36. **quality**　　37. **exaggerate**

38. **happened**　　39. **friends**

40. **ruins**　　41. **toddler**

42. **injured**　　43. **Saturday**

44. **fingers**　　45. **trapped**

46. **rescue**　　47. **removed**

48. **hospital**　　49. **attached**

50. **fortunately**

## An important note about the NAPLAN Online tests

The NAPLAN Online Numeracy test will be divided into different sections. Students will only have one opportunity to check their answers at the end of each section before proceeding to the next one. This means that after students have completed a section and moved onto the next they will not be able to check their work again. We have included reminders for students to check their work at specific points in the practice tests from now on so they become familiar with this process.

# NUMERACY TEST 1

This is the first Numeracy Test. You have 65 minutes to complete this test.

The NAPLAN Online Numeracy test consists of two parts.

The first part is the Non-calculator section consisting of 8 questions.

The second part is the Calculator Allowed section where students can use the onscreen calculator. There are 40 questions in this section.

If you aren't sure what to do, ask your teacher or your parents to help you. Don't be afraid to ask if it isn't clear to you.

Depending on the question, either write your answer in the box or colour in the circle with the correct answer. In most questions you will only colour in one circle. In a few questions you will be told there may be more than one answer so for those questions you might need to colour two, three, or more circles to match all the correct answers.

## Section 1: Non-calculator questions

**1.** There is a picture that covers some squares. How many pictures like this one are needed to cover all the area? (Hint: Use the size of the first picture to help you. Remember to include the picture that is shown in the final total.)

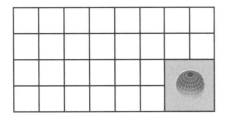

How many pictures are needed?

| 6 | 8 | 10 | 12 |
|---|---|----|----|
| ○ | ○ | ○  | ○  |

**2.** There are four shapes. They are called A, B, C and D. Part of each shape is coloured.

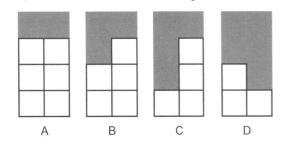

Which shape is coloured one-half?

| A | B | C | D |
|---|---|---|---|
| ○ | ○ | ○ | ○ |

**3.** Here is a pattern of some blocks.

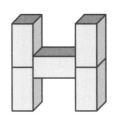

Which one of the four patterns below is the same as the one above? Is it A, B, C or D?

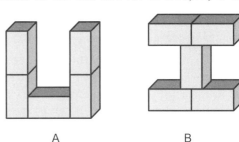

A          B

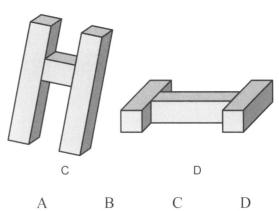

C          D

| A | B | C | D |
|---|---|---|---|
| ○ | ○ | ○ | ○ |

**4.** CS Lewis wrote the Narnia series, including *The Lion, the Witch and the Wardrobe*. He was born in 1898 and died in 1963.

Which sum would you use to show how old he was when he died?

○ 1898 + 1963

○ 1898 − 1963

○ 1963 − 1898

**5.** This chart shows the length of some objects.

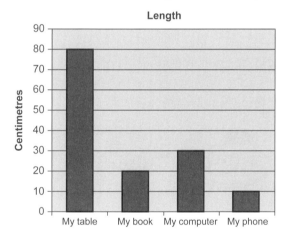

Which answer is correct?

○ My computer and phone together are the same length as my table.

○ My table is the same length as my book and my computer and my phone together.

○ My book and computer together are the same length as my table.

○ My book and phone together are the same length as my computer.

**6.** There are six spaces that have a number. We can spin the arrow and it will land on one of the spaces with a number.

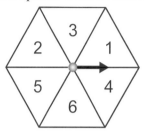

If I spin this arrow, what is the chance it will land on the space for the number 2.

○ 1 out of 6 chances    ○ 4 out of 6 chances

○ 6 out of 1 chances    ○ 2 out of 6 chances

**7.** Here is a prism.

How many separate faces does the shape have? (Hint: Also count the faces that you cannot see from the drawing.)

10          12          14          16

○           ○           ○           ○

**8.** Here is the time on a digital clock. It is in 24-hour time.

Which time is the same?

3:30 am    3:30 pm    4:30 am    4:30 pm

○          ○          ○          ○

This is the end of the part where you are not allowed to use a calculator.

It would be a good idea to check your answers to the questions in this section before moving on to the other questions.

## Section 2: Calculator Allowed questions

**9.** There is a pattern in these numbers. Write the number that is missing.

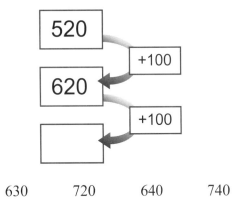

| 520 |
| 620 | +100 |
| | +100 |

630     720     640     740

○      ○      ○      ○

**10.** To answer this question write your answer in the space provided.

Use the table to answer the next question.

Flowers in home gardens

| Flower | Number |
|--------|--------|
| Roses | 13 |
| Tulips | 19 |
| Daisies | 16 |
| Lilies | 12 |

How many tulips and daisies are there?

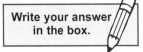

**Write your answer in the box.**

**11.** Look again at the table above. What is the average (or mean) number of flowers in the gardens?

16     17     12     15

○      ○      ○      ○

**12.** The question mark shows a missing number in this sum?

$$32 \times \boxed{?} = 288$$

Which number goes in the place of the question mark?

6     7     8     9

○      ○      ○      ○

**13.** This football costs $5.50. How much will four cost?

Fill in the number sentence below. Show how much four footballs cost.

$$\boxed{\phantom{xxx}} \times 4 = \$ \boxed{\phantom{xxx}}$$

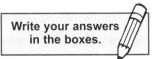

**Write your answers in the boxes.**

**14.** Here are some foods from a cafe. They are a slice of cake, some toast and fish. Their prices in the cafe are also shown.

$4.70      $3.20      $16.10

Here are four sums. They round off the prices and show a quick way to guess or estimate the price of the three foods.

Which is the best way?

○ $5 + $3 + $15

○ $5 + $3 + $16

○ $4 + $3 + $15

○ $4 + $4 + $16

Did you colour in one of the circles?

**15.** $684 - 169 =$ ☐

Write your answers in the box.

**16.** $5^2 + 9^2 = ?$

| 106 | 14 | 45 | 144 |
|:---:|:---:|:---:|:---:|
| ○ | ○ | ○ | ○ |

**It would be a good idea to check your answers to questions 9 to 16 before moving on to the other questions.**

**17.** $5.6 + 6.8 =$ ☐

**18.** $2104 \div 8 =$ ☐

**19.** Write one number in each space to complete this sum.

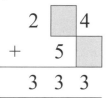

```
  2 □ 4
+   5 □
-------
  3 3 3
```

**20.** Here is a piece of wood. There is a tape under the wood.

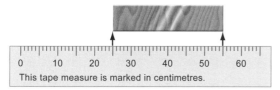

This tape measure is marked in centimetres.

How long is this piece of wood?

| 15 cm | 20 cm | 25 cm | 30 cm |
|:---:|:---:|:---:|:---:|
| ○ | ○ | ○ | ○ |

**21.** $\sqrt{4 + 5}$

| 5 | 9 | 3 | 45 |
|:---:|:---:|:---:|:---:|
| ○ | ○ | ○ | ○ |

**22.** Place brackets in this sum to make this number sentence correct. Write in the brackets.

$$24 + 6 \div 3 + 1 = 11$$

**23.** Speed is equal to the distance travelled divided by the time taken. To find the speed divide the distance by the time.

$$\text{Speed} = \frac{\text{Distance}}{\text{Time}}$$

For example, if the distance I covered was 100 km and it took me two hours, my speed would have been 50 km per hour ($100 \div 2 = 50$).

Here is a problem for you: If I travelled 150 km and the time taken was three hours, what was my speed?

☐ km/h

Write your answer in the box.

**24.** There are six nations in the imaginary kingdom of Acanoa. The total land size is 6 000 000 hectares. It varies from country to country.

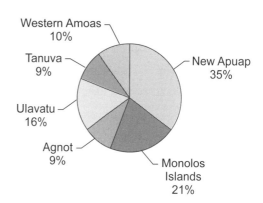

Which country has the second largest area?

- ○ Western Amoas
- ○ Monolos Islands
- ○ Ulavatu
- ○ Agnot
- ○ Tanuva
- ○ New Apuap

**25.** What is the perimeter (the distance around the outside edges) of this figure?

Note that some of the lengths are not shown in the figure.

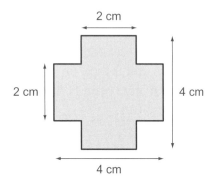

12 cm　14 cm　16 cm　18 cm　20 cm

○　　○　　○　　○　　○

**26.** Fibonacci numbers are a series of numbers. These are Fibonacci numbers:

1　1　2　3　5　8　13　21　44　55

What do you notice about these numbers?

○ Each number is made up of two odd numbers.

○ Each number is made up of the previous two added together.

○ Each number is made up of the previous three added together.

○ Each number is made up of the previous two multiplied together.

**27.** Which rule can be used to tell you whether a number is completely divisible by seven (without a remainder)?

○ Take the last digit of a number and see whether it is an odd number that is divisible by seven.

○ Take the last digit of the number, double it and subtract it from the rest of the number to see whether that is divisible by seven.

○ Take the last digit of the number, triple it and subtract it from the rest of the number to see whether that is divisible by seven.

○ Add up all the digits in a number and see if the total is divisible by seven.

**28.** Three cats all weigh the same and together the three of them weigh 15 kg. Four dogs also weigh the same and together the four of them weigh 32 kg.

You have just one cat and one dog. What would be the average weight of one cat and one dog?

5.5 kg　6 kg　6.5 kg　7 kg　7.5 kg

○　　○　　○　　○　　○

**29.** What is the area of the striped part of the figure?

The area of the blue squares is 27 square metres.

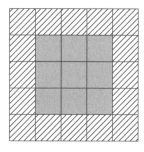

45 m² 　16 m² 　42 m² 　25 m² 　48 m²

○　　○　　○　　○　　○

**30.** A person paid $2.25 for some fruit. The price on the ticket was 1 kg for $9.

How much did they buy for $2.25?

○ 125 grams　　　○ 250 grams

○ 375 grams　　　○ 425 grams

**31.** Look at this rectangle. It is not drawn to scale.

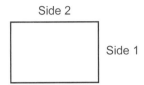

Side 2

Side 1

Perimeter = 26 cm
Area = 36 cm²

The perimeter of the rectangle is 26 cm and its area is 36 cm squared. What are the lengths of its two sides?

Side 1 [ ]

Side 2 [ ]

*Write your answers in the boxes.*

**32.** A box is one quarter full of cricket balls.

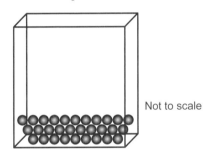

Not to scale

You put in another 60 cricket balls and now it is three-quarters full.

How many cricket balls does the box hold? [ ]

**It would be a good idea to check your answers to questions 17 to 32 before moving on.**

**33.** Pieces of wood are stacked one on top of the other to a height of 256 cm high. Each piece of wood is 1.28 cm in thickness. How many pieces of wood are there in the stack?

| 256 | 128 | 200 | 100 |
| :-: | :-: | :-: | :-: |
| ○ | ○ | ○ | ○ |

**34.** What is the size of the angle marked $x$ in the diagram?

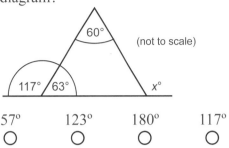

60°

(not to scale)

117° 63° $x°$

| 57° | 123° | 180° | 117° |
| :-: | :-: | :-: | :-: |
| ○ | ○ | ○ | ○ |

**35.** There is one team leader for every seven workers in a large factory. There are 560 employees.

How many are team leaders?

| 70 | 490 | 420 | 8 |
| :-: | :-: | :-: | :-: |
| ○ | ○ | ○ | ○ |

**36.** There are six entrants in a competition. How many games will need to be organised so that all entrants can play every other player in the competition?

| 6 | 36 | 30 | 15 |
| :-: | :-: | :-: | :-: |
| ○ | ○ | ○ | ○ |

**37.** A building has 4 levels underground, a ground floor and 53 levels above the ground. I enter a lift on the 4th level in the underground parking. I go up to the 31st floor. How many floors will I need to travel down to reach Level 4 underground again.

| 31 | 35 | 33 | 37 |
| :-: | :-: | :-: | :-: |
| ○ | ○ | ○ | ○ |

**38.** Find the angle $x$ in the diagram.

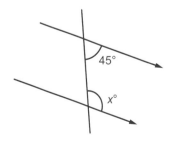

45°

$x°$

| 45° | 315° | 135° | 180° |
| :-: | :-: | :-: | :-: |
| ○ | ○ | ○ | ○ |

**39.** Each time that a liquid passes through a process its purity increases by one-fifth. How many times will it need to be processed for the purity to be more than one-half? (Hint: Assume that it is impure in the beginning.)

○ 3 times

○ 4 times

○ 5 times

○ 6 or more times

**40.** A couple have four children. There are 16 possible combinations of boys and girls. What is the probability that there are exactly three boys and one girl in that family?

○ 3 in 16

○ 4 in 16

○ 5 in 16

○ 8 in 16

**41.** A man and a bicycle rider are 6 km apart.

The man walks at 6 km per hour. The person on the bicycle rides at 12 km per hour.

After how many minutes will they meet?

○ 5 minutes     ○ 10 minutes

○ 15 minutes     ○ 20 minutes

○ 25 minutes     ○ 30 minutes

**42.** Which is the largest decimal number?

○ 14.0140     ○ 14.1400

○ 14.4     ○ 14.004

○ 1.4004

**43** This picture shows an original and its enlargement. It shows the height of the original and the height of the enlargement. The width of the enlargement is also shown, but not the width (x) of the original.

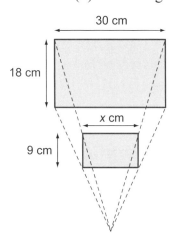

What is the length of *x*?

15 cm    9 cm    12 cm    18 cm    24 cm

○     ○     ○     ○     ○

**44.** Some numbers are triangular. This means that they have the pattern of a triangle. Here are some examples.

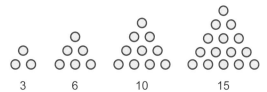

What would be the next triangular number?

22    25    27    21    24

○    ○    ○    ○    ○

**45.** Here is a series of numbers that follows a pattern. (Hint: Add the prior number to a cube.)

| 0 | 1 | 9 | 36 | ? | 225 |

Which number is missing in this series?

64      144      100      125

○      ○      ○      ○

**46.** How many three-digit numbers between 100 and 200 are divisible by nine?

| 9 | 10 | 11 | 12 |
|:---:|:---:|:---:|:---:|
| ○ | ○ | ○ | ○ |

**47.** Here are two charts that show how much the euro currency is worth in Australian dollars and US dollars.

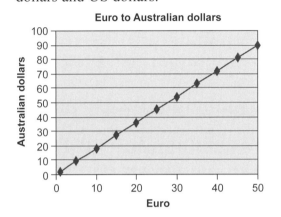

**Euro to Australian dollars**

**Euro to US dollars**

How much are US$70 worth in Australian dollars, using these charts?

[    ]

Write your answer in the box.

**48.** Two people play a game. Player 1 lost the first game and Player 2 lost the second time. After each game the loser of the game is meant to double the money of the other person. The loser gives money to the winner so that the winner's money is doubled.

After two games they both have $12. Each player lost one game.

How much money did they each have at the start?

PLAYER 1: $ [    ]

PLAYER 2: $ [    ]

Write your answers in the boxes.

# END OF TEST

Well done! You have completed the first Numeracy Test. Even if you don't practise any others, at least you have done a fair sample of the questions.

How did you go with these test questions? Some were harder than the sample questions. Check to see where you did well and where you had problems. Try to revise the questions that were hard for you.

Use the diagnostic chart on pages 33–34 to see which level of ability you reached. This is only an estimate. Don't be surprised if you answered some difficult questions correctly or even missed some easier questions.

There are now three more practice tests, each containing 48 questions. We will start to include new types of questions in each of these tests.

## Instructions

### Check the answers

As you check the answer for each question, mark it as correct (✓) or incorrect (✘). Mark any questions that you omitted or left out as incorrect (✘) for the moment.

Then look at how many you answered correctly in each level. Your level of ability is the point where you started having consistent difficulty with questions. For example, if you answer most questions correctly up to the Intermediate level and then get most questions wrong from then onwards, it is likely your ability is at an Intermediate level. You can ask your parents or your teacher to help you do this if it isn't clear.

We expect you to miss some easy questions and also to answer some hard questions correctly, but your ability level should be where you are starting to find the questions too hard. Some students will reach the top band—this means that their ability cannot be measured by these questions or even the NAPLAN Tests. They found it far too easy.

### Understanding the different levels

We have divided the questions into three levels of difficulty:

- Standard
- Intermediate
- Advanced.

For each question we have described the skill involved in answering the question. Then, depending on what sort of skill is involved, we have placed it into one of the three levels. It should make sense, especially when you go back and look at the type of question. The Standard level includes the easiest tasks and then they increase in difficulty.

Don't worry about the level of ability in which you are located. We expect students to be spread across all of the three bands. Also numeracy may or may not be your strongest subject.

The purpose of these practice tests is to help you be as confident as possible and perform to the best of your ability. The purpose of the NAPLAN Tests is to show what you know or can do. For the first time it allows the user to estimate his or her level of ability before taking the actual test and also to see if there is any improvement across the practice tests.

Remember that the levels of ability are only a rough guide. No claim is made that they are perfect. They are only an indicator. Your level might change as you do each practice test. We hope that these brief notes are of some help.

## Instructions

As you check the answer for each question, mark it as correct (✓) or incorrect (✗). Mark any questions that you omitted or left out as incorrect (✗) for the moment.

Then look at how many you answered correctly in each level. You will be able to see what level you are at by finding the point where you started having consistent difficulty with questions at a certain level. For example, if you answer most questions correctly up to the Intermediate level and then get most questions wrong from then onwards, it is likely your ability is at an Intermediate level. You can ask your parents or your teacher to help you do this if it isn't clear to you.

**Am I able to ...**

| | SKILL | ESTIMATED LEVEL | ✓ or ✗ |
|---|---|---|---|
| 1 | Measure area by counting grid squares? | Standard | |
| 2 | Use informal units to measure the area of a shape? | Standard | |
| 3 | Recognise a 3D model made from cubes from a different perspective? | Standard | |
| 4 | Recognise how to solve a difference in dates? | Standard | |
| 5 | Interpret data from column graphs to confirm a statement? | Standard | |
| 6 | Use chance to describe the outcome in a simple experiment? | Standard | |
| 7 | Identify the faces of a 3D model? | Standard | |
| 8 | Convert 24-hour time? | Standard | |
| 9 | Continue a number pattern involving counting by hundreds? | Standard | |
| 10 | Interpret data in two-way tables? | Standard | |
| 11 | Calculate the average of four numbers? | Standard | |
| 12 | Multiply a two-digit number by a single digit number? | Standard | |
| 13 | Solve everyday money problems involving multiplication? | Standard | |
| 14 | Select the best addition strategy for estimating a total? | Standard | |
| 15 | Solve a three-digit subtraction? | Standard | |
| 16 | Square and add numbers? | Standard | |
| 17 | Solve a problem with place values for decimals? | Intermediate | |
| 18 | Solve a division involving a four-digit number? | Intermediate | |
| 19 | Use problem-solving strategies to complete a number problem? | Intermediate | |
| 20 | Use a ruler to solve a length problem? | Intermediate | |
| 21 | Find the square root of a number less than 10? | Intermediate | |
| 22 | Insert parentheses into a number statement? | Intermediate | |
| 23 | Solve problems by applying knowledge of arithmetic operations? | Intermediate | |
| 24 | Interpret a sector graph? | Intermediate | |
| 25 | Calculate the perimeter of a composite rectangular shape? | Intermediate | |
| 26 | Find the pattern in a series of numbers? | Intermediate | |
| 27 | Check to see if a rule for division applies to a number? | Intermediate | |
| 28 | Find the average of a composite? | Intermediate | |

# CHECK YOUR SKILLS: NUMERACY TEST 1

| | SKILL | ESTIMATED LEVEL | ✓ or ✗ |
|---|---|---|---|
| 29 | Find the remaining area of a square figure? | Intermediate | |
| 30 | Convert a proportion of a price to the proportion of a quantity? | Intermediate | |
| 31 | Find the dimensions of a figure given the perimeter and area? | Advanced | |
| 32 | Solve a problem involving unknown fractions? | Advanced | |
| 33 | Divide a height in centimetres by a fraction of that height? | Advanced | |
| 34 | Apply knowledge of triangles to find angle size? | Advanced | |
| 35 | Solve a multi-step problem relating to proportions? | Advanced | |
| 36 | Determine the number of combinations of events? | Advanced | |
| 37 | Apply directed numbers? | Advanced | |
| 38 | Find a co-interior angle? | Advanced | |
| 39 | Use fractions of fractions in calculating quantities? | Advanced | |
| 40 | Find the combinations of three out of four binary objects? | Advanced | |
| 41 | Calculate the intersection of travel time and distance? | Advanced | |
| 42 | Use place value to compare decimals? | Standard | |
| 43 | Determine the dimensions of a figure that has been enlarged? | Intermediate | |
| 44 | Find the next number in a series? | Advanced | |
| 45 | Complete a number series? | Advanced | |
| 46 | Solve a number problem based on multiples of nine? | Advanced | |
| 47 | Convert a currency? | Advanced | |
| 48 | Solve a multi-stage problem? | Advanced | |
| | TOTAL | | |

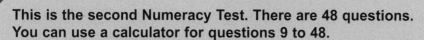

# NUMERACY TEST 2

This is the second Numeracy Test. There are 48 questions.
You can use a calculator for questions 9 to 48.

Allow around 65 minutes for this test.

Write the answer in the box or colour in the circle with the correct answer.
Colour in only one circle for each answer.

## Section 1: Non-calculator questions

**1.** Use the table to answer the next question.

| Threatened species | |
|---|---|
| **Species** | **Total threatened (approx.)** |
| Birds | 1200 |
| Mammals | 1100 |
| Fish | 800 |
| Reptiles | 300 |
| Amphibians | 150 |

In the graph below, draw in the column for Fish.

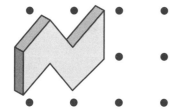

Draw your column in the third row.

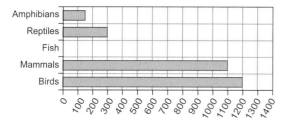

**2.** This is a drawing that covers some dots.

How many dots are covered by the drawing?

[    ] dots

**3.** There is a grid made up of squares. There is a coloured shape on this grid.

How many squares are covered by the coloured shape?

18 ○   14 ○   16 ○   28 ○

**4.** Here is a pattern of some blocks.

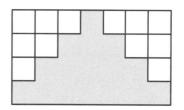

Which one of the four patterns below is the same as the one above? Is it A, B, C or D?

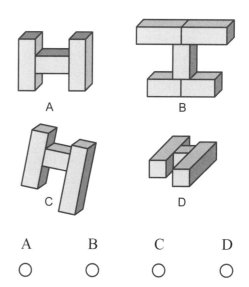

A   B   C   D
○   ○   ○   ○

**5.** The United States has an army of 502 000 and Russia has an army of 395 000.

Which sum would you use to show the difference between these armies?

○ 502 000 + 395 000

○ 502 000 − 395 000

○ 502 000 ÷ 395 000

○ 502 000 × 395 000

**6.** This table shows forecast weather for Sunday for capital cities throughout Australia.

It shows the temperature and a description.

| Forecast for Sunday | | |
|---|---|---|
| Sydney | 21° | Fine. Mostly sunny |
| Melbourne | 17° | Shower or two |
| Brisbane | 25° | Fine |
| Perth | 26° | Fine |
| Adelaide | 17° | Morning shower |
| Hobart | 13° | Shower or two, windy |
| Canberra | 16° | Fine and sunny |
| Darwin | 33° | Fine, high cloud |

Which answer is correct?

○ When the forecast is for a shower or two the temperatures are the same as when it is fine.

○ When the forecast is for fine and high cloud the temperature is highest.

○ When the forecast is just for fine the temperature could be lower than when there is a shower.

○ When the forecast is for a shower or two the temperatures are lower than when it is fine and sunny.

**7.** There are three rows. On each row there are some glasses (spectacles).

| Row | Objects |
|---|---|
| TOP | 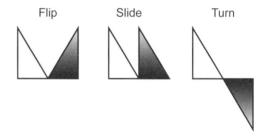 |
| MIDDLE | |
| BOTTOM | |

On which row (TOP, MIDDLE or BOTTOM) would I have the best chance of picking the glasses?

    TOP       MIDDLE    BOTTOM

    ○          ○          ○

**8.** We can flip, slide or turn shapes.

Here is an example. Look closely at what happens to the coloured shape.

| Flip | Slide | Turn |
|---|---|---|

Have we done a flip, a slide or a turn with this shape?

    FLIP       SLIDE      TURN

**This is the end of the part where you are not allowed to use a calculator.**

**It would be a good idea to check your answers to the questions in this section before moving on to the other questions.**

## Section 2: Calculator Allowed Questions

**9.** There is a pattern in these numbers. Write the number that is missing.

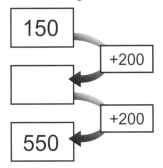

**10.** This chart shows how many women and men were in parliament in three countries.

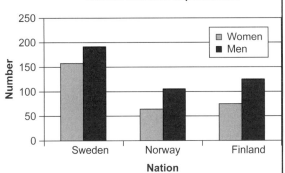

Use the information from the chart to fill in the missing part of this table.

|  | Sweden | Norway | Finland |
|---|---|---|---|
| Women | 158 | 64 |  |
| Men | 191 | 105 | 125 |

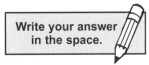

Write your answer in the space.

**11.** Here are the amounts spent on toys by some people in different countries.

|  | $ spent per person |
|---|---|
| American | 121 |
| Japanese | 69 |
| British | 115 |
| German | 64 |
| French | 71 |

What is the average amount in dollars that was spent by these people?

| 80 | 82 | 84 | 86 | 88 |
|---|---|---|---|---|
| ○ | ○ | ○ | ○ | ○ |

**12.** $34 \times 9 = ?$

| 346 | 306 | 316 | 276 |
|---|---|---|---|
| ○ | ○ | ○ | ○ |

**13.** Pong was one of the first computer games. It was like a type of table tennis and was developed in 1972. Pac-Man was a popular maze-type game that was developed in 1980.

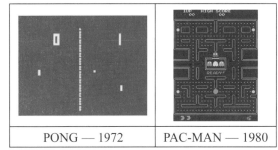

| PONG — 1972 | PAC-MAN — 1980 |
|---|---|

How many years were there from the development of Pong to that of Pac-Man?

| 6 | 8 | 10 | 12 |
|---|---|---|---|
| ○ | ○ | ○ | ○ |

**14.** Here is a piece of wood. It is to be cut into pieces that are 5 centimetres long.

This tape measure is marked in centimetres.

How many smaller pieces can be cut from it?

| 10 | 20 | 12 | 15 |
|---|---|---|---|
| ○ | ○ | ○ | ○ |

# NUMERACY TEST 2

**15.** An estimate is your best guess. It can be the closest answer to a question.

To do this, round off the numbers to end in 0. This way they are easy to add and also to guess. The answer is not perfectly accurate. It is an estimate.

Each chair = $47, Table = $73

Estimate the cost of this furniture by rounding off the cost of each item.

250     260     270     280

○      ○      ○      ○

**16.** At a school, children come by car or bus, or they walk.

$\frac{1}{3}$ of children travel to school by car.

$\frac{1}{4}$ of children come by bus.

The rest of the children walk.

What fraction of children walk to school?

$\frac{2}{7}$    $\frac{1}{3}$    $\frac{5}{12}$    $\frac{1}{6}$

○      ○      ○      ○

**17.** Find the perimeter of this shape.

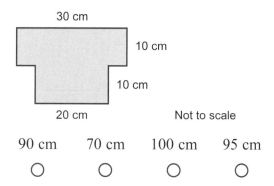

90 cm    70 cm    100 cm    95 cm

○      ○      ○      ○

**18.** Here are some Saturday activities of 300 people.

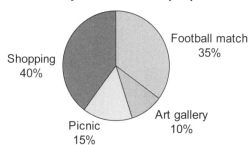

How many were at the football match?

35     85     105     100

○      ○      ○      ○

**19.** What number is halfway between 3.7 and 8.9?

6.2    6.3    6.4    6.5

○      ○      ○      ○

**20.** The question mark shows a missing number in this sum?

$$2556 \div \boxed{\ ?\ } = 142$$

Which number goes in the place of the question mark?

12     14     16     18

○      ○      ○      ○

It would be a good idea to check your answers to questions 9 to 16 before moving on to the other questions.

**21.** What is the circumference of this circle? The drawing shows one length to help you. (Hint: The formula for the circumference is $C = 2\pi r$.)

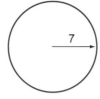

| 21 | 44 | 154 | 308 |
|----|----|-----|-----|
| ○  | ○  | ○   | ○   |

**22.** Here is a shape. There are tapes to measure two of the sides.

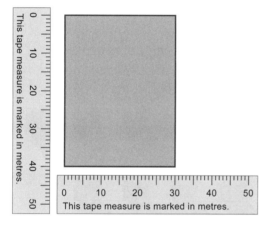

What is the perimeter of this shape?

| 150 m | 70 m | 120 m | 140 m |
|-------|------|-------|-------|
| ○     | ○    | ○     | ○     |

**23.** $3 - \dfrac{1}{4} = \boxed{\phantom{xxxx}}$

**Write your answer in the box.**

**24.** Here are four numbers. Three are multiples of four; one is a square number; one is divisible by both 3 and 5; one is a prime number.

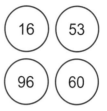

Which number is divisible by both 3 and 5?

| 16 | 53 | 96 | 60 |
|----|----|----|----|
| ○  | ○  | ○  | ○  |

**25.** Multiply these numbers.

$$
\begin{array}{r}
23.8 \\
\times \phantom{0}7 \\
\hline
\end{array}
$$

| 166.66 | 16.66 | 166.6 | 106.6 |
|--------|-------|-------|-------|
| ○      | ○     | ○     | ○     |

**26.** What is the area of this figure? Note that some of the lengths are not shown in the figure.

9 cm

3 cm

6 cm

4 cm

| 39 cm$^2$ | 648 cm$^2$ | 22 cm$^2$ | 36 cm$^2$ |
|-----------|------------|-----------|-----------|
| ○         | ○          | ○         | ○         |

**27.** Here is a map. It shows four towns on an island. The map is divided into sections. Each section is 20 km.

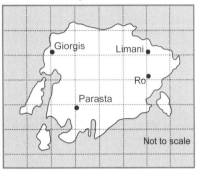

**Istigem Island**

Not to scale

How far is it from Giorgis to Limani to Ro to Parasta on this map? (Hint: You may have to guess some distances.)

- ○ 160 km
- ○ 180 km
- ○ 120 km
- ○ 200 km
- ○ 110 km

**28.** Here is a jar. An object is placed in the jar and the water rises.

By how much does the water increase in the second jar?

- ○ seven-fifths
- ○ one-fifth
- ○ two-fifths
- ○ three-fifths

**29.** A square number is any number that can be formed into a square of dots. Here are some square numbers.

What is the square number that is missing (the question mark is in its place)?

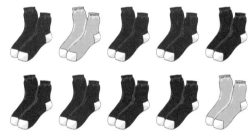

4    9    16    25    ?

- 39 ○
- 34 ○
- 33 ○
- 36 ○

**30.** Without looking, you picked a sock from a drawer at random (this means any sock). There are four pairs of black socks (8 socks), four pairs of blue socks (8 socks) and two pairs of grey socks (4 socks).

The first sock that you pick is grey. What is the chance that the next sock you pick will also be grey?

- ○ 3 out of 19
- ○ 4 out of 20
- ○ 19 out of 20
- ○ 4 out of 19
- ○ 3 out of 20

**31.** Five experienced workers take 120 days to finish a big job. Five new workers are added but they can only work half as fast. How long would it take the five experienced workers and the five new workers to finish a similar job?

- ○ 60 days
- ○ 70 days
- ○ 80 days
- ○ 90 days
- ○ 100 days

**32.** Look at this rectangle. It is not drawn to scale.

Side 2

Side 1

Perimeter = 24 cm
Area = 32 cm²

What are the lengths of its two sides?

Side 1 [        ]

Side 2 [        ]

> Write your answers in the boxes.

> **It would be a good idea to check your answers to questions 17 to 32 before moving on.**

**33.** This chart shows the number of male employees in different age groups.

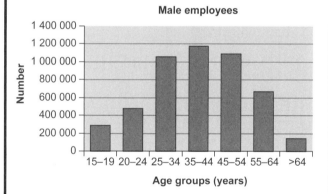

**Male employees**

The average number of male employees for the seven groups is just over 700 000.

How many age groups have more employees than the average number?

   1     2     3     4     5

   ○    ○    ○    ○    ○

**34.** Using the chart above, which group is the median for the number of employees?

  25–34  35–44  45–54  55–64  >64

    ○      ○     ○     ○    ○

**35.** A couple had four children. What is the probability that their first child is a girl and the others are boys?

  1 in 4   1 in 8   1 in 16  1 in 32  1 in 64

   ○      ○      ○      ○     ○

**36.** The cost of a tracksuit is $35 and the cost of a school blazer is $45. A school uniform shop buys 10 items of clothing and spends $380. How many tracksuits did the shop buy?

   3     4     5     6     7

   ○    ○    ○    ○    ○

**37.** What is 8 °C below 2 °C?

  −4 °C   −10 °C   −8 °C   −6 °C

   ○      ○     ○    ○

**38.** In this diagram, what is the size of the alternate angle to ∠EBC?

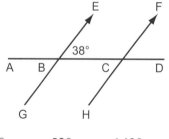

  38°     52°     142°    322°

  ○     ○     ○     ○

**39.** $\dfrac{5}{6} - \dfrac{2}{3} \times \dfrac{3}{4} + \dfrac{7}{12} = ?$

  $\dfrac{7}{12}$    $\dfrac{5}{12}$    $\dfrac{9}{12}$    $\dfrac{11}{12}$

  ○     ○     ○     ○

Did you colour in one of the circles?

**40.**

Half of the trees in an orchard are olive trees.

One-third of the trees are fig trees.

The rest are mixed types of fruit trees.

In the first week of the season the owner harvests one-quarter of the olive trees and one-quarter of the fig trees. What proportion of trees in the orchard still has to be harvested? (Remember to include the mixed types of trees.)

$\frac{5}{24}$     $\frac{15}{24}$     $\frac{19}{24}$     $\frac{21}{24}$

○      ○      ○      ○

**41.** Select a way of expanding 420 805.

○ $4 \times 100\,000 + 2 \times 10\,000 + 8 \times 100 + 5 \times 1$

○ $4 \times 10\,000 + 2 \times 1000 + 8 \times 100 + 5 \times 1$

○ $4 \times 100\,000 + 2 \times 1000 + 8 \times 100 + 5 \times 1$

○ $4 \times 1\,000\,000 + 2 \times 100\,000 + 8 \times 1000 + 5 \times 1$

**42.** Here is a factor tree. It shows the numbers that are multiplied together to give the number on top.

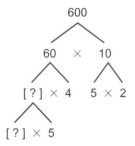

What numbers go in place of the question marks?

15, 4     15, 3     10, 4     10, 3

○      ○      ○      ○

**43.** Are there more, fewer or the same number of even numbers between 593 and 613 as there are odd numbers? Do not include 593 or 613.

Same     More     Fewer

○       ○       ○

**44.** What is $5\frac{1}{4}\%$ written as a decimal?

5.25     0.0525     0.00525     0.525

○      ○      ○      ○

Did you colour in one of the circles?

**45.** Insert <, > or = in place of the question mark (?) to make the statement true.

$$-(4 - 6) \; ? \; -(6 - 4)$$

     <         >         =

     ○         ○         ○

**46.** Select the group of years that are not leap years.

- ○ 1948, 1952, 1956, 1960
- ○ 1888, 1892, 1896, 1900
- ○ 2002, 2006, 2010, 2014
- ○ 1920, 1924, 1928, 1932

**47.** There are 24 forms of transport in this picture. There are buses, cars, aeroplanes, bicycles and ocean liners. Some are the same.

What fraction of the 24 methods of transport are bicycles?

   $\dfrac{24}{8}$       $\dfrac{16}{24}$       $\dfrac{1}{4}$       $\dfrac{1}{3}$

   ○        ○        ○        ○

**48.** A sporting knockout competition has 16 teams. Only the winner of each match goes to the next round. How many games are played to find the overall winner? (Remember to include the first matches.)

   8       15       16       12

   ○       ○       ○       ○

# END OF TEST

Well done! You have completed the second Numeracy Test. We tried to change the questions and some were a little harder.

How did you go with these test questions? Check to see where you did well and where you had problems. Try to revise the questions that were hard for you.

Use the diagnostic chart on pages 44–45 to see which level of ability you reached. This is only an estimate. Don't be surprised if you answered some difficult questions correctly or even missed some easier questions.

There are now two more practice tests, each containing 48 questions. We have included some new types of questions in these tests.

## Instructions

As you check the answer for each question, mark it as correct (✔) or incorrect (✘). Mark any questions that you omitted or left out as incorrect (✘) for the moment.

Then look at how many you answered correctly in each level. You will be able to see what level you are at by finding the point where you started having consistent difficulty with questions at a certain level. For example, if you answer most questions correctly up to the Intermediate level and then get most questions wrong from then onwards, it is likely your ability is at an Intermediate level. You can ask your parents or your teacher to help you do this if it isn't clear to you.

**Am I able to ...**

| | SKILL | ESTIMATED LEVEL | ✔ or ✘ |
|---|---|---|---|
| 1 | Convert data to a chart? | Standard | |
| 2 | Visualise missing dots? | Standard | |
| 3 | Use informal units to measure the area of a shape? | Standard | |
| 4 | Recognise a model made from cubes viewed from a different perspective? | Standard | |
| 5 | Recognise how to solve a difference? | Standard | |
| 6 | Interpret data from a chart to confirm a statement? | Standard | |
| 7 | Estimate the chances of selecting an object? | Standard | |
| 8 | Recognise the property of a shape that has been flipped? | Standard | |
| 9 | Continue a number pattern involving counting by 200? | Standard | |
| 10 | Interpret a table that accompanies a chart? | Standard | |
| 11 | Calculate the average of five numbers? | Standard | |
| 12 | Multiply a two-digit number by nine? | Standard | |
| 13 | Find the difference between two dates? | Standard | |
| 14 | Divide a length into smaller units? | Standard | |
| 15 | Use an estimate to describe the outcome? | Standard | |
| 16 | Convert fractions to a common unit to solve a problem? | Standard | |
| 17 | Find the perimeter of an irregular figure? | Intermediate | |
| 18 | Convert a proportion in a pie chart to a number? | Intermediate | |
| 19 | Find a number midway between two decimals? | Intermediate | |
| 20 | Solve a division involving a four-digit number? | Intermediate | |
| 21 | Find the circumference of a circle given the radius? | Intermediate | |
| 22 | Find the perimeter of a rectangle from a ruler that measures two sides? | Intermediate | |
| 23 | Subtract a fraction from a whole number? | Intermediate | |
| 24 | Find a multiple of three and five from a group of numbers? | Intermediate | |
| 25 | Multiply a decimal by a whole number? | Intermediate | |
| 26 | Calculate the area of an irregular shape? | Intermediate | |

| | SKILL | ESTIMATED LEVEL | ✓ or ✗ |
|---|---|---|---|
| 27 | Use a scale to determine distance on a grid? | Intermediate | |
| 28 | Determine the fraction of a quantity? | Intermediate | |
| 29 | Find the missing square of a number? | Advanced | |
| 30 | Describe the probability of a random selection? | Advanced | |
| 31 | Find a composite amount and apply it to a new situation? | Advanced | |
| 32 | Find the dimensions of a figure given the perimeter and area? | Advanced | |
| 33 | Find groups on a chart that are above the mean? | Advanced | |
| 34 | Find the median group from a chart? | Advanced | |
| 35 | Find the probability of a permutation and combination? | Advanced | |
| 36 | Solve a problem involving one unknown variable? | Advanced | |
| 37 | Subtract a positive number to give an answer below zero? | Advanced | |
| 38 | Recognise the size of an alternate angle? | Advanced | |
| 39 | Use order of operation for mixed fractions? | Advanced | |
| 40 | Apply fractions of fractions to solve a problem? | Advanced | |
| 41 | Write a number in expanded notation? | Standard | |
| 42 | Use a factor tree to find missing numbers? | Standard | |
| 43 | Compare even and odd numbers between two numerals? | Intermediate | |
| 44 | Convert a percentage to a decimal? | Intermediate | |
| 45 | Insert greater than, less than or equals to make a statement true? | Intermediate | |
| 46 | Identify a group of leap years? | Advanced | |
| 47 | Identify the simplest equivalent fraction? | Advanced | |
| 48 | Find the number of combinations in a sequence? | Advanced | |
| | **TOTAL** | | |

# NUMERACY TEST 3

This is the third Numeracy Test. There are 48 questions.
You can use a calculator in this test for questions 9 to 48.

Allow around 65 minutes for this test.

Write the answer in the box or colour in the circle with the correct answer.
Colour in only one circle for each answer.

## Section 1: Non-calculator questions

**1.** Here are some shapes. They are arranged in a pattern.

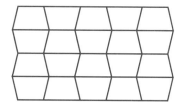

If you coloured in two-fifths of these shapes, how many would be coloured?

| 8 | 12 | 6 | 5 |
|---|----|----|---|
| ○ | ○ | ○ | ○ |

**2.** Here is a pattern of some blocks.

Which one of the four patterns below is the same as the one above? Is it A, B, C or D?

A

B

C

D

| A | B | C | D |
|---|---|---|---|
| ○ | ○ | ○ | ○ |

**3.** Which is another way of writing $4^3$?

- ○ $4 \times 3$
- ○ $4 \times 4 \times 4 \times 4$
- ○ $4 \times 4 \times 4$
- ○ $4 + 4 + 4$

**4.** Here is the time on a digital clock. It shows 24-hour time.

16:45

Which one of these is the same time?

| 6:45 pm | 4:45 am | 4:45 pm | 6:45 am |
|---------|---------|---------|---------|
| ○ | ○ | ○ | ○ |

Did you colour in one of the circles?

**5.** Here is part of a receipt from a shop. Four items were bought.

linkfrans
AS CHEAP AS IT GETS

WESTGARDEN
SHOP 458
ABN 93 496 2486
TAX INVOICE

| 1 FRESH BREAD | $3.19 |
| 1 SMALL MILK | $1.99 |
| 0.4 kg HAM | $2.82 |
| 0.6 kg CHEESE | $5.29 |
| 4 Items(s) SUB-TOTAL | $13.29 |
| Cash tendered | $20.00 |
| ROUND CASH | $13.30 |
| Change | $6.70 |

Tuesday 3–2–2020  #2285 L0004 Lina

THANK YOU
FOR SHOPPING AT LINKFRANS

Here are four sums. They round off the prices and show a quick way to guess or estimate the price of the four foods. Which is the best way?

○ $4 + $2 + $3 + $6

○ $3 + $1 + $2 + $5

○ $3 + $2 + $3 + $5

○ $3 + $1 + $3 + $5

**6.** This chart shows the rainfall for a suburb over more than a hundred years.

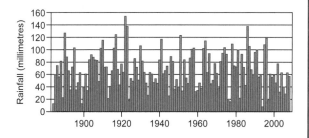

Which answer is correct?

○ The rainfall was more often above 120 mm than below 40 mm.

○ The rainfall was more often less than 40 mm than above 100 mm.

○ The rainfall was more often above 100 mm than above 60 mm.

○ The rainfall was more often less than 20 mm than above 100 mm.

**7.** A coin can land on its head or tail.

Someone tosses three coins. What is the chance they will all land on heads (heads for coin 1, heads for coin 2 and heads for coin 3)?

○ 3 out of 8 chances

○ 3 out of 6 chances

○ 1 out of 8 chances

○ 1 out of 6 chances

**8.** Have we done a flip horizontally, a slide or a flip vertically with this coloured shape?

○ FLIP HORIZONTAL

○ SLIDE

○ FLIP VERTICAL

---

**This is the end of the part where you are not allowed to use a calculator.**

**It would be a good idea to check your answers to the questions in this section before moving on to the other questions.**

## Section 2: Calculator Allowed questions

**9.** There is a pattern in these numbers. Write the number that is missing.

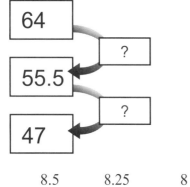

   8.75     8.5     8.25     8

   ○       ○       ○       ○

**10.** In one day around 350 000 people are born and about 155 000 people die. How many people are added to the world's population?

  195 000   185 000   205 000   405 000

    ○        ○       ○       ○

**11.** Here is a chart that shows the numbers of marriages and divorces in three different countries. (The figures are rounded.)

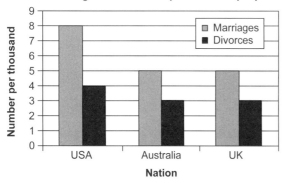

The chart was drawn from the table below but there is a number missing in the table. Look at the chart and find the number that is missing.

|            | USA | Australia | UK |
|------------|-----|-----------|----|
| Marriages  | 8   | 5         | 5  |
| Divorces   | ?   | 3         | 3  |

What figure should go in place of the question mark in the table?

   3      4      5      6

   ○      ○      ○      ○

**12.** Here is some wood and behind it is a tape measure which starts at the left-hand edge of the block.

About how long is this piece of wood?

  3.5 m    4 m    2.5 m    3 m

   ○      ○      ○      ○

**13** Which one of these is the same as

$$11 \times 7?$$

- ○ $10 + 1 \times 7$
- ○ $11 \times 3 + 4$
- ○ $10 \times 7 + 4 + 3$
- ○ $10 \times 7 + 11$

**14.** A number is multiplied by three and then six is subtracted. The answer is 18.

What is the number?
Write your answer in the rectangle.

**15.** The perimeter of this figure is 190 cm. What is the length of the side with the question mark?

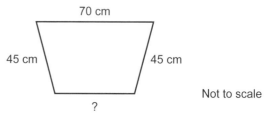

Not to scale

_____ cm

# NUMERACY TEST 3

**16.** A carton is 25 cm long, 20 cm wide and 10 cm deep. What is its capacity in cubic centimetres?

   50 cc      55 cc      500 cc    5000 cc

    ○         ○         ○         ○

> **It would be a good idea to check your answers to questions 9 to 16 before moving on to the other questions.**

**17.** At what number is the arrow pointing?

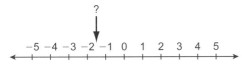

| | |
|---|---|
| ○ −2.0 | ○ −1.0 |
| ○ −1.25 | ○ −1.5 |
| ○ +1.5 | ○ +2.0 |
| ○ +1.0 | ○ +1.25 |

**18.** Complete this subtraction.

$$947 - 358$$

**Write your answer in the box.**

**19.** There is a number missing in this sum. Write your answer in the box.

$$\boxed{?} \times 5.1 = 31.926$$

**20.** The question mark shows a missing sign in this sum.

$$47.5 \boxed{?} 2.5 = 19$$

Which is the missing sign?

   +        −        ÷        ×

   ○        ○        ○        ○

**21.** There are signs missing in this sum. Use +, −, × or ÷ to fill the spaces and brackets if necessary. The spaces are shown with dots. Write your answers above the dots.

$$4 \ldots 20 \ldots 4 = 64$$

**22.** Add any five whole numbers in a row. Here are examples of five numbers in a row:

$$1 + 2 + 3 + 4 + 5 \text{ or } 2 + 3 + 4 + 5 + 6$$
$$\text{or } 20 + 21 + 22 + 23 + 24$$
$$\text{or even } 98 + 99 + 100 + 101 + 102.$$

Choose the best answer.

- ○ The average is sometimes the middle number.
- ○ The average is always the middle number.
- ○ The average is never the middle number.

**23.** A parcel of paperback books weighs 3750 grams. Each paperback book weighs 150 grams. Which sum should we use to work out how many books are in the parcel?

- ○ $3750 \div 150$
- ○ $150 \div 3750$
- ○ $3750 - 150$
- ○ $3750 \times 150$

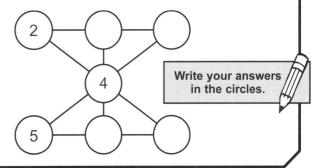

Did you colour in one of the circles?

**24.** In this puzzle only the numbers from 1 to 7 are used. Each row, column and diagonal where there is a line adds up to 12. Part of the puzzle has been completed for you.

Fill in the numbers 1, 3, 6 and 7 to complete the diagram. Remember that every line has to add up to 12.

**Write your answers in the circles.**

# NUMERACY TEST 3

**25.** A book is $33 but the shop will sell it for $30 to a customer.

What fraction does the customer save?

$\dfrac{1}{9}$     $\dfrac{1}{10}$     $\dfrac{1}{11}$     $\dfrac{1}{12}$

○       ○       ○       ○

**26.** Here is a map. It shows three suburbs in a town. The map is divided into sections. Each section or square is 1 km.

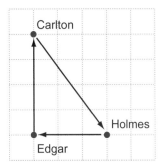

How far is it from Edgar to Carlton, then from Carlton to Holmes and Holmes to Edgar on this map? (Hint: First find Carlton to Holmes; note that this is a right-angled triangle.)

14 km   12 km   15 km   16 km   19 km

○     ○     ○     ○     ○

**27.** In a group of teenagers there are 18 girls and 9 boys.

What is the fraction of teenagers in the group who are boys?

$\dfrac{18}{9}$     $\dfrac{1}{2}$     $\dfrac{18}{27}$     $\dfrac{1}{3}$

○       ○       ○       ○

**28.** An old clock is always 20 minutes fast. Here is the time shown by the clock in the afternoon:

Which is the correct digital time in the afternoon when the clock shows the above time?

3:20     2:40     2:20     3:40

○       ○       ○       ○

**29.** The train left Central Station at 10:15 am and arrived at Woy Woy at 11:37 am. How long did that trip take?

○ 1 hr 22 min     ○ 1 hr 12 min

○ 11 hr 37 min     ○ 1 hr 30 min

**30.** The average acceleration is measured in metres per second per second ($m/s^2$). It is the change in velocity divided by the time interval. Velocity is like speed. Here is an example of how it is calculated.

$$\text{Acceleration} = \frac{\text{Change of velocity}}{\text{Time}}$$

For example, if a car moves from stop to 7 m/s in 5 seconds, its average acceleration is:

$$\text{Acceleration} = \frac{\text{Change of velocity}}{\text{Time}}$$
$$= \frac{7 - 0}{5}$$
$$= 1.4 \text{ m/s}^2$$

If a car accelerates from 6 m/s to 12 m/s in 2 seconds, what is the car's average acceleration?

3 $m/s^2$    6 $m/s^2$    9 $m/s^2$    12 $m/s^2$

○       ○       ○       ○

**31.** If $\frac{3}{4}$ of a number is 360, what is the number?

| 600 | 240 | 480 | 270 |
| ○ | ○ | ○ | ○ |

**32.** This pattern is made up of octagon shapes. The chart shows how many lines are needed to draw 1, 2, 3 and 4 shapes. It does not show 7 shapes.

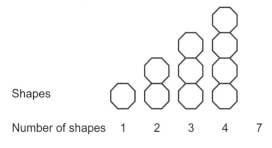

Shapes

| Number of shapes | 1 | 2 | 3 | 4 | 7 |
| Number of lines | 8 | 15 | 22 | 29 | ? |

How many lines would be needed to draw the pattern for seven octagon shapes?

| 51 | 49 | 48 | 50 |
| ○ | ○ | ○ | ○ |

**It would be a good idea to check your answers to questions 17 to 32 before moving on.**

**33.**

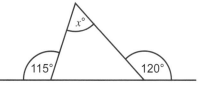

What is the value of the angle ($x°$) in the triangle?

| 65° | 60° | 45° | 55° |
| ○ | ○ | ○ | ○ |

**34.** Here are some details of the size and shape of a 50-cent coin.

| Standard weight | Length of shortest diameter or of diameter | Thickness |
|---|---|---|
| 15.5 grams | 31.6 mm | 2.8 mm |

How much would 31 kg of 50 cent coins be worth?

| $1000 | $100 | $10,000 | $750 |
| ○ | ○ | ○ | ○ |

**35.** In how many ways can you express 50 as the sum of two prime numbers? Write your answer in the space provided.

**Write your answer in the box.**

**36.** Which fraction is between $\frac{2}{3}$ and $\frac{5}{6}$?

| $\frac{3}{4}$ | $\frac{7}{12}$ | $\frac{39}{60}$ | $\frac{41}{48}$ |
| ○ | ○ | ○ | ○ |

**37.** A person spends $\frac{2}{3}$ of the time awake. They spend $\frac{3}{8}$ of the time that they are awake at their job. How many hours do they work in a day?

| 5 hrs | 6 hrs | 7 hrs | 8 hrs |
| ○ | ○ | ○ | ○ |

Did you colour in one of the circles?

**38.** Find the value of the unknown angle.

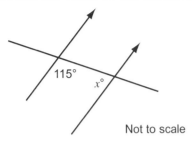

115°

x°

Not to scale

65°  60°  45°  55°

○  ○  ○  ○

**39.** How many three-digit numbers are divisible evenly by 33?

30  33  27  36

○  ○  ○  ○

**40.** In how many ways can four people be chosen from a group of 10 and arranged in a line?

400  2400  2700  5040

○  ○  ○  ○

**41.** How much is shown in coins?

$3.65  $3.85  $3.95  $3.75

○  ○  ○  ○

**42** Some books were sold for $42. A goods and services tax is 10%. How much is paid after tax?

$44.20  $46.20  $48.20  $44.40

○  ○  ○  ○

**43.** What is the perimeter of this shape? Note that one length is not shown.

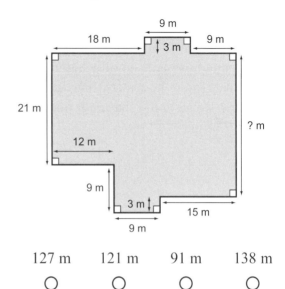

127 m  121 m  91 m  138 m

○  ○  ○  ○

**44.** Here are the ingredients in a recipe. It is a recipe for 12 thick slices of basic white bread.

*Ingredients*

- Melted butter, for greasing and brushing
- 500 g plain flour
- 2 sachets dried yeast
- 1 teaspoon salt
- 375 mL lukewarm water

How much water is needed if you want to make 60 thick slices of bread?

○ 1.785 litres　　l　1.587 litres

○ 1.875 litres　　l　1.758 litres

**45.** A pole that is 20 metres high casts a shadow of 15 metres. Another pole casts a shadow of 7.5 metres.

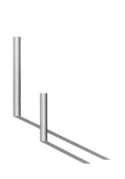

How tall is the pole with a shadow of 7.5 metres?

2.5 m    5 m    7.5 m    10 m    12.5 m

◯     ◯     ◯     ◯     ◯

**46.** A school library had 20 books for each student in the school. There were 3600 books in that library. How many students were in that school?

60      120      180      240

◯      ◯      ◯      ◯

**47.** In Tasmania people were asked this question: 'If a State election were held tomorrow, which political party would you be likely to vote for?'

Here are their answers:

| FEBRUARY 2009 | |
|---|---|
| **Political party** | **Voting intentions** |
| Labor | 340 |
| Liberal | 290 |
| Greens | 150 |
| Independent | ? |
| Undecided | 200 |
| TOTAL | 1000 |

Adapted from EMRS State Voting Poll Intentions, February 2009

What percentage of voters is Independent?

[      ] %

**Write your answer in the box.**

**48.**

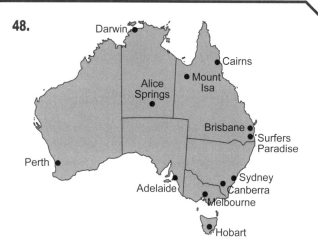

The distance from Surfers Paradise to Sydney is around 950 km.

The distance from Canberra to Melbourne is around 650 km.

The distance from Surfers Paradise to Melbourne is 1890 km.

What is the distance from Sydney to Canberra?

[      ] km

**Write your answer in the box.**

# END OF TEST

Well done! You have completed the third Numeracy Test. We tried to change the questions and some were a little harder. Don't worry if you didn't finish it in time as we added some new types of questions.

How did you go with these test questions? Check to see where you did well and where you had problems. Try to revise the questions that were hard for you.

Use the diagnostic chart on pages 54–55 to see which level of ability you reached. This is only an estimate. Don't be surprised if you answered some difficult questions correctly or even missed some easier questions.

There is now one last practice test, which contains 48 questions.

## Instructions

As you check the answer for each question, mark it as correct (✓) or incorrect (✗). Mark any questions that you omitted or left out as incorrect (✗) for the moment.

Then look at how many you answered correctly in each level. You will be able to see what level you are at by finding the point where you started having consistent difficulty with questions at a certain level. For example, if you answer most questions correctly up to the Intermediate level and then get most questions wrong from then onwards, it is likely your ability is at an Intermediate level. You can ask your parents or your teacher to help you do this if it isn't clear to you.

**Am I able to ...**

| | SKILL | ESTIMATED LEVEL | ✓ or ✗ |
|---|---|---|---|
| 1 | Find the fraction of a shape? | Standard | |
| 2 | Recognise a model viewed from a different perspective? | Standard | |
| 3 | Recognise the meaning of a number cubed? | Standard | |
| 4 | Convert from 24-hour time to analog time? | Standard | |
| 5 | Round off amounts to estimate a total? | Standard | |
| 6 | Read and compare data from a distribution? | Standard | |
| 7 | Use chance to describe the outcome in a simple experiment? | Standard | |
| 8 | Recognise the property of a shape that has been flipped? | Standard | |
| 9 | Continue a number pattern involving counting by 8.5? | Standard | |
| 10 | Interpret data in a subtraction problem? | Standard | |
| 11 | Find a missing value in a table from a chart? | Standard | |
| 12 | Estimate the length from a ruler? | Standard | |
| 13 | Carry out the correct order of operations? | Standard | |
| 14 | Reverse arithmetical process to find a number? | Standard | |
| 15 | Determine the perimeter when one side is not listed? | Standard | |
| 16 | Calculate the volume of a carton? | Standard | |
| 17 | Locate a negative number on a number line? | Standard | |
| 18 | Solve a three-digit subtraction? | Standard | |
| 19 | Multiply decimals with numbers after the decimal point? | Intermediate | |
| 20 | Insert a missing sign or operation in a sum? | Intermediate | |
| 21 | Use problem-solving strategies to complete a number sentence? | Intermediate | |
| 22 | Find the pattern for the mean of consecutive numbers? | Intermediate | |
| 23 | Provide a calculation for finding the quantity in a collection? | Intermediate | |
| 24 | Complete vertical, horizontal and diagonal additions of numbers? | Intermediate | |
| 25 | Calculate a saving after a discount? | Intermediate | |
| 26 | Find the perimeter of a right-angled triangle with an unknown hypotenuse? | Intermediate | |
| 27 | Find the fraction of a group? | Intermediate | |

| | SKILL | ESTIMATED LEVEL | ✓ or ✗ |
|---|---|---|---|
| 28 | Adjust an analogue time to a digital time? | Intermediate | |
| 29 | Find the time taken to travel? | Advanced | |
| 30 | Substitute values in a formula? | Advanced | |
| 31 | Find a whole number given the fraction? | Advanced | |
| 32 | Calculate the numbers of sides in a shape using a formula? | Advanced | |
| 33 | Find an angle in a triangle given two external angles? | Advanced | |
| 34 | Solve a problem with multiple steps? | Advanced | |
| 35 | Show that an even number is the sum of two prime numbers? | Advanced | |
| 36 | Locate an intermediate fraction? | Advanced | |
| 37 | Find a fraction of a fraction in a problem? | Advanced | |
| 38 | Find a co-interior angle on a parallel line? | Advanced | |
| 39 | Find the number of three digit numbers in a range? | Advanced | |
| 40 | Find the number of ways each position may be filled from a group? | Advanced | |
| 41 | Recognise the value of some coins? | Standard | |
| 42 | Calculate a percentage and the final price? | Standard | |
| 43 | Calculate the perimeter of a diagram? | Intermediate | |
| 44 | Increase the ratio to find the quantity required? | Intermediate | |
| 45 | Solve a problem involving a relation between two quantities? | Intermediate | |
| 46 | Determine the number of items from the ratio of a quantity? | Advanced | |
| 47 | Insert a value in a two-way table and calculate a percentage? | Advanced | |
| 48 | Calculate a total distance from the components? | Advanced | |
| | **TOTAL** | | |

This is the fourth Numeracy Test. There are 48 questions.

You can use a calculator in this test for questions 9 to 48.

Allow around 65 minutes for this test.

Write the answer in the box or colour in the circle with the correct answer.
Colour in only one circle for each answer.

## Section 1: Non-calculator questions

**1.** Which of these events is most likely if I throw a dice?

- ○ It would land with one dot on top.
- ○ It would land with one or two dots on top.
- ○ It would land with four dots on top.
- ○ It would land with one, two or four dots on top.

**2.** What is the proper fraction for $\frac{7}{2}$?

$3$     $3\frac{1}{4}$     $3\frac{1}{2}$     $3\frac{1}{4}$

○      ○      ○      ○

**3.** Which expression is true?

- ○ $43579 > 24634$
- ○ $43579 < 24634$
- ○ $43579 = 24634$
- ○ $24634 \neq 24634$

**4.**

242°

What sort of angle is this?

- ○ It is an obtuse angle.
- ○ It is an acute angle.
- ○ It is a reflex angle.
- ○ It is a right angle.

**5.** Here is a pattern of symbols.

☆, ☆☆, ☆☆☆, ☆☆☆☆☆, ☆☆☆☆☆☆☆☆, **?**

Which pattern comes next in the series?

- ○ ☆☆☆☆☆☆ ☆☆☆☆☆☆
- ○ ☆☆☆☆☆ ☆☆☆☆☆☆☆☆
- ○ ☆☆☆☆☆☆☆ ☆☆☆☆☆☆☆☆
- ○ ☆☆☆☆☆☆☆☆ ☆☆☆☆☆☆☆☆☆☆

**6.** Here are some blocks.

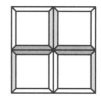

Which one of the four rotated patterns below is the same as the one shown? Is it A, B, C or D?

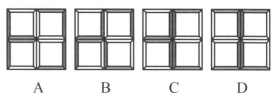

A      B      C      D

○      ○      ○      ○

Did you colour in one of the circles?

**7.** The volume of this cube is 216 cm³. What is the length of its sides?

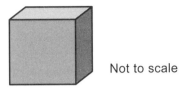

Not to scale

| 4 cm | 6 cm | 8 cm | 12 cm |
|:---:|:---:|:---:|:---:|
| ○ | ○ | ○ | ○ |

**8.** What number is in place of the question mark in this triangle of numbers?

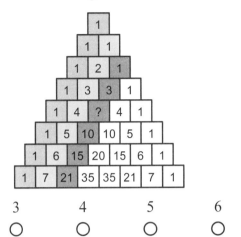

| 3 | 4 | 5 | 6 |
|:---:|:---:|:---:|:---:|
| ○ | ○ | ○ | ○ |

---

**This is the end of the part where you are not allowed to use a calculator.**

**It would be a good idea to check your answers to the questions in this section before moving on to the other questions.**

## Section 2: Calculator Allowed questions

**9.** What percentage of this figure is coloured?

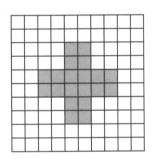

| 15% | 20% | 25% | 30% |
|:---:|:---:|:---:|:---:|
| ○ | ○ | ○ | ○ |

**10.** Here is a sum that is made up of shapes. Each shape is a number. Only one of the numbers is given.

$$\triangle = 7$$
$$\blacksquare - \triangle = \triangle \times \triangle$$

Which number does the ■ equal?

| 49 | 56 | 65 | 63 |
|:---:|:---:|:---:|:---:|
| ○ | ○ | ○ | ○ |

**11.** Many patients recovering from surgery died of infections before British surgeon Joseph Lister used antiseptics in 1865.

He was born in 1827 and died in 1912. How old was he when he died?

Source: Art Today

| 83 | 85 | 87 | 89 |
|:---:|:---:|:---:|:---:|
| ○ | ○ | ○ | ○ |

**12.** The distance between Sydney and Los Angeles in California is about 12 000 km. About how long would an A380 travelling at 900 km per hour take to fly from Sydney to California?

- ○ 13.0 hours
- ○ 13.1 hours
- ○ 13.3 hours
- ○ 13.5 hours

**13.** On this indicator, how far is it from Maroubra to the City?

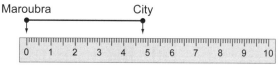

Scale : 1 cm = 2 km

| 9.6 km | 10.8 km | 4.8 km | 9.0 km |
| :-: | :-: | :-: | :-: |
| ◯ | ◯ | ◯ | ◯ |

**14.** The toner for a printer costs $65.50.

If you pay for the toner with a $100 bill, how much change would you receive?

| $33.50 | $35.50 | $35.00 | $34.50 |
| :-: | :-: | :-: | :-: |
| ◯ | ◯ | ◯ | ◯ |

**15.** A boy cut a rope that was 14.5 m long into 2.9 m lengths. How many lengths did he cut?

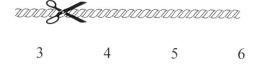

| 3 | 4 | 5 | 6 |
| :-: | :-: | :-: | :-: |
| ◯ | ◯ | ◯ | ◯ |

**16.** Which two numbers should be subtracted to give an answer that can be rounded up to 75?

- ◯ 99 − 29
- ◯ 103 − 29
- ◯ 182 − 103
- ◯ 107 − 29

**17.** $35 - 7 \times 3 =$ ⬚

> **Write your answer in this box.**

**18.** This is a chart that shows how much water a household used per day.

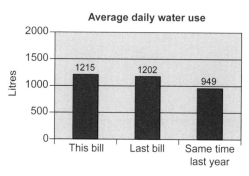

By how much has their water use changed in this bill from the same time last year?

- ◯ 13 litres
- ◯ 266 litres
- ◯ 253 litres
- ◯ 366 litres

**19.** Find the area of this figure.

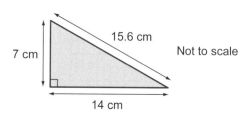

Not to scale

| 49 cm² | 36.6 cm² | 98 cm² | 196 cm² |
| :-: | :-: | :-: | :-: |
| ◯ | ◯ | ◯ | ◯ |

**20.** Complete this number sentence.

$$46.6 + 208.4 = \boxed{\phantom{xx}} + 30.3$$

> **Write your answer in the box.**

---

**It would be a good idea to check your answers to questions 9 to 16 before moving on to the other questions.**

**21.** What is the size of angle PQR?

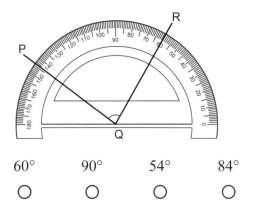

60°　　90°　　54°　　84°

○　　○　　○　　○

**22.** The path from the corner of Holmes Street and Anzac Parade to Edgar Street is shown by the dotted line. Follow the arrow.

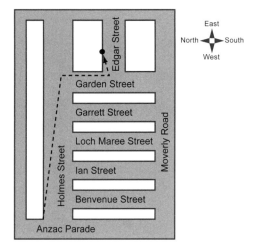

In what direction is someone travelling from the beginning at Anzac Parade to the finish at Edgar Street?

South　South-east　East　West

○　　○　　○　　○

**23.** Some tiles will be used to make a pattern. Each tile is 0.2 m diagonally. The distance to be tiled is 3.6 m.

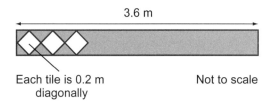

3.6 m

Each tile is 0.2 m diagonally　　Not to scale

How do we work out how many white tiles will be needed to fill the pattern?

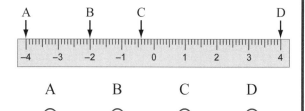

○ 3.6 ÷ 2　　○ 3.6 × 2

○ 3.6 ÷ 0.2　　○ 3.6 × 0.2

**24.** Which of the letters below is pointing to −0.4?

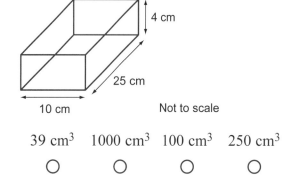

A　　B　　C　　D

○　　○　　○　　○

**25.** This is a rectangular prism. What is the volume of this figure?

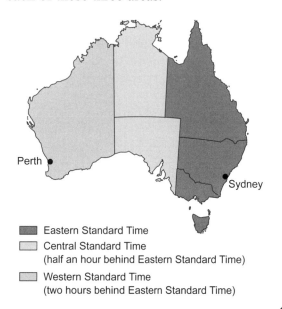

4 cm
25 cm
10 cm　　Not to scale

39 cm³　1000 cm³　100 cm³　250 cm³

○　　○　　○　　○

**26.** This map shows the three different time zones in Australia. The time is different in each of these three areas.

Perth

Sydney

■ Eastern Standard Time
□ Central Standard Time (half an hour behind Eastern Standard Time)
□ Western Standard Time (two hours behind Eastern Standard Time)

If it is 4:00 pm in Perth (Western Standard Time), what would be the time in Adelaide (Central Standard Time)? (Hint: Find Eastern Standard Time first.)

2:00 pm    5:30 pm    6:00 pm    2:30 pm

◯     ◯     ◯     ◯

**27.** Here is a shape. It contains squares. Some of the squares are all white, some are all grey, and some are half grey and half white.

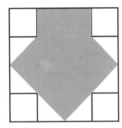

What proportion of the squares is half grey and half white?

$\frac{6}{8}$      $\frac{16}{6}$      $\frac{3}{8}$      $\frac{10}{16}$

◯     ◯     ◯     ◯

**28.** The price of a game after a 25% discount was $207. What was the price before the discount?

$277     $286     $267     $276

◯     ◯     ◯     ◯

**29.** How many four-digit numbers can you make using the numerals 1, 2, 3 and 4? Each numeral can only be used once in each number.

20     24     16     36

◯     ◯     ◯     ◯

Did you colour in one of the circles?

**30.** There are three soccer fields at my school. There is a 10-metre distance between each field. The perimeter of the three fields is 730 metres.

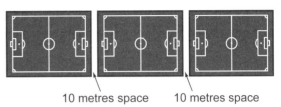

10 metres space     10 metres space

If the length of each soccer field at my school is 100 metres, what is its width?

◯   40 metres

◯   45 metres

◯   50 metres

◯   55 metres

**31.** Here is a series of numbers.

What would be the next number?

40     41     42     43

◯     ◯     ◯     ◯

**32.** You toss three 50-cent coins at once. What are the chances of throwing two tails and one head (in any order)?

1 in 8     1 in 4     1 in 6     3 in 8

◯     ◯     ◯     ◯

**It would be a good idea to check your answers to questions 17 to 32 before moving on.**

**33.** To relieve famine in a country, 80 000 tonnes of food were sent.

If 15% of the food was spoilt and then 10% of what was left was damaged, how much food was left for famine relief?

○ 61 200 tonnes

○ 62 100 tonnes

○ 68 000 tonnes

○ 60 120 tonnes

**34.** Here is a credit account for a household. The amount for accommodation is not shown.

### SIVA EXPRESS CARD

**MONTHLY ACCOUNT**

| | |
|---|---|
| Hardware | $ 29.50 |
| Books | $ 50.00 |
| Air travel | $ 211.00 |
| Accommodation | ? |
| Total amount due | $ 534.67 |

How much is the accommodation cost?

$ [ ]    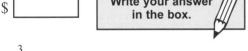 **Write your answer in the box.**

**35.** If $\frac{3}{4}$ of half a number is 960, what is the number?

| 2880 | 1280 | 1920 | 2560 |
|---|---|---|---|
| ○ | ○ | ○ | ○ |

**36.** A coach wants to set a rope around the edge of a field. He uses around 332.84 metres of rope.

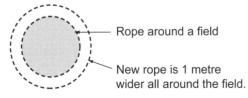

Rope around a field

New rope is 1 metre wider all around the field.

The manager of the team now says it should be 1 metre wider all round the field.

About how much more rope will be needed? (Hint: Use pi or $\pi = 3.14$.)

○ about 6.28 metres

○ about 60.28 metres

○ about 20.28 metres

○ about 16.28 metres

**37.** 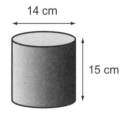 (?) × (?) + 9 = 45

What number goes in the symbol (?) with the question mark?

| −4 | −5 | −6 | −7 |
|---|---|---|---|
| ○ | ○ | ○ | ○ |

**38.** What is the volume of this cylinder?

14 cm

15 cm

| 660 cm³ | 210 cm³ | 735 cm³ | 2310 cm³ |
|---|---|---|---|
| ○ | ○ | ○ | ○ |

**39.** What is the total number of degrees in the interior angles of any pentagon?

| 180° | 360° | 540° | 720° |
|---|---|---|---|
| ○ | ○ | ○ | ○ |

**40.** Imagine a box with an ant at one corner. The ant wants to travel to the opposite corner by the most direct path. It must travel across the top of the box at some stage. The top of the box is the light area. It cannot travel along the ground or under the box. (Hint: It does not have to travel along an edge.)

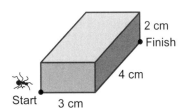

What is the shortest possible path?

   7.8 cm     6.5 cm     4.9 cm     3.8 cm

     ◯         ◯         ◯         ◯

**41.** 6.84,  6.42,  6.00,  5.58,  5.16, ...

What rule is followed in this number pattern?

- ◯ The numbers increase by 0.46.
- ◯ The numbers decrease by 0.42.
- ◯ The numbers decrease by 0.44.
- ◯ The numbers decrease by 0.48.

**42.** Here is a sum with some numbers missing.

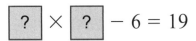

What number should be in place of the question mark?

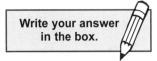

**43.** Here is an electricity bill. It shows how much energy was used and the cost.

| Meter | Energy used (kilowatt hour) | Rate | Cost |
|---|---|---|---|
| Off-peak | 240 | 5 cents | $12.00 |
| Shoulder energy | 800 | 10 cents | $80.00 |
| Peak energy | ? | 30 cents | |
| TOTAL | | | $242.00 |

How much peak energy was used? This belongs where the question mark is in the table. (Hint: First find the cost of peak energy used.)

   400      500      600      700

   ◯        ◯        ◯        ◯

**44.** What is 8.8 divided by 0.2?

   4.4        44        5.4        54

   ◯        ◯        ◯        ◯

**45.** The temperature is measured at different points on Mt Everest. The temperature at Summit 1 is 17° colder than at the base. The temperature at Summit 2 is 3° colder than at Summit 1.

In April the temperature was −12 °C at the base camp. What was the temperature at Summit 2?

  −29 °C    −30 °C    −31 °C    −32 °C

   ◯        ◯        ◯        ◯

**46.** There are two cars that are 375 kilometres apart. They are heading towards each other on the same road. The first car is travelling at 30 kilometres per hour; the second car is travelling at 45 kilometres per hour.

After how long will they meet?

| 5 hours | 6 hours | 7 hours | 8 hours |
|---------|---------|---------|---------|
| ○ | ○ | ○ | ○ |

**47.** We can add the numbers in order, like this:

$1 + 2 = 3$
$1 + 2 + 3 = 6$
$1 + 2 + 3 + 4 = 10$
$1 + 2 + 3 + 4 + 5 = 15$, and so on.

What is the sum of all the numbers from 1 to 100? (Hint: You need to work out a way of doing this. Try to work out how to do this with the first few numbers up to 10.)

| 10 100 | 5050 | 100 100 | 9500 |
|--------|------|---------|------|
| ○ | ○ | ○ | ○ |

**48.** Complete the table below. Use the rule that $y = 4x^2 + 2x + 3$. Replace the $x$ in the equation with the value in the top line. Two sections have been done for you.

| $x$ | −3 | −2 | 0 | +2 | +3 |
|-----|----|----|----|----|----|
| $y$ | 33 | | | | 45 |

# END OF TEST

Well done! You have completed the final Numeracy Test. It means you have answered or attempted over 190 Numeracy questions.

How did you go with these test questions? Check to see where you did well and where you had problems. Try to revise the questions that were hard for you.

Use the diagnostic chart on pages 64–65 to see which level of ability you reached. This is only an estimate. Don't be surprised if you answered some difficult questions correctly or even missed some easier questions.

This is the last Numeracy Test. We will start to look at literacy tasks in the sections that follow. Now take a well-earned rest.

## Instructions

As you check the answer for each question, mark it as correct (✓) or incorrect (✗). Mark any questions that you omitted or left out as incorrect (✗) for the moment.

Then look at how many you answered correctly in each level. You will be able to see what level you are at by finding the point where you started having consistent difficulty with questions at a certain level. For example, if you answer most questions correctly up to the Intermediate level and then get most questions wrong from then onwards, it is likely your ability is at an Intermediate level. You can ask your parents or your teacher to help you do this if it isn't clear to you.

**Am I able to ...**

|  | SKILL | ESTIMATED LEVEL | ✓ or ✗ |
|---|---|---|---|
| 1 | Determine the likelihood of an event? | Standard | |
| 2 | Convert an improper fraction? | Standard | |
| 3 | Choose a number that is greater than another? | Standard | |
| 4 | Identify a reflex angle? | Standard | |
| 5 | Complete the pattern in a series? | Standard | |
| 6 | Match a rotated shape with an original pattern? | Standard | |
| 7 | Find the length of one side when the volume of a cube is known? | Standard | |
| 8 | Find the pattern in a triangle of numbers? | Standard | |
| 9 | Find the percentage of a grid that is coloured? | Standard | |
| 10 | Substitute values into a sum? | Standard | |
| 11 | Calculate difference in years between two dates? | Standard | |
| 12 | Find time taken to travel a distance? | Standard | |
| 13 | Convert a length in centimetres to a scale distance in kilometres? | Standard | |
| 14 | Subtract an amount to find the change? | Standard | |
| 15 | Divide a decimal length into decimal sections? | Standard | |
| 16 | Subtract two numbers and round the result? | Standard | |
| 17 | Complete multiplication before subtraction? | Standard | |
| 18 | Subtract quantities from a chart? | Standard | |
| 19 | Find the area of a triangle? | Intermediate | |
| 20 | Complete a number sentence involving decimals? | Intermediate | |
| 21 | Determine the angle? | Intermediate | |
| 22 | Indicate the direction of travel? | Intermediate | |
| 23 | Know how to find the number of items in a quantity? | Intermediate | |
| 24 | Locate a point on the number line? | Intermediate | |
| 25 | Calculate the volume of a rectangular prism? | Intermediate | |
| 26 | Calculate an intermediate time difference? | Intermediate | |
| 27 | Find the fraction of a figure that is shaded? | Intermediate | |
| 28 | Restore an original price after discount? | Intermediate | |
| 29 | Form numbers from a combination of four digits? | Advanced | |

| | SKILL | ESTIMATED LEVEL | ✓ or ✗ |
|---|---|---|---|
| 30 | Find the width when the perimeter is known? | Advanced | |
| 31 | Find the pattern in a series of numbers? | Advanced | |
| 32 | Calculate the probability of occurrence? | Advanced | |
| 33 | Solve a percentage problem involving multiple reductions? | Advanced | |
| 34 | Calculate a household account? | Advanced | |
| 35 | Find a number from a fraction? | Advanced | |
| 36 | Calculate the circumference of a circle enlarged by one metre? | Advanced | |
| 37 | Solve an incomplete problem involving multiplication? | Advanced | |
| 38 | Find the volume of a cylinder? | Advanced | |
| 39 | Determine the sum of the angles in a pentagon? | Advanced | |
| 40 | Visualise a three-dimensional path as a right-angled triangle? | Advanced | |
| 41 | Find the rule in a number pattern? | Standard | |
| 42 | Complete the missing numbers in a sum? | Standard | |
| 43 | Calculate the missing values in a table? | Intermediate | |
| 44 | Divide a decimal number by a decimal? | Advanced | |
| 45 | Calculate two differences involving negative numbers? | Advanced | |
| 46 | Compute two travelling times to determine the point of meeting? | Advanced | |
| 47 | Determine the formula for the sum of a series of numbers? | Advanced | |
| 48 | Substitute the value for $x$ in an equation? | Advanced | |
| | TOTAL | | |

## An important note about the NAPLAN Online tests

The NAPLAN Online Reading test will be divided into different sections. Students will only have one opportunity to check their answers at the end of each section before proceeding to the next one. This means that after students have completed a section and moved onto the next they will not be able to check their work again. We have included reminders for students to check their work at specific points in the practice tests from now on so they become familiar with this process.

# READING TEST 1

This is the first Reading Test. There are 50 questions.

Allow around 65 minutes for this test. Take a short break if necessary.

In this test you will need to read a text. Then read each question and colour in the circle with the correct answer.

Read *Welcome to the Barossa* and answer questions 1 to 6.

## Welcome to the Barossa

The Barossa Valley is a well-known wine region in Australia. It was settled more than 160 years ago by farmers who practised a European tradition of  wine growing. The original settlers were migrants from Prussia, in modern Germany, and parts of Poland. They started with small vineyards. They first settled in the town called Lyndoch around 1840 and then in Bethany in 1842.

The Barossa's main wine varieties include Shiraz, Grenache, Semillon and Riesling. There are many cellar doors where visitors can taste the wine or enjoy a meal.

The Barossa Valley is around 30 kilometres long and has become a major tourist attraction for visitors to South Australia. It is about 75 kilometres north from Adelaide and takes about an hour and fifteen minutes by car. There are picturesque country towns and villages along the way. The traveller will see many historic churches and interesting stone buildings that form part of this beautiful scene.

1. In which state of Australia is the Barossa Valley?
   ○ South Australia
   ○ New Zealand
   ○ Victoria
   ○ Western Australia

2. Where would you find Prussia?
   ○ in modern-day Holland
   ○ in modern-day South Australia
   ○ in modern-day Germany
   ○ in modern-day Barossa

3. What does this text mainly describe?
   ○ It describes a tourist destination.
   ○ It outlines the history of a region.
   ○ It describes the geography of the Barossa.
   ○ It provides directions for travelling to a region.

4. Which one of the following is described as a wine variety?
   ○ Lyndoch          ○ Bethany
   ○ Shiraz           ○ Barossa

5. From this description, what type of industry would you expect to see in the Barossa Valley?
   ○ fishing industry
   ○ tourist industry
   ○ manufacturing industry
   ○ finance industry

**6.** In *Welcome to the Barossa*, a cellar door is a

○ door to a storeroom in a vineyard.

○ strong wooden door for a vineyard.

○ place in a vineyard for tasting and buying wines.

○ basement in a vineyard.

**Read *Save the environment* and answer questions 7 to 13.**

## Save the environment

Here are some tips for saving energy and at the same time saving our planet. It is all part of being 'green'. We can all take an active part in fighting climate change. You will not only save energy, you will also save money, help others and ensure a cleaner environment.

### Save electricity

Start by switching off any lights when you leave a room at work or at home. It is useless to have empty rooms with lights on for many hours. In Germany even the escalators will stop when there is no one using them. The escalator can sense when you first step onto it.

Whether you live in an apartment or in a house you can save energy by using a clothesline rather than a drier.

Also check your refrigerator because it uses a great deal of electricity keeping food fresh. Here is a neat trick. If the seal on your refrigerator door at home is not tight, the refrigerator will be working extra hard trying to keep things cool. Just take a piece of paper and see if you can insert it under the door seal. If you can slide it in, it means that the door seal probably needs examining and maybe replacing.

### Ride to school or work

Much of our energy use each day is travelling to and from school or work. It is better for our health to walk but this is not always possible if the distance from home to school or work is considerable. We can use public transport more often and think about cycling. This is increasing in popularity. Too many people use cars unnecessarily.

### Buy and use only what you need

In Australia some families throw away many items, from food to clothing and household appliances. Often we buy much more than we will ever need. This is wasteful. At the same time it is so sad that some people are starving while many others throw away food. Maybe a good way to start is by having a shopping list and buying only what is on the list. Otherwise you can easily be tempted to buy much more than is needed for your daily life.

Also, there are two other things you can do. First, why not list any items you no longer need and want to give away on the web? There are websites for people who want to give away items free to others. This way everyone benefits. To save the planet you need to conserve. Second, be prepared to restore and repair things rather than just throw them away.

There are many small ways in which we can all help to make this a greener planet and slow down the effects of climate change. It starts with each one of us.

**7.** According to the text, how can we fight climate change?

- ○ by helping others
- ○ through conservation
- ○ by saving money

**8.** In the first paragraph it says 'You will not only save energy, you will also save money'. Who is the 'You' in this sentence?

- ○ someone who saves money
- ○ someone who saves energy
- ○ someone who is reading the text
- ○ everyone in the whole world

**9.** What is the main idea in this text?

- ○ to save energy and to save money
- ○ to save energy and to save lives
- ○ to save energy and to save the environment
- ○ to save energy and to save time

**10.** What is the aim of the author?

- ○ to convince the reader to consume fewer resources
- ○ to convince the reader to make savings
- ○ to convince the reader to make big changes in lifestyle
- ○ to convince the reader to help others

**11.** How many different ways of saving electricity are listed?

| 3 | 4 | 5 | 6 |
|---|---|---|---|
| ○ | ○ | ○ | ○ |

**12.** What does the author recommend to reduce the use of energy for transport?

- ○ using energy efficient escalators
- ○ a ban on cars
- ○ using energy-efficient cars
- ○ using more public transport

**13.** What are the three main methods that the author outlines for reducing overconsumption?

- ○ buying things you need, using a shopping list and listing items on the web
- ○ limiting purchases, sharing unwanted items and repairing items
- ○ using a shopping list, listing items on the web and giving them away free

Read *The heavenly bodies* and answer questions 14 to 20.

## The heavenly bodies

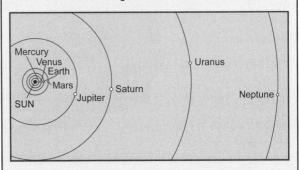

The heavenly bodies fall into two very distinct classes so far as their relation to our Earth is concerned; the one class, a very small one, comprises a sort of colony of which the Earth is a member. These bodies are called *planets*, or wanderers. There are eight of them, including the Earth, and they all circle round the sun. Their names, in the order of their distance from the sun, are Mercury, Venus, Earth, Mars, Jupiter, Saturn, Uranus, Neptune, and of these Mercury, the nearest to the sun, is rarely seen by the naked eye. Uranus is practically invisible, and Neptune quite so. These eight planets, together with the sun, constitute, as we have said, a sort of little colony; this colony is called the Solar System.

The second class of heavenly bodies are those which lie *outside* the solar system. Every one of those glittering points we see on a starlit night is at an immensely greater distance from us than is any member of the Solar System. Yet the members of this little colony of ours, judged by terrestrial standards, are at enormous distances from one another. If a shell were shot in a straight line from one side of Neptune's orbit to the other it would take five hundred years to complete its journey. Yet this distance, the greatest in the Solar System as now known (excepting the far swing of some of the comets), is insignificant compared to the distances of the stars. One of the nearest stars to the earth that we know of is Alpha Centauri, estimated to be some twenty-five million millions of miles away. Sirius, the brightest star in the firmament, is double this distance from the Earth.

From *The Outline of Science*, vol. 1, by J Arthur Thomson, GP Putnam's Sons and The Knickerbocker Press, 1922. Please note that when this was written in 1922, the planet Pluto had not been included.

**14.** What are the separate classes of heavenly bodies?

- ○ those in the solar system and the eight planets
- ○ planets and wanderers
- ○ those in the solar system and those outside
- ○ the colony and the stars

**15.** Which planet is rarely visible?

- ○ Mercury
- ○ Uranus
- ○ Neptune

Did you colour in one of the circles?

**16.** What is the main idea outlined in the second paragraph?

- ○ There are many heavenly bodies and these fall into two classes.
- ○ There are heavenly bodies outside the solar system and these are quite distant.
- ○ The distances within our solar system are quite small compared with the distances to other stars.
- ○ The distance from Earth to Neptune is vast and would take around 500 years at a great speed.

**17.** Which statement is correct?

- ○ The brightness of a star is related to its distance from Earth.
- ○ The brightness of a star is not related to its distance from Earth.

**It would be a good idea to check your answers to questions 1 to 17 before moving on to the other questions.**

**18.** The solar system is described as a colony. The description is a

- ○ simile.          ○ metaphor.
- ○ genre.          ○ allegory.

**19.** The nearest star system to the earth is

- ○ Alpha Centauri.
- ○ Southern Cross.
- ○ Sirius.
- ○ Neptune.

**20.** The *distinct classes* referred to is

- ○ inside or outside the solar system.
- ○ the planets or wanderers.
- ○ the close or far distance of a star.
- ○ the glittering points on a starlit night.

**Read *Pride and Prejudice* and answer questions 21 to 28.**

## Pride and Prejudice

From *Watercolour Illustrations* by CE Brock, 1907, www.mollands.net/etexts/prideandprejudice/pnpillus.html

It is a truth universally acknowledged, that a single man in possession of a good fortune, must be in want of a wife.

However little known the feelings or views of such a man may be on his first entering a neighbourhood, this truth is so well fixed in the minds of the surrounding families, that he is considered the rightful property of some one or other of their daughters.

'My dear Mr. Bennet,' said his lady to him one day, 'have you heard that Netherfield Park is let at last?'

Mr. Bennet replied that he had not.

'But it is,' returned she; 'for Mrs. Long has just been here, and she told me all about it.'

Mr. Bennet made no answer.

'Do you not want to know who has taken it?' cried his wife impatiently.

'*You* want to tell me, and I have no objection to hearing it.'

This was invitation enough.

'Why, my dear, you must know, Mrs. Long says that Netherfield is taken by a young man of large fortune from the north of England; that he came down on Monday in a chaise

and four to see the place, and was so much delighted with it, that he agreed with Mr. Morris immediately; that he is to take possession before Michaelmas, and some of his servants are to be in the house by the end of next week.'

'What is his name?'

'Bingley.'

'Is he married or single?'

'Oh! Single, my dear, to be sure! A single man of large fortune; four or five thousand a year. What a fine thing for our girls!'

From *Pride and Prejudice* by Jane Austen, 1813

**21.** What is Mrs Bennet thinking?
- ○ She thinks that Mr Bingley wants to marry one of her daughters.
- ○ She is pleased that Netherfield Park will be occupied by a rich person.
- ○ She is thinking that she will marry one of her daughters to Mr Bingley.

**22.** Why is the opening sentence important?
*It is a truth universally acknowledged, that a single man in possession of a good fortune, must be in want of a wife.*
- ○ This sentence describes what follows in the text.
- ○ This sentence outlines the story.
- ○ This sentence describes what is going to happen in the story.
- ○ This sentence reflects an idea that is part of the story.

**23.** What is Netherfield Park?
- ○ a playing field
- ○ a public area for enjoyment
- ○ a house
- ○ a park

**24.** Mr Bennet said to his wife, '*You* want to tell me ...' Why is the word *You* in italics? (Italic is a special font that is different from the normal font used in the text—it looks like sloping writing.)

- ○ Mrs Bennet is in a hurry to leave.
- ○ Mr Bennet wants to emphasise something.
- ○ Mrs Bennet is frustrated with his disinterest.
- ○ It is a special pronoun.

**25.** What is Michaelmas?

- ○ a person
- ○ a season of the year
- ○ another name for Netherfield
- ○ another name for Mr Morris

**26.** What is a *chaise and four*?

- ○ a type of car with a four-cylinder engine
- ○ a type of chair carried by four men
- ○ a type of carriage drawn by four horses
- ○ a search and hunt by four gentlemen

**27.** Which word could best be used to describe this text?

- ○ historical
- ○ romantic
- ○ suspense
- ○ comedy
- ○ factual

Did you colour in one of the circles?

**28.** Mrs Bennet is **most** concerned to

- ○ annoy Mr Bennet.
- ○ engage in gossip about the new resident of Netherfield.
- ○ find a husband for her daughters.
- ○ spread rumours.

**Read *Ancient furniture* and answer questions 29 to 36.**

## Ancient furniture

The first reference to woodwork is to be found in the Book of Genesis, in the instructions given to Noah to make an Ark of gopher wood, 'to make a window,' to 'pitch it within and without with pitch,' and to observe definite measurements. From the specific directions thus handed down to us, we may gather that mankind had acquired at a very early period of the world's history a knowledge of the different kinds of wood, and of the use of tools.

We know, too, from the bas reliefs and papyri in the British Museum, how advanced were the Ancient Egyptians in the arts of civilization, and that the manufacture of comfortable and even luxurious furniture was not neglected. In them, the Hebrews must have had excellent workmen for teachers and taskmasters, to have enabled them to acquire sufficient skill and experience to carry out such precise instructions as were given for the erection of the Tabernacle, some 1,500 years before Christ—as to the kinds of wood, measurements, ornaments, fastenings ('loops and taches'), curtains of linen, and coverings of dried skins. We have only to turn for a moment to the 25th chapter of Exodus to be convinced that all the directions there mentioned were given to a people who had considerable experience in the methods of carrying out work, which must have resulted from some generations of carpenters, joiners, weavers, dyers, goldsmiths, and other craftsmen.

From *Illustrated History of Furniture: From the earliest to the present time* by Frederick Litchfield, Truslove & Hanson Ltd, 1893 (1922)

**29.** Where does the author say that we can read about the first knowledge of different kinds of wood in a very early period in history?

- ○ Genesis
- ○ British Museum
- ○ Egyptian papyrus
- ○ 25th Chapter of Exodus

**30.** What is *Genesis*?

- ○ the first book of the Bible
- ○ an ancient Egyptian book
- ○ a book written by Noah
- ○ a history of furniture

**31.** How might we guess that Noah had an understanding of woodworking at a very early period of the world's history?

- ○ Noah used gopher wood.
- ○ Noah made a window.
- ○ Noah used pitch or tar to make the Ark watertight.
- ○ Noah used measurements.

**32.** To what fact does the illustration with the text refer?

- ○ the woodworking skills of Hebrew workmen
- ○ the bas reliefs in the British Museum
- ○ the furniture of the Ancient Egyptians
- ○ the construction of the Tabernacle

**33.** About how many years ago would the Tabernacle have been constructed?

| 1500 | 2500 | 3500 | 4500 |
|:---:|:---:|:---:|:---:|
| ○ | ○ | ○ | ○ |

**34.** What evidence is provided in the 25th Chapter of Exodus?

- ○ The construction of the Tabernacle, with its wood, measurements, ornaments, fastenings, curtains of linen and coverings of dried skins, provides evidence in Chapter 25 that the Egyptians had developed skills over many generations.
- ○ The construction of the Ark, with its detailed directions, provides evidence in Chapter 25 that Noah had developed skills over many generations.
- ○ The construction of the Tabernacle, with its detailed directions, provides evidence in Chapter 25 that the Egyptians had developed skills over many generations.
- ○ The construction of the Tabernacle, with its wood, measurements, ornaments, fastenings, curtains of linen and coverings of dried skins, provides evidence in Chapter 25 that the Hebrews had developed skills over many generations.

**35.** What is the writer's overall point of view?

- ○ The papyri provide evidence of manufacturing the Ark or boats.
- ○ The Old Testament provides evidence that mankind had acquired the skill of making chairs from an early period of history.
- ○ There is evidence from an early period of history that mankind had acquired the skill of woodworking.

**36.** What are papyri?

- ○ writing parchments
- ○ a form of Egyptian writing
- ○ another name for the books of the Bible
- ○ bas reliefs in the British Museum

**It would be a good idea to check your answers to questions 18 to 36 before moving on to the other questions.**

**Read *A scandal in Bohemia* and answer questions 37 to 43.**

## A scandal in Bohemia

Illustration by Sidney Paget, from 'A scandal in Bohemia', *Strand Magazine*, 1891, www.arthes.com/holmes/scan/default.html

To Sherlock Holmes she is always *the* woman. I have seldom heard him mention her under any other name. In his eyes she eclipses and predominates the whole of her sex. It was not that he felt any emotion akin to love for Irene Adler. All emotions, and that one particularly, were abhorrent to his cold, precise but admirably balanced mind. He was, I take it, the most perfect reasoning and observing machine that the world has seen, but as a lover he would have placed himself in a false position. He never spoke of the softer passions, save with a gibe and a sneer. They were admirable things for the observer—excellent for drawing the veil from men's motives and actions. But for the trained reasoner to admit such intrusions into his own delicate and finely adjusted temperament was to introduce a distracting factor which might throw a doubt upon all his mental results. Grit in a sensitive instrument, or a crack in one of his own high-power lenses, would not be more disturbing than a strong emotion

in a nature such as his. And yet there was but one woman to him, and that woman was the late Irene Adler, of dubious and questionable memory.

I had seen little of Holmes lately. My marriage had drifted us away from each other. My own complete happiness, and the home-centred interests which rise up around the man who first finds himself master of his own establishment, were sufficient to absorb all my attention, while Holmes, who loathed every form of society with his whole Bohemian soul, remained in our lodgings in Baker Street, buried among his old books, and alternating from week to week between cocaine and ambition, the drowsiness of the drug, and the fierce energy of his own keen nature. He was still, as ever, deeply attracted by the study of crime, and occupied his immense faculties and extraordinary powers of observation in following out those clues, and clearing up those mysteries which had been abandoned as hopeless by the official police.

From *The Adventures of Sherlock Holmes* by Sir Arthur Conan Doyle, George Newnes Ltd, 1892

**37.** Who was described as *the most perfect reasoning and observing machine*?

○ the doctor

○ the woman

○ the detective

○ the narrator

**38.** In this text what is the meaning of *a balanced mind*?

○ A balanced mind means that both sides of the brain are the same.

○ A balanced mind means someone who has decided what to do.

○ A balanced mind is one that is precise and measures every detail.

○ A balanced mind is one that is happy about what is occurring.

**39.** What is the meaning of the word *gibe*?

○ a type of ape

○ to talk quickly

○ a sneer

○ a type of bribe

**40.** Why was the soul of Sherlock Holmes described as *Bohemian*?

○ He lived in a rough part of London.

○ He liked books.

○ He took cocaine.

○ He had an unconventional life.

○ He was a detective.

**41.** What is the main purpose of these few paragraphs from 'A scandal in Bohemia'?

○ The paragraphs are an introduction to a true detective story.

○ The paragraphs are an introduction to a fictional detective story.

○ The paragraphs outline the plot of a crime that occurred in London.

○ The paragraphs come at the conclusion to a true crime.

**42.** How does the author describe Holmes?

○ as a questionable character

○ as completely happy

○ as temperamental

○ as someone without emotions

**43.** What is the meaning of the word *abhorrent*?

○ disgusting    ○ desirable

○ scary    ○ balanced

**Read *Marseilles—the arrival* and answer questions 44 to 50.**

## Marseilles—the arrival

Source: www.gutenberg.org/files/28510/28510-h/
images/091.jpg

On the 24th of February, 1815, the look-out at Notre-Dame de la Garde signalled the three-master, the Pharaon from Smyrna, Trieste, and Naples.

As usual, a pilot put off immediately, and rounding the Chateau d'If, got on board the vessel between Cape Morgion and Rion island.

Immediately, and according to custom, the ramparts of Fort Saint-Jean were covered with spectators; it is always an event at Marseilles for a ship to come into port, especially when this ship, like the Pharaon, has been built, rigged, and laden at the old Phocee docks, and belongs to an owner of the city.

The ship drew on and had safely passed the strait, which some volcanic shock has made between the Calasareigne and Jaros islands; had doubled Pomegue, and approached the harbour under topsails, jib, and spanker, but so slowly and sedately that the idlers, with that instinct which is the forerunner of evil, asked one another what misfortune could have happened on board. However, those experienced in navigation saw plainly that if any accident had occurred, it was not to the vessel herself, for she bore down with all the evidence of being skilfully handled, the anchor a-cockbill, the jib-boom guys already eased off, and standing by the side of the pilot, who was steering the Pharaon towards the narrow entrance of the inner port, was a young man, who, with activity and vigilant eye, watched every motion of the ship, and repeated each direction of the pilot.

The vague disquietude which prevailed among the spectators had so much affected one of the crowd that he did not await the arrival of the vessel in harbour, but jumping into a small skiff, desired to be pulled alongside the Pharaon, which he reached as she rounded into La Reserve basin.

When the young man on board saw this person approach, he left his station by the pilot, and, hat in hand, leaned over the ship's bulwarks.

He was a fine, tall, slim young fellow of eighteen or twenty, with black eyes, and hair as dark as a raven's wing; and his whole appearance bespoke that calmness and resolution peculiar to men accustomed from their cradle to contend with danger.

'Ah, is it you, Dantes?' cried the man in the skiff. 'What's the matter? and why have you such an air of sadness aboard?'

'A great misfortune, M. Morrel,' replied the young man,—'a great misfortune, for me especially! Off Civita Vecchia we lost our brave Captain Leclere.'

'And the cargo?' inquired the owner, eagerly.

'Is all safe, M. Morrel; and I think you will be satisfied on that head. But poor Captain Leclere—'

From *The Count of Monte Cristo*, by Alexandre Dumas, Pere, Chapman & Hall, 1846

**44.** What does the author encourage the reader to think about?
- ○ the return of the vessel
- ○ some misfortune
- ○ the loss of the cargo
- ○ the man jumping into the skiff

**45.** What is the name of the vessel entering the harbour?
- ○ Notre-Dame de la Garde
- ○ Chateau d'If
- ○ Smyrna
- ○ Pharaon

**46.** Where did the pilot board the vessel?
- ○ after Cape Morgion
- ○ between Smyrna, Trieste and Naples
- ○ at Chateau d'If
- ○ at Notre-Dame de la Garde

**47.** What factor made the arrival of the ship such a special event?
- ○ The date of arrival was 24 February 1815.
- ○ It was a three-master.
- ○ The ship was locally built and owned.
- ○ It was the custom for spectators to watch a ship come into port.

**48.** What features are described and linked together in the fourth paragraph of the text?
- ○ the measured and slow-moving entrance of the ship into the port, indicating some probable misfortune
- ○ the details of the accident to the ship, indicating some obvious misfortune
- ○ the skilful handling of the ship, indicating how it impressed the onlookers
- ○ the actions of the pilot and how the ship safely entered the harbour to the admiration of all

**49.** Who owned the cargo in the *Pharaon*?

- ○ the pilot
- ○ Dantes
- ○ Morrel
- ○ Captain Leclere

**50.** In what sense is the word *disquietude* used?

- ○ to describe the uneasiness of the situation
- ○ to describe the loud reactions of the onlookers
- ○ to describe the sound of the ship entering the harbour
- ○ to describe the peacefulness of the scene

Did you colour in one of the circles?

# END OF TEST

Well done! You have completed the first Reading Test. Some questions were quite challenging.

How did you find these questions? We hope that you found them interesting. Revise anything that was hard for you. There are further questions in the next Reading Test. The next test contains some different questions. Take a long break before doing any more tests.

Use the diagnostic chart on pages 77–78 to see which level of ability you reached. This is only an estimate. Don't be surprised if you answered some difficult questions correctly or even missed some easier questions.

Please note that multiple interpretations are possible for the levels of difficulty of these tasks. Also, some questions involve skills from different levels. This is only an initial guide to the approximate level of the reading skill assessed.

# CHECK YOUR SKILLS: READING TEST 1

## Instructions

As you check the answer for each question, mark it as correct (✔) or incorrect (✘). Mark any questions that you omitted or left out as incorrect (✘) for the moment.

Then look at how many you answered correctly in each level. You will be able to see what level you are at by finding the point where you started having consistent difficulty with questions at a certain level. For example, if you answer most questions correctly up to the Intermediate level and then get most questions wrong from then onwards, it is likely your ability is at an Intermediate level. You can ask your parents or your teacher to help you do this if it isn't clear to you.

**Am I able to ...**

| | SKILL | ESTIMATED LEVEL | ✔ or ✘ |
|---|---|---|---|
| 1 | Locate directly stated information? | Standard | |
| 2 | Locate directly stated information? | Standard | |
| 3 | Find the main idea in a text? | Standard | |
| 4 | Identify a relevant detail? | Standard | |
| 5 | Infer from a text? | Standard | |
| 6 | Define a phrase? | Intermediate | |
| 7 | Link ideas in a text? | Standard | |
| 8 | Identify the reference to a personal pronoun? | Standard | |
| 9 | Note the main idea in a text? | Standard | |
| 10 | State the author's aim? | Standard | |
| 11 | List the ideas in a section of the text? | Standard | |
| 12 | Clarify the key ideas in a message? | Standard | |
| 13 | Summarise the reasons? | Standard | |
| 14 | Find information from two separate paragraphs? | Standard | |
| 15 | Locate directly stated information? | Standard | |
| 16 | Infer the main idea? | Standard | |
| 17 | Conclude the truth or falsity of a statement? | Intermediate | |
| 18 | Identify a metaphor? | Advanced | |
| 19 | Deduce a fact? | Standard | |
| 20 | Make a distinction? | Intermediate | |
| 21 | Infer the reason? | Intermediate | |
| 22 | Interpret the opening sentence? | Intermediate | |
| 23 | Identify a name? | Standard | |
| 24 | Identify the use of a word in italics? | Intermediate | |
| 25 | Define a term? | Advanced | |
| 26 | Find the meaning of a term? | Advanced | |
| 27 | Describe the type of text? | Intermediate | |
| 28 | Make an inference? | Advanced | |
| 29 | Find the source for a statement? | Standard | |

| | SKILL | ESTIMATED LEVEL | ✓ or ✗ |
|---|---|---|---|
| 30 | Explain some information? | Intermediate | |
| 31 | Find the reason for a statement? | Intermediate | |
| 32 | Relate an illustration to a statement? | Intermediate | |
| 33 | Calculate a date from a textual description? | Intermediate | |
| 34 | Provide evidence from the text? | Intermediate | |
| 35 | Determine the writer's overall point of view? | Intermediate | |
| 36 | Define a term? | Intermediate | |
| 37 | Identify a person in a text? | Standard | |
| 38 | Interpret descriptive language? | Intermediate | |
| 39 | Define a word? | Advanced | |
| 40 | Interpret a description of a person? | Advanced | |
| 41 | State the purpose of the paragraphs in a text? | Advanced | |
| 42 | Describe a character? | Advanced | |
| 43 | Define a word in the text? | Advanced | |
| 44 | Describe the author's aim? | Advanced | |
| 45 | Indicate a fact in the text? | Standard | |
| 46 | Identify the location of an event and its sequence? | Intermediate | |
| 47 | Relate an effect to two causes? | Intermediate | |
| 48 | Link the author's description of an action with a sense of foreboding? | Advanced | |
| 49 | Infer ownership from details in the text? | Intermediate | |
| 50 | Define a word in terms of what it describes? | Advanced | |
| | TOTAL | | |

# READING TEST 2

This is the second Reading Test. There are 50 questions.

Allow around 65 minutes for this test. Take a short break if necessary.

In this test you will need to read a text. Then read each question and colour in the circle with the correct answer.

---

**Read this letter that appeared in the *Sydney Morning Herald* and answer questions 1 to 4.**

## Finally, a taste of freedom

At last that thing called *MasterChef* is over and life can resume some normality ('Cooking up a storm', smh.com.au, July 19). I will be able to watch the news on SBS or ABC and I will be able to sit down to a meal without some wannabe chef at home commenting on the presentation or the flavour.

James Anthony, Maroubra
July 20, 2009

**1.** Who wrote this letter?
- ○ the editor
- ○ a reader
- ○ a journalist
- ○ a newspaper reporter

**2.** What is the writer stating in this letter?
- ○ The writer is pleased that a popular show has ended.
- ○ The writer is sad that a popular show has ended.
- ○ The writer is angry that a popular show has ended.

**3.** What conflict is mentioned in the letter?
- ○ The conflict is between the *MasterChef* show and sitting down to a meal.
- ○ The conflict is between watching the news on the ABC or on SBS.
- ○ The conflict is between the time of the *MasterChef* show and the time for other shows.
- ○ The conflict is between the presentation and the flavour of the food.

**4.** What is the writer's purpose in this letter?
- ○ to influence other readers
- ○ to complain to other readers
- ○ to entertain other readers
- ○ to inform other readers

---

**Read these four sentences or paragraphs and answer question 5.**

**A** More than 60 000 walked through the doors at the Eastfield Shopping Mall at Westlands to cash in on bargains being offered in all stores at its annual sale.

**B** 'Just as in previous years, we have many one-off bargains,' Mr Furbish said.

**C** The Shopping Mall Manager, Mr Noel Furbish, said more than 1000 people were lined up outside the doors of the mall when it opened at 7.30 am.

**D** Children's and women's clothing were the biggest sellers of the day, with strong sales of electrical goods.

**5.** Which is the correct order for these paragraphs?
- ○ ABCD
- ○ ABDC
- ○ ACDB
- ○ ACBD
- ○ ADBC
- ○ ADCB

**Read** *A bank debit card* **and answer questions 6 to 10.**

## A bank debit card

A debit card is like a credit card but you don't have to make separate payments. It uses the funds in your personal bank account directly when you make a purchase.

It gives you the best of both worlds. It means that you can use it as a credit card and you still have a personal account. You do not owe anything and you do not have to pay any interest on the purchases you make. The money is drawn directly from your account at the time of purchase.

You can use your debit card wherever credit cards are accepted. You can:

- make purchases at stores in Australia and around the world
- withdraw cash at ATMs
- pay bills
- make purchases over the Internet using your card number.

**6.** What does the text describe?
- ○ a credit card
- ○ a deposit-only card
- ○ a business card
- ○ a debit card

**7.** How could a debit card be described?
- ○ A debit card allows you to borrow when you make a purchase.
- ○ A debit card withdraws from your account when you make a purchase.
- ○ A debit card puts money in your account when you make a purchase.
- ○ A debit card deposits to your account when you make a purchase.

**8.** What is the meaning of the phrase *the best of both worlds*?
- ○ You can enjoy a debit card in Australia and overseas.
- ○ The debit card has two benefits.
- ○ The debit card can be used in this life and in a future life.
- ○ You can use the card as a credit card and at ATMs.
- ○ There are advantages and disadvantages of using a debit card.

**9.** What happens when you use a debit card for a purchase?
- ○ You pay for something in cash.
- ○ You pay at a later time.
- ○ The money comes out of your account.

**10.** How does a debit card help users?
- ○ The debit card lets you use only the funds you have.
- ○ The debit card gives you a credit card.
- ○ The debit card allows you to borrow.

Did you colour in one of the circles?

**Read this table about the details of an airline's fleet and answer questions 11 to 15.**

| Aircraft | Fleet statistics | Details |
|---|---|---|
| Embraer 170 | Maximum guests 78<br>Maximum take-off weight 37,200 kg<br>Maximum range 3704 km<br>Typical cruising speed 840 km/h | Wing span (with winglets) 26 m<br>Overall length 29.9 m<br>Tail height 9.82 m<br>Interior cabin width 2.74 m |
| Embraer 190 | Maximum guests 104<br>Maximum take-off weight 51,800 kg<br>Maximum range 4260 km<br>Typical cruising speed 840 km/h | Wing span (with winglets) 28.72 m<br>Overall length 36.25 m<br>Tail height 10.57 m<br>Interior cabin width 2.74 m |
| Boeing 737-700 | Maximum guests 144<br>Maximum take-off weight 70,143 kg<br>Maximum range 6038 km<br>Typical cruising speed 833.7 km/h | Wing span (with winglets) 34.3 m<br>Overall length 33.6 m<br>Tail height 12.5 m<br>Interior cabin width 3.4 m |

| Aircraft | Fleet statistics | Details |
|---|---|---|
| Boeing 737-800 | Maximum guests 180<br>Maximum take-off weight 78,240 kg<br>Maximum range 5449 km<br>Typical cruising speed 833.7 km/h | Wing span (with winglets) 34.3 m<br>Overall length 39.5 m<br>Tail height 12.5 m<br>Interior cabin width 3.4 m |
| Boeing 777-300ER | Maximum guests 350<br>Maximum take-off weight 351,534 kg<br>Maximum range 14,685 km<br>Typical cruising speed 892 km/h | Wing span (with winglets) 64.8 m<br>Overall length 73.9 m<br>Tail height 18.7 m<br>Interior cabin width 5.86 m |

**11.** Which aircraft has a wing span of 34.3 m?

- ○ Embraer 190
- ○ Boeing 737-700
- ○ Boeing 777-300ER

**12.** Why is the lowest cruising speed described as typical?

- ○ This is the speed at which it normally flies.
- ○ This is the speed at which it always flies.
- ○ This is the speed at which it must fly.
- ○ This is the highest speed at which it could fly.

**13.** Which aircraft could travel the 7797 km from Sydney to Tokyo?

- ○ Embraer 170
- ○ Embraer 190
- ○ Boeing 737-700
- ○ Boeing 737-800
- ○ Boeing 777-300ER

**14.** Which aircraft is third highest in the number of passengers it can carry, third highest in the weight it can carry, second highest in the maximum range and lowest in the typical cruising speed?

○ Embraer 170

○ Embraer 190

○ Boeing 737-700

○ Boeing 737-800

○ Boeing 777-300ER

**15.** Which word completes the meaning?

Maximum is to minimum as utmost is to _____.

○ small          ○ slight

○ furthest       ○ least

○ most

**It would be a good idea to check your answers to questions 1 to 15 before moving on to the other questions.**

Read *An introduction to GPS* and answer questions 16 to 20.

## An introduction to GPS

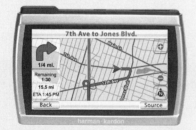

In Australia the letters GPS can stand for 'Greater Public Schools' but they are now more likely to bring to mind the new navigational Global Positioning System. There are other navigation systems, including those produced by Russia, Europe, China and India.

GPS was once an expensive novelty and was considered a luxury, but it is now common and is best known for its use in cars. Some mobile phones have navigation systems and some systems even allow mobile phones to be tracked.

In a complex or new environment GPS can help you find locations and can give you directions about where to turn and how to proceed. Some sophisticated systems even let you know about speed zones, red light cameras and speed cameras. It is also possible for some to determine altitude, as well as other aspects of location.

By 2009 these navigational systems were in common use and readily available from retailers. Many people are not aware that the GPS—like an early version of the Internet—was developed by the United States Department of Defence. GPS was made available for civilian use in the 1990s. President Reagan made it available for common benefit and use following the shooting down of a commercial airline flight in 1983.

The system works through a series of 24–32 satellites that circle the earth. They transmit microwave signals that are picked up by the car navigation units. These use the signals from at least two satellites to fix a position and this information is used with mapping software to give directions. The signals can be used to determine location, speed, direction and time.

**16.** What is GPS?

○ a tracking system

○ a navigational system

○ a mobile satellite system

**17.** In which regions would GPS operate?

- ○ mainly in the eastern regions of Australia
- ○ mainly in the western regions of Australia
- ○ mainly in the northern regions of Australia
- ○ mainly in the southern regions of Australia
- ○ throughout Australia

**18.** From your reading of the text, decide which sentence is correct.

- ○ The letters GPS have an ambiguous meaning.
- ○ The letters GPS have an unambiguous meaning.

**19.** Why are two satellites necessary to pinpoint a position?

- ○ It is necessary to have two locations.
- ○ It is necessary to have two lines intersect.
- ○ It is necessary to have two parallel lines.

**20.** Which statement is correct?

- ○ It has taken around 25 years since its release to the public for GPS to become widely available.
- ○ It has taken around 15 years since its release to the public for GPS to become widely available.
- ○ It has taken around 10 years since its release to the public for GPS to become widely available.

Did you colour in one of the circles?

**Read this email and answer questions 21 to 25.**

**James Turner**
From: James Turner [turner@magil.edu.au]
Sent: Mon 23/11/2020 1:57 PM
To: 'nick.antony@imgal.ac.uk'
Subject: Reverend Stephen motor vehicle accident

Dear Dr Antony

I returned last night from a conference in New Zealand and went this morning to Royal North Shore Hospital to see your uncle Rev. Stephen, who was injured as a passenger in a motor vehicle accident, fracturing fibia and tibula. I believe there was no loss of consciousness. There may be some spinal injury.

He was airlifted to the hospital on Friday evening and operated on that night. Fortunately the actions of Dr Eugene prevented the loss of too much blood. He is in a serious but stable condition. Given his age and other conditions there were major concerns.

Mary and Angelena managed to see him momentarily while I was parking the car. There are two priests from his parish at the hospital. They are keeping a vigil and are restricting the visitors as he was not able to rest yesterday.

This is my news—I was not certain whether anyone has spoken to you. My apologies for any delay but as I said, I found out only on Saturday, when in Wellington.

I believe that your friend Professor Pontingsee is in frequent contact with Dr Eugene. No doubt he would have an even more up-to-date report on Rev. Stephen's condition. Given the difference in our time zones I thought I would write first rather than phone.

James Turner

**21.** What best describes the main purpose of the email?

- ○ The email is a message about medical treatment.
- ○ The email conveys some serious news.
- ○ The email is an apology for a delay in writing.
- ○ The email provides some information about a car accident.

**22.** About how many people (visitors and others) are mentioned as being at the hospital?

| 7 | 5 | 4 | 3 |
|---|---|---|---|
| ○ | ○ | ○ | ○ |

**23.** From where was the message sent and to where was it sent?

- ○ The writer sent the email from Australia to the UK.
- ○ The writer sent the email from the UK to Australia.
- ○ The writer sent the email within Australia.
- ○ The writer sent the email from New Zealand to the UK.

**24.** Which feature in this message is most important?

- ○ The email reports some news.
- ○ The email outlines some facts.
- ○ The email informs the reader.
- ○ The email provides some background.

**25.** What medical aspect was of concern in the message?

- ○ The patient was an important person who had a car accident and needed treatment.
- ○ The patient was likely to die.
- ○ The patient had fractured his tibia and fibula and lost considerable blood.
- ○ The patient was old and had other medical problems.

---

**Read the poem *Pan in Wall Street* and answer questions 26 to 33.**

**This poem was written in 1867 by Edmund Clarence Stedman. It is about the stock exchange and the world outside it. The author sees an organ-grinder playing his tunes in Wall Street, New York, among the buildings where enormous financial transactions are made. Look at the notes that follow the poem to give you some further information.**

## Pan in Wall Street

Just where the Treasury's[1] marble front
Looks over Wall Street's[2] mingled nations;
Where Jews and Gentiles most are wont
To throng for trade and last quotations[3];
Where, hour by hour, the rates of gold
Outrival, in the ears of people,
The quarter-chimes, serenely tolled
From Trinity's[4] undaunted steeple,—

Even there I heard a strange, wild strain
Sound high above the modern clamor,
Above the cries of greed and gain,
The curbstone[5] war, the auction's hammer;
And swift, on Music's misty ways,
It led, from all this strife for millions.
To ancient, sweet-do-nothing[6] days
Among the kirtle-robed Sicilians[7].

And as it stilled the multitude,
And yet more joyous rose, and shriller,
I saw the minstrel where he stood
At ease against a Doric pillar[8]:
One hand a droning organ played,
The other held a Pan's-pipe[9] (fashioned
Like those of old) to lips that made
The reeds give out that strain impassioned.

'Twas Pan himself had wandered here
A-strolling through this sordid city,
And piping to the civic ear
The prelude of some pastoral ditty[10]!
The demigod had crossed the seas,—
From haunts of shepherd, nymph, and satyr,
And Syracusan[11] times,—to these
Far shores and twenty centuries later.

A ragged cap was on his head;
But—hidden thus—there was no doubting
That, all with crispy locks o'erspread,
His gnarlèd horns were somewhere sprouting;
His club-feet, cased in rusty shoes,
Were crossed, as on some frieze you see them,
And trousers, patched of divers hues,
Concealed his crooked shanks beneath them.

He filled the quivering reeds with sound,
And o'er his mouth their changes shifted,
And with his goat's-eyes looked around
Where'er the passing current drifted;
And soon, as on Trinacrian[12] hills
The nymphs and herdsmen ran to hear him,
Even now the tradesmen from their tills,
With clerks and porters, crowded near him.

The bulls and bears[13] together drew
From Jauncey Court[14] and New Street Alley,
As erst, if pastorals be true,
Came beasts from every wooded valley;
And random passers stayed to list,—
A boxer Ægon[15], rough and merry,
A Broadway Daphnis[16], on his tryst
With Nais[17] at the Brooklyn Ferry.

A one-eyed Cyclops[18] halted long
In tattered cloak of army pattern,
And Galatea[19] joined the throng,—
A blowsy apple-vending slattern;
While old Silenus[20] staggered out
From some new-fangled lunch-house handy,
And bade the piper, with a shout,
To strike up Yankee Doodle Dandy!

A newsboy and a peanut-girl
Like little Fauns[21] began to caper;
His hair was all in tangled curl,
Her tawny legs were bare and taper;
And still the gathering larger grew,
And gave its pence and crowded nigher,
While aye the shepherd-minstrel blew
His pipe, and struck the gamut higher.

O heart of Nature, beating still
With throbs her vernal passion taught her,—
Even here, as on the vine-clad hill,
Or by the Arethusan[22] water!
New forms may fold the speech, new lands
Arise within these ocean-portals,
But Music waves eternal wands,—
Enchantress of the souls of mortals!

So thought I,—but among us trod
A man in blue, with legal baton,
And scoffed the vagrant demigod,
And pushed him from the step I sat on.
Doubting I mused upon the cry,
'Great Pan is dead!'—and all the people
Went on their ways:—and clear and high
The quarter sounded from the steeple.

# READING TEST 2

**NOTES**

1. the Treasury—the Sub-Treasury Building.

2. Wall Street—an old street in New York faced by the Stock Exchange and the offices of the wealthiest bankers and brokers.

3. last quotations—the latest information on stock values given out before the Stock Exchange closes.

4. Trinity—the famous old church that stands at the head of Wall Street.

5. curbstone war (also kerb stone)—the clamorous quoting, auctioning, and bidding of stock out on the street curb (kerb), where the 'curb brokers'—brokers who do not have seats on the Stock Exchange—do business.

6. sweet-do-nothing—a translation of an Italian expression, *dolce far niente*.

7. Sicilians—Theocritus (3rd century BCE), the Greek pastoral poet, wrote of the happy life of the shepherds and shepherdesses in Sicily.

8. Doric pillar—a heavy marble pillar, such as was used in the architecture of the Dorians in Greece.

9. Pan's pipe—Pan was the Greek god of shepherds, and patron of fishing and hunting. He is represented as having the head and body of a man, with the legs, horns, and tail of a goat. It was said that he invented the shepherd's pipe or flute, which he made from reeds plucked on the bank of a stream.

10. pastoral ditty—a poem about shepherds and the happy outdoor life. The word *pastoral* comes from the Latin *pastor*, shepherd.

11. Syracusan times—Syracuse was an important city in Sicily. See the note on Sicilians, above.

12. Trinacrian hills—Trinacria is an old name for Sicily.

13. bulls and bears—a bull, on the Stock Exchange, is one who operates in expectation of a rise in stocks; a bear is a person who sells stocks in expectation of a fall in the market.

14. Jauncey Court—the Jauncey family were prominent in the early New York days. This court was probably named after them.

15. Ægon—usually spelled Ægaeon; another name for Briareus, a monster with a hundred arms.

16. Daphnis—in Greek myth, a shepherd who loved music.

17. Nais—in Greek myth, a happy young girl, a nymph.

18. Cyclops—one of a race of giants having but one eye—in the middle of the forehead. These giants helped Vulcan at his forge under Aetna.

19. Galatea—a sea-nymph beloved by the Cyclops Polyphemus.

20. Silenus—the foster-father and companion of Bacchus, god of wine. In pictures and sculpture Silenus is usually represented as intoxicated.

21. Fauns—fabled beings, half goat and half man.

22. Arethusan water—Arethusa, in Greek myth, was a wood-nymph, who was pursued by the river Alpheus. She was changed into a fountain, and ran under the sea to Sicily, where she rose near the city of Syracuse. Shelley has a poem on Arethusa.

From *Modern Prose and Poetry; For Secondary Schools*, edited with notes, study helps and reading lists by Margaret Ashmun, Riverside Press, 1914, pp. 43–46

**26.** What does the poet contrast?

- ○ the serenity of Trinity with the sordid Wall Street
- ○ the organ-grinder with Pan
- ○ the serenity of the ancient world with busy America
- ○ the curbstone war with the auction's hammer

**27.** How is the idea of Pan emphasised?

- ○ through playing an organ and holding a pipe like those in ancient times
- ○ through the demigod that had crossed the seas
- ○ through the clothing that hid his horns, clubbed feet and shanks
- ○ by the fact that he filled the quivering reeds with sound

**28.** Who was the man in blue?

- ○ the organ grinder with a composer's baton
- ○ the vagrant demigod
- ○ a policeman
- ○ Great Pan
- ○ the shepherd-minstrel
- ○ someone from the stock exchange
- ○ a street cleaner
- ○ a thug

**29.** Who are the mingled nations?

○ the one-eyed Cyclops

○ Sicilians

○ Jews and Gentile

○ clerks and porters

**30.** What was the *strange, wild strain*?

○ a sound

○ a war

○ a hammer

○ cries of greed and gain

**31.** How does the poet describe the city?

○ sordid

○ pastoral

○ marble

○ modern

**32.** A minstrel is a

○ nymph.

○ herdsman.

○ musician.

○ shepherd.

○ tradesperson.

○ clerk.

○ porter.

○ beast.

○ passer-by.

*Did you colour in one of the circles?*

**33.** Doric pillars are to ▨▨▨▨ as Trinacrian hills are to ▨▨▨▨ .

○ Greece, Sicily

○ marble front, Wall Street

○ Broadway, Brooklyn Ferry

**It would be a good idea to check your answers to questions 16 to 33 before moving on to the other questions.**

Read *First scene—the duel* and answer questions 34 to 43.

## First scene—the duel

THE doctors could do no more for the Dowager Lady Berrick.

When the medical advisers of a lady who has reached seventy years of age recommend the mild climate of the South of France, they mean in plain language that they have arrived at the end of their resources. Her ladyship gave the mild climate a fair trial, and then decided (as she herself expressed it) to 'die at home.' Traveling slowly, she had reached Paris at the date when I last heard of her. It was then the beginning of November. A week later, I met with her nephew, Lewis Romayne, at the club.

'What brings you to London at this time of year?' I asked.

'The fatality that pursues me,' he answered grimly. 'I am one of the unluckiest men living.'

He was thirty years old; he was not married; he was the enviable possessor of the fine old country seat, called Vange Abbey; he had no poor relations; and he was one of the handsomest men in England. When I add that I am, myself, a retired army officer, with a wretched income, a disagreeable wife, four ugly children, and a burden of fifty years on my back, no one will be surprised to hear that I answered Romayne, with bitter sincerity, in these words:

'I wish to heaven I could change places with you!'

'I wish to heaven you could!' he burst out, with equal sincerity on his side. 'Read that.'

From *The Black Robe*, by Wilkie Collins, Belford Clarke & Co., 1881

**34.** In what type of text would you expect to find this scene?

○ a novel

○ a book on history

○ a book on medicine

○ a non-fiction book

**35.** What is the meaning of the words *arrived at the end of their resources* in this story?

○ The doctors did not have any more medical supplies.

○ The hospital did not have any more medical supplies.

○ The doctors could not do anything more for her.

○ The doctors and the hospital needed more resources.

**36.** Where does this scene take place?

○ Paris

○ south of France

○ Vange Abbey

○ London

**37.** When did the events at the club occur?

○ the first week of November

○ the second week of November

○ the third week of November

○ the fourth week of November

**38.** What is the tone or sense of the phrase *The fatality that pursues me*?

○ bleak

○ fatal

○ unlucky

○ uninviting

**39.** Why are four semicolons used in this sentence?
*He was thirty years old; he was not married; he was the enviable possessor of the fine old country seat, called Vange Abbey; he had no poor relations; and he was one of the handsomest men in England.*

○ It is a list.

○ It is a long sentence.

○ These are separate clauses.

**40.** What is a *fine old country seat* in this text?

○ an abbey

○ a valuable chair

○ an antique chair

○ a place of residence

**41.** Why did the retired army officer respond *with bitter sincerity*?

○ He compared himself with Romayne.

○ He was sorry for Romayne.

○ He was jealous of Romayne.

○ He was impolite to Romayne.

○ He admired Romayne.

**42.** What is the aim of the author in this introduction?

○ The author is setting the scene for a dispute between Romayne and the retired army officer.

○ The author is setting the scene for a confrontation between Romayne and the retired army officer.

○ The author is setting the scene for a duel between Romayne and the retired army officer.

○ The author is setting the scene for a tragedy following the discussion between Romayne and the retired army officer.

**43.** What is the justification for the bitter response by Romayne?

○ the comparison with the wealth and position of the retired army officer

○ the poor health of the Dowager Lady Berrick

○ the fatality that occurred

○ what he handed the retired army officer

---

**Read *Economy* and answer questions 44 to 50. This text was written by Henry Thoreau in 1854. It describes the writer's stay in a cabin near Walden Pond, a woodland area of Massachusetts.**

---

## Economy

When I wrote the following pages, or rather the bulk of them, I lived alone, in the woods, a mile from any neighbour, in a house which I had built myself, on the shore of Walden Pond, in Concord, Massachusetts, and earned my living by the labour of my hands only. I lived there two years and two months. At present I am a sojourner in civilized life again.

I should not obtrude my affairs so much on the notice of my readers if very

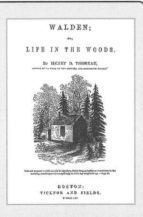

particular inquiries had not been made by my townsmen concerning my mode of life, which some would call impertinent, though they do not appear to me at all impertinent, but, considering the circumstances, very natural and pertinent.

Some have asked what I got to eat; if I did not feel lonesome; if I was not afraid; and the like. Others have been curious to learn what portion of my income I devoted to charitable purposes; and some, who have large families, how many poor children I maintained. I will therefore ask those of my readers who feel no particular interest in me to pardon me if I undertake to answer some of these questions in this book.

In most books, the I, or first person, is omitted; in this it will be retained; that, in respect to egotism, is the main difference. We commonly do not remember that it is, after all, always the first person that is speaking. I should not talk so much about myself if there were anybody else whom I knew as well. Unfortunately, I am confined to this theme by the narrowness of my experience.

From *Walden* by Henry David Thoreau, Ticknor & Fields, 1854

**44.** In which section of the book is this extract?

○ the conclusion

○ the introduction

○ the contents

○ the middle

**45.** How is the author portrayed in this text?

○ as a loner

○ as an egotist

○ as a vacationer

○ as an autobiographer

**46.** Why is the author telling this story?

○ He lived alone in the woods.

○ Others had enquired about his life.

○ He lived sincerely.

○ He wanted to talk about himself.

**47.** What is the best way to consider this work?

○ as a description of a time of personal discovery

○ as a travel diary over a period of two years and two months

○ as a do-it-yourself book on how to live alone

**48.** Which sentence is **not** correct?

○ Thoreau's aim was to live as a hermit.

○ Thoreau had neighbours.

○ Thoreau's aim was to be self-sufficient.

○ Thoreau's cabin was in the wilderness.

**49.** The last paragraph of this text discusses the style of writing. Which is correct?

○ The book is written in the first person singular.

○ The book is written in the first person plural.

○ The book is written in the second person singular.

○ The book is written in the second person plural.

○ The book is written in the third person singular.

○ The book is written in the third person plural.

**50.** Which sentence is correct?

○ *Walden* emphasises the value of closeness to nature.

○ *Walden* indicates aspects of contemporary life.

○ *Walden* outlines a permanent experiment.

○ *Walden* describes a simpler life.

# END OF TEST

**Well done! You have completed the second Reading Test.**

**How did you find these questions?** We hope that you found them interesting. Revise anything that was hard for you. There are further questions in the next Reading Test. The next test contains some different questions. Now take a long break before doing any more tests.

**Use the diagnostic chart on pages 91–92 to see which level of ability you reached. This is only an estimate. Don't be surprised if you answered some difficult questions correctly or even missed some easier questions.**

**Please note that multiple interpretations are possible for the levels of difficulty of these tasks. Also, some questions involve skills from different levels. This is only an initial guide to the approximate level of the reading skill assessed.**

## Instructions

As you check the answer for each question, mark it as correct (✓) or incorrect (✗). Mark any questions that you omitted or left out as incorrect (✗) for the moment.

Then look at how many you answered correctly in each level. You will be able to see what level you are at by finding the point where you started having consistent difficulty with questions at a certain level. For example, if you answer most questions correctly up to the Intermediate level and then get most questions wrong from then onwards, it is likely your ability is at an Intermediate level. You can ask your parents or your teacher to help you do this if it isn't clear to you.

**Am I able to ...**

| | SKILL | ESTIMATED LEVEL | ✓ or ✗ |
|---|---|---|---|
| 1 | Identify the author of a letter to the editor? | Standard | |
| 2 | Outline the content of a letter? | Standard | |
| 3 | Report the conflict that exists in a letter? | Standard | |
| 4 | Indicate the purpose of a letter? | Standard | |
| 5 | Find the correct order of four sentences? | Standard | |
| 6 | Identify the topic? | Standard | |
| 7 | State the meaning of a product? | Standard | |
| 8 | Interpret a phrase? | Advanced | |
| 9 | State what happens? | Intermediate | |
| 10 | State the nature of a product? | Intermediate | |
| 11 | Find information in a table? | Standard | |
| 12 | Explain the meaning of an adverb in context? | Intermediate | |
| 13 | Deduce an answer from details provided? | Standard | |
| 14 | Identify a product from its details? | Intermediate | |
| 15 | Complete an analogy? | Intermediate | |
| 16 | Identify the purpose of an object? | Standard | |
| 17 | State the area of use of a system? | Intermediate | |
| 18 | Understand the meaning of *ambiguous* and *unambiguous*? | Advanced | |
| 19 | Make a deduction from given facts and known principles? | Advanced | |
| 20 | Estimate a time frame from information that is given? | Standard | |
| 21 | State the purpose of an email? | Intermediate | |
| 22 | Identify the number of characters in a message? | Intermediate | |
| 23 | Find the address of the source and recipient of a message? | Intermediate | |
| 24 | State the main feature of a message? | Intermediate | |
| 25 | Select the main feature of the message? | Intermediate | |
| 26 | Find contrasts in a poem? | Advanced | |
| 27 | State the way an idea is emphasised? | Advanced | |
| 28 | Identify a character in a poem? | Intermediate | |
| 29 | Define a phrase? | Advanced | |

| | SKILL | ESTIMATED LEVEL | ✓ or ✗ |
|---|---|---|---|
| 30 | Define a phrase? | Advanced | |
| 31 | Categorise a description? | Intermediate | |
| 32 | Interpret a word? | Intermediate | |
| 33 | Draw an analogy? | Advanced | |
| 34 | Indicate the type of text? | Intermediate | |
| 35 | Interpret a phrase? | Advanced | |
| 36 | State the location in a story? | Intermediate | |
| 37 | Locate the time of an event? | Intermediate | |
| 38 | Identify the tone of a phrase? | Intermediate | |
| 39 | State the reason for the use of semicolons? | Intermediate | |
| 40 | Interpret a figurative phrase? | Advanced | |
| 41 | Interpret the way language is used? | Advanced | |
| 42 | Infer the author's aim? | Advanced | |
| 43 | Find the reason for a response? | Advanced | |
| 44 | Determine the location within a text? | Intermediate | |
| 45 | Portray a character? | Advanced | |
| 46 | Find the reason for a story? | Advanced | |
| 47 | Identify correct statements about the author? | Advanced | |
| 48 | Indicate the author's aim? | Advanced | |
| 49 | State the person and number of the style of writing? | Advanced | |
| 50 | State the content of an account? | Advanced | |
| | **TOTAL** | | |

# READING TEST 3

This is the third Reading Test. There are 50 questions.

Allow around 65 minutes for this test. Take a short break if necessary.

In this test you will need to read a text. Then read each question and colour in the circle with the correct answer.

---

**Read these four sentences from the tourist brochure *Clovelly to Cronulla* and answer questions 1 to 9.**

## Clovelly to Cronulla
### Golden cliffs and beaches

A. Along the way are some of the best coastal views in Sydney and places of intriguing history and beauty.

B. This is the jumping off point for the Royal National Park's Coast Track from Bundeena to Otford and the Federation Track to Melbourne.

C. The second 13 kilometre section runs from Cook's Landing Place at Kurnell, birthplace of European Australia, via the spectacular coastline of the Kurnell Peninsula and the Aboriginal middens at Boat Harbour, to the golden sweep of Cronulla Beach and eventually Gunamatta Bay Wharf.

D. The first 17 kilometre section of this walk takes you along the cliffs and coastal reserves from Clovelly to La Perouse.

From *Walking Coastal Sydney*, Walking Volunteers and Sydney Coastal Councils Group, 2008

1. Which is the correct order for these sentences?
   - ○ DABC
   - ○ DACB
   - ○ DBCA
   - ○ DBAC
   - ○ DCAB
   - ○ DCBA

2. What type of information is contained in these sentences?
   - ○ information for tourists
   - ○ information about beaches
   - ○ information about coastal walks
   - ○ information about Sydney

3. Which word in these four sentences means the same as *fascinating*?
   - ○ intriguing
   - ○ jumping
   - ○ spectacular
   - ○ birthplace

4. Which is the longest section of the walk?
   - ○ Clovelly to La Perouse
   - ○ Cook's Landing Place to Gunamatta Bay Wharf

5. What is the length of the walk from Clovelly to Cronulla?
   - ○ 17 kilometres
   - ○ less than 17 kilometres
   - ○ more than 17 kilometres

---

6. The start of the Royal National Park Coast Track is at
   - ○ Clovelly.
   - ○ La Perouse.
   - ○ Woolooware.
   - ○ Cronulla.

7. On the map where is the birthplace of European Australia?
   - ○ Botany Bay
   - ○ Maroubra Bay
   - ○ Bate Bay
   - ○ Long Bay

8. In the space write the word in the text that means 'the first people of Australia who inhabited it from the earliest times or before the arrival of colonists'?

   [                    ]

9. A [        ] is a place where people left the remains of their meals.
   - ○ birthplace
   - ○ midden
   - ○ coastal reserve
   - ○ landing place

**Read *It's easy to save electricity when you know how* and answer questions 10 to 16.**

## It's easy to save electricity when you know how

If we are efficient in our use of electricity, we can extend our supply of energy and help the environment. Being energy efficient is one of the easiest things any household can do. We can also reduce our electricity bills. It is as simple as using electricity more carefully.

Here are five things we can all do at home:

1. Switch off—Most households have appliances that use electricity even when they are on 'standby'. This can amount to over 10% of the total electricity used in a typical home. Appliances with a standby mode include DVD players, televisions, air conditioners and clocks. Switch off appliances at the wall.

| | Average standby energy use (watts) | Annual cost (approx.) |
|---|---|---|
| Television | 10 | $13 |
| Clock radio | 4 | $5 |
| VCR | 8 | $10 |
| Stereo | 10 | $13 |
| Mobile phone charger | 1 | $1 |
| Personal computer | 2 | $2 |
| Computer monitor | 5 | $7 |
| Printer | 8 | $10 |
| Microwave oven | 4 | $5 |
| Cordless phone | 3 | $4 |

Source: Sustainable Energy Authority Victoria, 2002

2. Save on hot water—Hot water systems are the biggest energy user in the average home. The average cost for a system is $56–$78 per month. Reduce costs by installing an economical water-saving shower head!

3. Cold wash, natural dry—It is possible to use cold water in the laundry. On sunny days the clothes drier can be rested and clothes hung outside. The hourly cost for a clothes drier is 35c and 13c for a washing machine.

4. Smarter heating—To save energy the temperature of a heated room in winter should be around 18–20 °C. During the cold months, gas heating is more effective than electric heaters.

5. Keep the heat in—Insulate homes and ensure that doors and windows are draught proof. This is a cheap and easy way to improve the insulation in your home. Cover windows with blinds or curtains to avoid heat loss. Close doors to rooms that are not in use.

Adapted from EnergyAustralia brochure, undated

10. Who is the main audience for this information?
   ○ parents
   ○ electricity companies
   ○ consumers
   ○ environmentalists

11. What is the number of the energy saving tip that recommends appliances are switched off at the wall?
   ○ 1
   ○ 2
   ○ 3
   ○ 4
   ○ 5

12. From the information given, what appears to be the major household user of electricity?
   ○ televisions on standby
   ○ clothes driers
   ○ washing machines
   ○ hot water systems

13. Which statement is emphasised most in the text?
   ○ Energy costs are increasing.
   ○ There are simple steps everyone can take to be more energy efficient.
   ○ People will be surprised at the different ways to reduce energy costs.
   ○ Saving electricity will extend the world's supply of energy.

14. Around one-tenth of the total electricity in a typical home is used by
   ○ standby.
   ○ hot-water systems.
   ○ cold wash, natural dry.
   ○ smarter heating.

15. This article tries to convince the reader to save electricity by
   ○ only providing facts about electricity use.
   ○ proving it has been done.
   ○ showing different ways to save.
   ○ convincing people to help the environment.

16. Which recommendation for the things we can do to save electricity at home involves spending money?
   ○ switching off appliances on standby
   ○ saving on hot water
   ○ resting the clothes drier
   ○ insulating homes

Did you colour in one of the circles?

**It would be a good idea to check your answers to questions 1 to 16 before moving on to the other questions.**

**Read *Faster and more agile than ever before* and answer questions 17 to 19.**

## Faster and more agile than ever before

The new GTX. Discover astounding performance.

An impressive car never stops improving. The new German designed 155 kW GTX is now assembled in Australia from imported components. From next year it will be exported to the Asia–Pacific region.

You will be impressed by the new styling, which is available in a range of modern colours. Leather seats, air conditioning, cruise control, electric windows, six front-and-rear airbags, ABS, automatic windscreen wipers and GPS are all standard options. We were the first company to design a hatchback and we are still the leading carmaker in this field.

The body is galvanised and guaranteed against rust for 10 years. Our 5-year 70,000 km warranty gives you peace of mind. You can also feel secure with our five-star ANCAP safety rating.

Beyond the external features look closely at the most modern technologies, such as our new differential lock system. It controls the stability of the car while you focus on the traffic. The pressure on each wheel is controlled to give you more grip and the right amount of steering direction.

Don't delay—visit your local dealer for a test drive or contact us at www.flog.com.au.

**17.** Which feature of the car is indicated in this advertisement?

- ○ It will impress the reader.
- ○ It is available for a test drive.
- ○ It has a five-star ANCAP safety rating.
- ○ This company developed the first hatchback.

**18.** Which statement about the GTX is correct?

- ○ The GTX is exported.
- ○ The GTX is imported.
- ○ The GTX is locally built.
- ○ The GTX is assembled locally.

**19.** Which aspect provides the purchaser with an assurance of quality?

- ○ the galvanised body
- ○ the German design
- ○ the new styling
- ○ the leading designer

**Read *When I heard the learn'd astronomer* and answer questions 20 to 23.**

## When I heard the learn'd astronomer

When I heard the learn'd astronomer,
When the proofs, the figures, were ranged
   in columns before me,
When I was shown the charts and diagrams,
   to add, divide and measure them,
When I sitting heard the astronomer where
   he lectured with much applause in the
   lecture-room,
How soon unaccountable I became tired
   and sick,
Till rising and gliding out I wander'd off
   by myself,
In the mystical moist night-air, and from
   time to time,
Look'd up in perfect silence at the stars.

*Walt Whitman*

From *Modern Prose And Poetry; For Secondary Schools*, edited with notes, study helps and reading lists by Margaret Ashmun, The Riverside Press, 1914, p. 115

**20.** What happened to the poet?

○ He became tired because there was too much applause.

○ He became tired because he was probably bored.

○ He became tired because the proofs were arranged in columns.

○ He became tired because he wanted to be by himself.

**21.** What did the poet learn from the stars when he was alone out of doors?

○ He saw the details of the astronomy that was described.

○ He relaxed under the stars in the mystical and moist night air.

○ He saw the beauty of the night sky for himself.

**22.** Which statement is correct?

○ The poet writes that the subject of astronomy is interesting.

○ The poet considers that proofs, figures, charts and diagrams are interesting.

○ The poet thinks that the reality of nature is interesting.

○ The poet thinks that wandering off to watch the stars is interesting.

**23.** What does this poem have to say?

○ A lecture by an expert is boring.

○ It is important to be alone and have some time for yourself.

○ Data and information are important for a real experience.

○ Theory is no substitute for a real experience.

---

Read *The eve of the war* and answer questions 24 to 32.

## The eve of the war

No one would have believed in the last years of the nineteenth century that this world was being watched keenly and closely by intelligences greater than man's and yet as mortal as his own; that as men busied themselves about their various concerns they were scrutinised and studied, perhaps almost as narrowly as a man with a microscope might scrutinise the transient creatures that swarm and multiply in a drop of water. With infinite complacency men went to and fro over this globe about their little affairs, serene in their assurance of their empire over matter. It is possible that the infusoria under the microscope do the same. No one gave a thought to the older worlds of space as sources of human danger, or thought of them only to dismiss the idea of life upon them as impossible or improbable. It is curious to recall some of the mental habits of those departed days. At most terrestrial men fancied there might be other men upon Mars, perhaps inferior to themselves and ready to welcome a missionary enterprise. Yet across the gulf of space, minds that are to our minds as ours are to those of the beasts that perish, intellects vast and cool and unsympathetic, regarded this earth with envious eyes, and slowly and surely drew their plans against us. And early in the twentieth century came the great disillusionment.

The planet Mars, I scarcely need remind the reader, revolves about the sun at a mean distance of 140,000,000 miles, and the light and heat it receives from the sun is barely half of that received by this world.

It must be, if the nebular hypothesis has any truth, older than our world; and long before this earth ceased to be molten, life upon its surface must have begun its course. The fact that it is scarcely one seventh of the volume of the earth must have accelerated its cooling to the temperature at which life could begin. It has air and water and all that is necessary for the support of animated existence.

Yet so vain is man, and so blinded by his vanity, that no writer, up to the very end of the nineteenth century, expressed any idea that intelligent life might have developed there far, or indeed at all, beyond its earthly level. Nor was it generally understood that since Mars is older than our earth, with scarcely a quarter of the superficial area and remoter from the sun, it necessarily follows that it is not only more distant from time's beginning but nearer its end.

From The Project Gutenberg e-book of *The War of the Worlds* by HG Wells

**24.** What type of writing is this likely to be?
- ○ information about science and other planets
- ○ science fiction
- ○ a historical novel
- ○ a story about war

**25.** What is the tone of this writing?
- ○ This is written in a serious style.
- ○ This is written in a scientific style.
- ○ This is written in a newspaper style.
- ○ This is written in a pessimistic style.

**26.** When did these events occur?
- ○ around 1800
- ○ around 1850
- ○ around 1900
- ○ around 1940

**27.** What does this text say at the outset?
- ○ that people were complacent about being watched by aliens
- ○ that people were concerned about being watched by aliens
- ○ that people imagined they were watched by aliens
- ○ that people were unaware they were being watched by aliens

**28.** What was the result of not giving any thought to the idea of life on other planets?
- ○ People fancied that there might be life on Mars, perhaps inferior to themselves.
- ○ People were ready to welcome a missionary enterprise.
- ○ People thought that Martians regarded this earth with envious eyes.
- ○ People were greatly disillusioned by what happened.

**29.** How did the Martians regard the earth?
- ○ in an unsympathetic way
- ○ in an envious way
- ○ with a superior intellect
- ○ in an inferior way

**30.** What is the message of the second paragraph?
- ○ The second paragraph is a reminder about Mars.
- ○ The second paragraph is about the vanity of people who underestimated Mars.
- ○ The second paragraph is a reminder that life was possible on Mars.
- ○ The second paragraph is a history of Mars.

**31.** What is the cause of people's vanity?

- ○ They are conceited.
- ○ They did not think that there were greater intelligences.
- ○ They overlooked the potential danger.
- ○ They forgot that Mars is older than earth.

**32.** What is the meaning of the word *superficial* in the last paragraph?

- ○ cursory
- ○ artificial
- ○ insincere
- ○ surface
- ○ trivial

> **It would be a good idea to check your answers to questions 17 to 32 before moving on to the other questions.**

> **Read *Plant cell structure* and answer questions 33 to 39.**

## Plant cell structure

If we make a thin slice across the stem of a rapidly growing plant,—e.g. geranium, begonia, celery,—mount it in 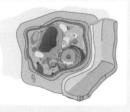 water, and examine it microscopically, it will be found to be made up of numerous cavities or chambers separated by delicate partitions. Often these cavities are of sufficient size to be visible to the naked eye, and examined with a hand lens the section appears like a piece of fine lace, each mesh being one of the chambers visible when more strongly magnified. These chambers are known as 'cells,' and of them the whole plant is built up.

In order to study the structure of the cell more exactly we will select such as may be examined without cutting them. A good example is furnished by the common spiderwort plant. Attached to the base of the stamens are delicate hairs composed of chains of cells, which may be examined alive by carefully removing a stamen and placing it in a drop of water under a cover glass.

Each cell is an oblong sac, with a delicate colourless wall which chemical tests show to be composed of cellulose, a substance closely resembling starch. Within this sac, and forming a lining to it, is a thin layer of colourless matter containing many fine granules. Bands and threads of the same substance traverse the cavity of the cell, which is filled with a deep purple homogeneous fluid. This fluid, which in most cells is colourless, is called the cell sap, and is composed mainly of water. Imbedded in the granular lining of the sac is a roundish body, which itself has a definite membrane, and usually shows one or more roundish bodies within, besides an indistinctly granular appearance. This body is called the nucleus of the cell, and the small one within it, the nucleolus.

The membrane surrounding the cell is known as the cell wall, and in young plant cells is always composed of cellulose.

The granular substance lining the cell wall is called 'protoplasm,' and with the nucleus constitutes the living part of the cell. If sufficiently magnified, the granules within the protoplasm will be seen to be in active streaming motion. This movement, which is very evident here, is not often so conspicuous, but still may often be detected without difficulty.

From The Project Gutenberg e-book of *Elements of Structural and Systematic Botany* by Douglas Houghton Campbell

**33.** How many steps were described in the method for observing cells?

○ 1      ○ 2

○ 3      ○ 4

○ 5      ○ 6

**34.** What is the name of the cavities or chambers in the stem of a plant?

○ partitions    ○ cells

○ spiderwort    ○ cellulose

○ sacs

**35.** Which items are parts of a cell? (You may colour in more than one circle.)

○ protoplasm    ○ cell wall

○ nucleus       ○ granules

○ stamen

**36.** Why is the cell sap called *homogeneous*?

○ It is purple.    ○ It is varied.

○ It is uniform.   ○ It is colourless.

**Look at this diagram of a cell. Use the information in the text *Plant cell structure* to answer the next three questions.**

**37.** What is the name of the section marked A?

○ nucleolus    ○ nucleus

○ sac         ○ cellulose

**38.** What is the name of the section marked B?

○ nucleolus    ○ protoplasm

○ nucleus      ○ chamber

**39.** What is the name of the section marked C?

○ cellulose

○ protoplasm

○ cell sap

○ cell wall

**Read the text below and answer questions 40 to 42.**

A Lion had come to the end of his days and lay sick unto death at the mouth of his cave, gasping for breath. The animals, his subjects, came round him and drew nearer as he grew more and more helpless. When they saw him on the point of death they thought to themselves: 'Now is the time to pay off old grudges.' So the Boar came up and drove at him with his tusks; then a Bull gored him with his horns; still the Lion lay helpless before them: so the Ass, feeling quite safe from danger, came up, and turning his tail to the Lion kicked up his heels into his face. 'This is a double death,' growled the Lion.

From The Second Project Gutenberg e-text of *Aesop's Fables*, 10th edition

**40.** What is the title of the fable?

- ○ The Lion's Share
- ○ The Lion, the Fox, and the Beasts
- ○ The Sick Lion
- ○ Lion in Love
- ○ The Ass in the Lion's Skin
- ○ The Lion and the Statue

**41.** What is the meaning of this story?

- ○ Only cowards insult dying majesty.
- ○ Injuries may be forgiven, but not forgotten.
- ○ Gratitude and greed do not go together.
- ○ You may share the labours of the great, but you will not share the spoils.

**42.** Why is this a parable?

- ○ It describes what could have been a true story with a meaning.
- ○ It is an animal legend but with a sense of truthfulness.
- ○ It is a fable that did not happen.
- ○ It describes one thing through an image of another.

Read *The origin of species* and answer questions 43 to 50.

## The origin of species

I will here give a brief sketch of the progress of opinion on the Origin of Species. Until recently the great majority of naturalists believed that species were immutable productions, and had been separately created. This view has been ably maintained by many authors.

Some few naturalists, on the other hand, have believed that species undergo modification, and that the existing forms of life are the descendants by true generation of pre existing forms.

Passing over allusions to the subject in the classical writers (Aristotle, in his 'Physicae Auscultationes' (lib.2, cap.8, s.2), after remarking that rain does not fall in order to make the corn grow, any more than it falls to spoil the farmer's corn when threshed out of doors, applies the same argument to organisation; and adds (as translated by Mr. Clair Grece, who first pointed out the passage to me), 'So what hinders the different parts (of the body) from having this merely accidental relation in nature? as the teeth, for example, grow by necessity, the front ones sharp, adapted for dividing, and the grinders flat, and serviceable for masticating the food; since they were not made for the sake of this, but it was the result of accident. And in like manner as to other parts in which there appears to exist an adaptation to an end. Wheresoever, therefore, all things together (that is all the parts of one whole) happened like as if they were made for the sake of something, these were preserved, having been appropriately constituted by an internal spontaneity; and whatsoever things were not thus constituted, perished and still perish.' We here see the principle of natural selection shadowed forth, but how little Aristotle fully comprehended the principle, is shown by his remarks on the formation of the teeth.), the first author who in modern times has treated it in a scientific spirit was Buffon. But as his opinions fluctuated greatly at different periods, and as he does not enter on the causes or means of the transformation of species, I need not here enter on details.

Lamarck was the first man whose conclusions on the subject excited much attention. This justly celebrated naturalist first published his views in 1801; he much enlarged them in 1809 in his 'Philosophie Zoologique', and subsequently, 1815, in the Introduction to his 'Hist. Nat. des Animaux sans Vertebres'. In these works he up holds the doctrine that all species, including man, are descended from other species. He first did the eminent service of arousing attention to the probability of all change in the organic, as well as in the inorganic world, being the result of law, and not of miraculous interposition. Lamarck seems to have been chiefly led to his conclusion on the gradual change of species, by the difficulty of distinguishing species and varieties, by the almost perfect gradation of forms in certain groups, and by the analogy of domestic productions.

From *The Origin of Species by means of Natural Selection; or, the Preservation of Favoured Races in the Struggle for Life* by Charles Darwin, 6th edn, John Murray, 1859

**43.** What is the principle of natural selection?
- ○ the difficulty of distinguishing species and varieties
- ○ the almost perfect gradation of forms
- ○ the transformation of a species
- ○ the adaptation of a species to a purpose

**44.** Who understood completely the principle of natural selection?
- ○ Aristotle
- ○ Buffon
- ○ Lamarck
- ○ Clair Grece

**45.** In this text who is giving the outline of the progress of opinion on the origin of species?
- ○ Buffon
- ○ Clair Grece
- ○ Aristotle
- ○ Lamarck
- ○ It is not stated specifically.

**46.** Complete the comparison.

Creationism is to evolution as species were separately created is to _____.

- ○ existing forms of life descended from pre-existing life forms
- ○ species are immutable creations
- ○ the probability of all change in the organic is of miraculous interposition

**47.** Up to the time this was written, how many naturalists believed in natural selection?
- ○ none
- ○ a few
- ○ about half
- ○ the majority
- ○ all

**48.** What does the principle of natural selection imply?
- ○ Humans were created by God.
- ○ There is miraculous intervention in the world.
- ○ There is a purposeful adaptation.
- ○ There is an accidental relationship in nature.

**49.** What do you think would be the modern reaction to the evolution of species?

- ○ The evolution of species is still likely to be controversial.
- ○ The evolution of species is still likely to be unpopular.
- ○ The evolution of species is still likely to be religious.

**50.** Look at this cartoon illustration of Charles Darwin.

What is the meaning behind this illustration?

- ○ This is an illustration of the author as nothing more than a foolish animal.
- ○ The illustration ridicules the author's supposed view that humans have evolved from apes.
- ○ This is a cartoon of the author, who looks like a hairy monkey.
- ○ The illustration indicates that the author has reverted to an earlier species.

# END OF TEST

**Well done! You have completed the third Reading Test.**

**How did you find these questions? We hope that you found them interesting. Revise anything that was hard for you. There are further questions in the final Reading Test.**

**Use the diagnostic chart on pages 104–105 to see which level of ability you reached. This is only an estimate. Don't be surprised if you answered some difficult questions correctly or even missed some easier questions.**

**Please note that multiple interpretations are possible for the levels of difficulty of these tasks. Also, some questions involve skills from different levels. This is only an initial guide to the approximate level of the reading skill assessed. No claim is made that this will be identical to the scores a student will receive in the actual tests, as the assessors will use a complex scoring system to estimate a student's level of ability.**

## Instructions

As you check the answer for each question, mark it as correct (✓) or incorrect (✗). Mark any questions that you omitted or left out as incorrect (✗) for the moment.

Then look at how many you answered correctly in each level. You will be able to see what level you are at by finding the point where you started having consistent difficulty with questions at a certain level. For example, if you answer most questions correctly up to the Intermediate level and then get most questions wrong from then onwards, it is likely your ability is at a Intermediate level. You can ask your parents or your teacher to help you do this if it isn't clear to you.

**Am I able to ...**

| | SKILL | ESTIMATED LEVEL | ✓ or ✗ |
|---|---|---|---|
| 1 | Determine the order of sentences? | Intermediate | |
| 2 | Analyse the information? | Standard | |
| 3 | Define the meaning of a word? | Standard | |
| 4 | Locate a detail? | Standard | |
| 5 | Deduce a fact from information that is given? | Standard | |
| 6 | Comprehend an outcome? | Standard | |
| 7 | Relate textual information and information from a map? | Standard | |
| 8 | Find the meaning of a word in the text? | Intermediate | |
| 9 | Select a possible meaning for an unusual word in the text? | Advanced | |
| 10 | Describe the audience for some information? | Standard | |
| 11 | Locate a fact? | Standard | |
| 12 | Deduce a major cost from the information given? | Standard | |
| 13 | Identify the emphasis in a text? | Intermediate | |
| 14 | Translate a quantitative detail to a general statement? | Intermediate | |
| 15 | Infer the purpose of the text? | Advanced | |
| 16 | Deduce information that is not readily apparent? | Advanced | |
| 17 | Select a feature in an advertisement? | Intermediate | |
| 18 | Check a fact? | Standard | |
| 19 | Find the feature that is evidence of the quality of a product? | Standard | |
| 20 | Describe a reaction to a scene from a poem? | Standard | |
| 21 | Describe a feeling in a scene from a poem? | Intermediate | |
| 22 | Find a correct statement about a poem? | Intermediate | |
| 23 | Summarise a poem's outcome? | Intermediate | |
| 24 | Describe the type of text? | Intermediate | |
| 25 | Interpret the style? | Advanced | |
| 26 | Locate the date of the events? | Standard | |
| 27 | Judge people's responses in the narrative? | Intermediate | |
| 28 | Indicate an outcome? | Intermediate | |
| 29 | Judge a response of one group to another? | Standard | |

| | SKILL | ESTIMATED LEVEL | ✓ or ✗ |
|---|---|---|---|
| 30 | State the purpose of a paragraph? | Standard | |
| 31 | Outline the reason for a response in the text? | Advanced | |
| 32 | Define a term that is not used in its ordinary meaning? | Advanced | |
| 33 | Indicate the number of steps in an operation? | Standard | |
| 34 | Locate a fact? | Standard | |
| 35 | State the components of a biological component? | Intermediate | |
| 36 | State the meaning of a word in context? | Advanced | |
| 37 | Locate a section in a diagram from a verbal description? | Intermediate | |
| 38 | Locate a section in a diagram from a verbal description? | Intermediate | |
| 39 | Locate a section in a diagram from a verbal description? | Intermediate | |
| 40 | Select a title? | Advanced | |
| 41 | Find the meaning of an allegory? | Advanced | |
| 42 | Indicate the nature of a parable? | Advanced | |
| 43 | State a principle? | Advanced | |
| 44 | Identify the person holding a view? | Advanced | |
| 45 | Nominate an author for a text? | Advanced | |
| 46 | Solve an analogy? | Advanced | |
| 47 | Find the number of adherents for a point of view? | Intermediate | |
| 48 | Explain a principle? | Advanced | |
| 49 | Estimate the popularity or contentiousness of a view? | Advanced | |
| 50 | Find the meaning of an illustration? | Advanced | |
| | **TOTAL** | | |

# READING TEST 4

This is the final Reading Test. There are 50 questions.

Allow around 65 minutes for this test. Take a short break if necessary.

In this test you will need to read a text. Then read the question and colour in the circle with the correct answer.

Read *Miracle man falls 47 floors* and answer questions 1 to 9.

## Miracle man falls 47 floors

Alcides Moreno, 37, is a native of Ecuador. He is a window cleaner who, together with his brother, fell 47 storeys from the roof of a New York skyscraper on 7 December 2007. This was a distance of some 152 metres. One doctor told the *New York Post*, 'Fifty per cent of people who fall four to five storeys die. By the time you reach 10 or 11 storeys, just about everyone dies.' Both legs and his right arm and wrist were broken in several places. He had severe injuries to his chest, his abdomen and his spinal column. His brain was bleeding. It was a major medical catastrophe requiring 24 pints of blood transfusion (twice his body volume). Yet Mr Moreno survived and he spoke on Christmas Day. His wife said, 'Thank God for the miracle that we had. He keeps telling me that it just wasn't his time.' The hospital's chief of surgery, Dr Philip Barie, also remarked, 'If you are a believer in miracles, this would be one.' Mr Moreno was discharged from the New York Presbyterian Hospital on 18 January 2008.

1. Where would you expect to read this text?
   ○ in a novel
   ○ in a newspaper
   ○ in a medical magazine

2. What was the expected probability of surviving this fall?

   | 0% | 1% | 50% | 100% |
   |----|----|-----|------|
   | ○ | ○ | ○ | ○ |

3. What is the meaning of *native* in the first sentence?
   ○ an inhabitant
   ○ a resident
   ○ a national
   ○ an indigenous person

4. To whom did his wife express appreciation?
   ○ Mr Moreno
   ○ New York Presbyterian Hospital
   ○ Dr Philip Barie
   ○ God

5. Which word is different in meaning from *miracle*?

   | normal | wonder | marvel |
   |--------|--------|--------|
   | ○ | ○ | ○ |

6. Mr Moreno says that he was saved by
   ○ his natural powers
   ○ a physical effect
   ○ a supernatural cause
   ○ a law of nature.

7. What is the main purpose of this text?
   ○ to describe Mr Moreno's recovery
   ○ to support miracles
   ○ to educate readers about falling
   ○ to state an opinion

**8.** Dr Barie remarked, 'If you are a believer in miracles …' mainly because

- ○ not everyone believes in miracles.
- ○ Mr Moreno survived an individual catastrophe.
- ○ almost everyone who falls that distance dies.

**9.** *Discharged from hospital* means

- ○ dying in hospital.
- ○ paying fees to a hospital.
- ○ leaving hospital.

Read *Australian cruiser destroyed the 'Emden'* and answer questions 10 to 16.

## Australian cruiser destroyed the *Emden*

The Battle of Cocos was a naval battle that took place in November 1914 during World War I. It took place in the Cocos (Keeling) Islands in the northeast Indian Ocean.

Over a period of three months, the German light cruiser SMS *Emden* had sunk 28 Allied merchant vessels and two warships. In November 1914 it had attacked a communication station on Direction Island. It was then engaged several hours later by HMAS *Sydney*, an Australian light cruiser. The battle was the first naval engagement for the Royal Australian Navy.

Captain Glossop was commander of HMAS *Sydney*, which destroyed the *Emden*. He received the following message from the First Lord of the Admiralty: 'Warmest congratulations on the brilliant entry of the Australian Navy into the war, and the signal service rendered to the Allied cause and to peaceful commerce by the destruction of the "Emden".'

HMAS *Melbourne*

While it fell to HMAS *Sydney* to bring the *Emden* to action, another vessel of the Australian Navy, the *Melbourne*, also joined in the pursuit. The Admiralty stated that a 'large combined operation by fast cruisers against the "Emden" has been for some time in progress. In this search, which covered an immense area, the British cruisers have been aided by French, Russian, and Japanese vessels working in harmony. HMAS Melbourne and Sydney were also included in these movements.'

Adapted from *The Illustrated War News*, 18 November 1914, no. 15

**10.** What is the meaning of this text?

- ○ It summarises the ship-to-ship engagement of the Royal Australian Navy.
- ○ It is about HMAS *Melbourne*.
- ○ It describes a naval battle.
- ○ It summarises the naval Battle of Cocos.

**11.** Vessels from which nations were involved in the search for SMS *Emden*?

- ○ France, Russia and Japan
- ○ Britain, France, Russia and Japan
- ○ Australia, Britain, France, Russia and Japan
- ○ Germany, Australia, Britain, France, Russia and Japan

**12.** Why did the first Lord of the Admiralty congratulate Commander Glossop?

○ Commander Glossop was congratulated because he worked with the British, French, Russian and Japanese vessels.

○ Commander Glossop was congratulated because the battle was an outstanding achievement by the Royal Australian Navy.

○ Commander Glossop was congratulated because HMAS *Melbourne* and HMAS *Sydney* worked together.

○ Commander Glossop was congratulated because he destroyed SMS *Emden*.

**13.** What was 'the Allied cause' referred to in the third paragraph?

○ the war being fought by Britain and other nations

○ the naval battle against the Germans

○ the reasons for the war against Germany

○ the cooperation by many nations in the fighting

**14.** What do the letters *HMAS* represent in this text?

○ Heavy Merchant Australian Ship

○ His Majesty's Australian Ship

○ His Majesty's Admiralty Ship

**15.** SMS is to ▓▓▓▓▓▓ as HMAS is to ▓▓▓▓▓▓

○ German, Australian

○ Emden, Royal Australian Navy

○ cruiser, light cruiser

**16.** This sea battle occurred in

○ World War I.

○ World War II.

○ the Vietnam War.

○ the Korean War.

---

It would be a good idea to check your answers to questions 1 to 16 before moving on to the other questions.

Read *Christopher Columbus (1436–1506)* and answer questions 17 to 23.

## Christopher Columbus (1436–1506)

While living in Lisbon, Columbus made up his mind to try to do what no other man, at that time, dared attempt,—that was to cross the Atlantic Ocean. He thought that by doing so he could get directly to Asia and the Indies, which, he believed, were opposite Portugal and Spain. If successful, he could open up a very profitable trade with the rich countries of the East, from which spices, drugs, and silk were brought to Europe. The people of Europe could not reach those countries directly by ships, because they had not then found their way round the southern point of Africa.

*This map shows how Columbus hoped to reach Asia and the East Indies.*

### Columbus tries to get help in carrying out his plans

Columbus was too poor to fit out even a single ship to undertake such a voyage as he had planned. He asked the king of Portugal to furnish some money or vessels toward it, but he received no encouragement. At length he determined to go to Spain and see if he could get help there.

On the southern coast of Spain there is a small port named Palos. Within sight of the village of Palos, and also within plain sight

---

of the ocean, there was a convent—which is still standing—called the Convent of Saint Mary.

One morning a tall, fine-looking man, leading a little boy by the hand, knocked at the door of this convent and begged for a piece of bread and a cup of water for the child. The man was Columbus,—whose wife was now dead,—and the boy was his son.

It chanced that the guardian of the convent noticed Columbus standing at the door. He liked his appearance, and coming up, began to talk with him. Columbus frankly told him what he was trying to do. The guardian of the convent listened with great interest; then he gave him a letter to a friend who he thought would help him to lay his plans before Ferdinand and Isabella, the king and queen of Spain.

**Columbus gets help for his great voyage**
Columbus left his son at the convent, and set forward on his journey full of bright hopes. But Ferdinand and Isabella could not then see him; and after waiting a long time, the traveller was told that he might go before a number of learned men and tell them about his proposed voyage across the Atlantic.

After hearing what Columbus had to say, these men thought that it would be foolish to spend money in trying to reach the other side of the ocean.

People who heard what this captain from Lisbon wanted to do began to think that he had lost his reason, and the boys in the streets laughed at him and called him crazy. Columbus waited for help seven years; he then made up his mind that he would wait no longer. Just as he was about to leave Spain, Queen Isabella, who had always felt interested in the brave sailor, resolved to aid him. Two rich sea-captains who lived in Palos also decided to take part in the voyage.

With the assistance which Columbus now got he was able to fit out three small vessels. He went in the largest of the vessels—the only one which had an entire deck—as admiral or commander of the fleet.

From *The Beginner's American History* by DH Montgomery, Ginn & Company, 1893

17. What was the unprecedented decision Columbus made?
   ○ to travel to Asia around Africa
   ○ to seek help from the king of Portugal
   ○ to open up profitable trade routes
   ○ to reach the Indies by sailing west

18. In which direction did Columbus plan to sail?
   ○ south        ○ north
   ○ west         ○ east

19. What was the first step that Columbus took to get help in carrying out his plans?
   ○ He asked the king of Portugal.
   ○ He went to Spain to see if he could get help.
   ○ He went to the village of Palos.
   ○ He went to see the king and queen of Spain.

20. How was Columbus able to put his plans before the king and queen of Spain?
   ○ He visited Ferdinand and Isabella.
   ○ He received a letter of introduction.
   ○ He spoke with learned men.
   ○ He left his son at the convent.

21. What did Columbus suffer before getting help for his great voyage?
   ○ the need to reach the other side of the ocean
   ○ impatience    ○ ridicule
   ○ the loss of his reason

**22.** Why might the people at that time have not believed Columbus?

- ○ They did not believe in the charts he had prepared and the details of his plans.
- ○ They knew that it was not possible to travel to Asia as America was in the way.
- ○ They thought he was entirely crazy.
- ○ They believed that the world was flat and that to travel west would mean to fall over the edge.

**23.** What does the text tell us about the character of Columbus?

- ○ He was pushy and stubborn.
- ○ He was correct and determined.
- ○ He was brave and resolute.
- ○ He was impatient and convincing.

**Read the following text and answer questions 24 to 33.**

There was no possibility of taking a walk that day. We had been wandering, indeed, in the leafless shrubbery an hour in the morning; but since dinner (Mrs. Reed, when there was no company, dined early) the cold winter wind had brought with it clouds so sombre, and a rain so penetrating, that further out-door exercise was now out of the question.

I was glad of it: I never liked long walks, especially on chilly afternoons: dreadful to me was the coming home in the raw twilight, with nipped fingers and toes, and a heart saddened by the chidings of Bessie, the nurse, and humbled by the consciousness of my physical inferiority to Eliza, John, and Georgiana Reed.

The said Eliza, John, and Georgiana were now clustered round their mama in the drawing-room: she lay reclined on a sofa by the fireside, and with her darlings about her (for the time neither quarrelling nor crying) looked perfectly happy. Me, she had dispensed from joining the group; saying, 'She regretted to be under the necessity of keeping me at a distance; but that until she heard from Bessie, and could discover by her own observation, that I was endeavouring in good earnest to acquire a more sociable and childlike disposition, a more attractive and sprightly manner— something lighter, franker, more natural, as it were—she really must exclude me from privileges intended only for contented, happy, little children.'

'What does Bessie say I have done?' I asked.

'Jane, I don't like cavillers or questioners; besides, there is something truly forbidding in a child taking up her elders in that manner. Be seated somewhere; and until you can speak pleasantly, remain silent.'

A breakfast-room adjoined the drawing-room, I slipped in there. It contained a bookcase: I soon possessed myself of a volume, taking care that it should be one stored with pictures. I mounted into the window-seat: gathering up my feet, I sat cross-legged, like a Turk; and, having drawn the red moreen curtain nearly close, I was shrined in double retirement.

Folds of scarlet drapery shut in my view to the right hand; to the left were the clear panes of glass, protecting, but not separating me from the drear November day. At intervals, while turning over the leaves of my book, I studied the aspect of that winter afternoon. Afar, it offered a pale blank of mist and cloud; near a scene of wet lawn and storm-beat shrub, with ceaseless rain sweeping away wildly before a long and lamentable blast.

From *Jane Eyre: an Autobiography* by Charlotte Bronte, Service & Paton, 1897

**24.** In the first paragraph the writer tells us that there were cold winter winds. What other clue in the first paragraph indicates indirectly that it is winter?

- ○ the dark clouds on the horizon
- ○ the leafless shrubs
- ○ the penetrating rain

**25.** What time is probably referred to in the first paragraph?

- ○ It is after dinner.
- ○ It is before dinner.
- ○ It is dinner time.

**26.** In the second paragraph what is the meaning of *chidings*?

- ○ reprimands
- ○ praise
- ○ punishments
- ○ lectures

**27.** What is the name of the person relating the story?

- ○ Mrs Reed  ○ Bessie
- ○ Eliza  ○ Jane
- ○ John  ○ Georgiana

**28.** Why was the person in the story said to be excluded from the group?

- ○ Mrs Reed said she was not sociable.
- ○ Mrs Reed was not her mother.
- ○ She had annoyed Bessie.
- ○ Mrs Reed said she was insolent.

**29.** What did Mrs Reed resent?

- ○ being interrupted by a child
- ○ being spoken to rudely by a child
- ○ being challenged by a child
- ○ being ordered around by a child

**30.** What is a *caviller*?

- ○ someone who quibbles
- ○ someone who is arrogant
- ○ someone who is evasive with another
- ○ someone who lies

**31.** Where did the conversation (in paragraphs 3–5) between Mrs Reed and the girl take place?

- ○ in the dining room
- ○ in the drawing room
- ○ in the breakfast room
- ○ in the library

**32.** What was one thing the girl did not do when she went into the room by herself?

- ○ She reclined on a sofa by the window.
- ○ She selected a picture book from the library.
- ○ She sat by the window.
- ○ She saw the mist and the cloud.

**33.** How would you imagine that the girl was treated in that household?

- ○ She was treated as a cheeky member of that family.
- ○ She was excluded from all the family activities.
- ○ She was treated as an outsider who did not belong to that family.
- ○ She was treated differently from her other siblings.

Did you colour in one of the circles?

It would be a good idea to check your answers to questions 17 to 33 before moving on to the other questions.

**Read *The four traditional castes* and answer questions 34 to 41.**

## The four traditional castes

The well-known traditional theory of caste is that the Aryans were divided from the beginning of time into four castes: Brahmans or priests, Kshatriyas or warriors, Vaishyas or merchants and cultivators, and Sudras (also Shudra) or menials and labourers, all of whom had a divine origin, being born from the body of Brahma—the Brahmans from his mouth, the Kshatriyas from his arms, the Vaishyas from his thighs, and the Sudras from his feet. Intermarriage between the four castes was not at first entirely prohibited, and a man of any of the three higher ones, provided that for his first wife he took a woman of his own caste, could subsequently marry others of the divisions beneath his own. In this manner the other castes originated. Thus the Kaivarttas or Kewats were the offspring of a Kshatriya father and Vaishya mother, and so on. Mixed marriages in the opposite direction, of a woman of a higher caste with a man of a lower one, were reprobated as strongly as possible, and the offspring of these were relegated to the lowest position in society; thus the Chandals, or descendants of a

Sudra father and Brahman mother, were of all men the most base. It has been recognised that this genealogy, though in substance the formation of a number of new castes through mixed descent may have been correct, is, as regards the details, an attempt made by a priestly law-giver to account, on the lines of orthodox tradition, for a state of society which had ceased to correspond to them.

From *The Tribes and Castes of the Central Provinces of India* by RV Russell & RBH Lai, Macmillan and Co., 1916

**34.** In which caste were the traders?
- ○ Brahmans
- ○ Sudras
- ○ Kshatriyas
- ○ Vaishyas

**35.** Which caste originated from the mouth of Brahma?
- ○ Brahmans
- ○ Sudras
- ○ Kshatriyas
- ○ Vaishyas

**36.** Which country used this caste system?
- ○ Tibet
- ○ Pakistan
- ○ Afghanistan
- ○ India

**37.** Which word rhymes best with *caste*?
- ○ haste      ○ waste
- ○ last       ○ taste
- ○ class      ○ fracas
- ○ farce      ○ pass

**38.** Which caste is best represented by this picture of a priest?

- ○ Brahman
- ○ Sudra
- ○ Kshatriya
- ○ Vaishya

**39.** From your reading of this text, which is the best definition for a caste?

- ○ A caste is a type of social group.
- ○ A caste is a description of people.
- ○ A caste is a group in which people work.
- ○ A caste is a state of society.

**40.** In this text what appears to be the chief basis for the division into castes?

- ○ father
- ○ occupation
- ○ intermarriage
- ○ religion

**41.** What could be a correct replacement for the word *genealogy* in the text?

- ○ genetics
- ○ history
- ○ offspring
- ○ family tree
- ○ mixed descent

**Read the following text and answer questions 42 to 50.**

This book is intended not to raise fears but to record facts. We wish to describe with pen and pencil those features of England which are gradually disappearing, and to preserve the memory of them. It may be said that we have begun our quest too late; that so much has already vanished that it is hardly worthwhile to record what is left. Although much has gone, there is still, however, much remaining that is good, that reveals the artistic skill and taste of our forefathers, and recalls the wonders of old-time. It will be our endeavour to tell of the old country houses that Time has spared, the cottages that grace the village green, the stern grey walls that still guard some few of our towns, the old moot halls and public buildings. We shall see the old-time farmers and rustics gathering together at fair and market, their games and sports and merry-makings, and whatever relics of old English life have been left for an artist and scribe of the twentieth century to record.

Our age is an age of progress. *Altiora peto* is its motto. The spirit of progress is in the air, and lures its votaries on to higher flights. Sometimes they discover that they have been following a mere will-o'-the-wisp, that leads them into bog and quagmire whence no escape is possible. The England of a century, or even of half a century ago, has vanished, and we find ourselves in the midst of a busy, bustling world that knows no rest or peace. Inventions tread upon each other's heels in one long vast bewildering procession. We look back at the peaceful reign of the pack-horse, the rumbling wagon, the advent of the merry coaching days, the 'Lightning' and the 'Quicksilver,' the chaining of the rivers with locks and bars, the network of canals that spread over the whole country; and then the first shriek of the railway engine startled the echoes of the countryside, a poor powerless thing that had to be pulled up the steep gradients by a chain attached to a big stationary engine at the summit. But it was the herald of the doom of the old-world England. Highways and coaching roads, canals and rivers, were abandoned and deserted. The old coachmen, once lords of the road, ended their days in the poorhouse, and steam, almighty steam, ruled everywhere.

Now the wayside inns wake up again with the bellow of the motor-car, which like a hideous monster rushes through the old-world villages, startling and killing old slow-footed rustics and scampering children, dogs and hens, and clouds of dust strive in very mercy to hide the view of the terrible rushing demon. In a few years' time the air will be conquered, and aeroplanes, balloons, flying-machines and air-ships, will drop down upon us from the skies and add a new terror to life.

From *Vanishing England* by PH Ditchfield & F Roe, Methuen & Co., 1910

**42.** What is the overall purpose of the text?
- ○ It provides a historical sketch of England.
- ○ It provides a geographical sketch of England.
- ○ It provides a political sketch of England.
- ○ It provides a social sketch of England.
- ○ It provides an environmental sketch of England.
- ○ It provides an archaeological sketch of England.

**43.** Which sentence is correct?
- ○ This text is the work of an author and a separate illustrator.
- ○ This text is the work of one author and illustrator combined.
- ○ This text is the work of an author and a photographer.
- ○ This text is the work of an artist and an illustrator.
- ○ This text is the work of a person who both wrote the text and drew the pictures.

**44.** What will not be described in this book?
- ○ old country houses
- ○ vintage motor cars
- ○ moot halls
- ○ public buildings
- ○ canals
- ○ farmers

**45.** What is the meaning of the word *rustics* in the first paragraph?
- ○ corroded machinery
- ○ shopkeepers
- ○ country folk
- ○ city folk

**46.** *Altiora peto* is a Latin expression. It means something like 'aim higher'. To what did the writer apply this expression?

- ○ our present-day progress
- ○ the better times in days gone by
- ○ the future
- ○ the time of writing

**47.** Why has this text been written?

- ○ to describe the culture and traditions of England
- ○ to outline the progress in English life
- ○ to highlight a changing lifestyle in the English countryside
- ○ to preserve aspects of English life that are vanishing

**48.** What is the meaning of the word *will-o'-the-wisp* in the second paragraph?

- ○ something deliberate
- ○ a small person
- ○ something that misleads
- ○ a small bundle

**49.** In the second paragraph where it refers to the spirit of progress and its votaries, to what is the word *votaries* referring?

- ○ those who vote for progress
- ○ those who worship progress
- ○ those who admire progress
- ○ those who note the modern progress
- ○ those who benefit from progress

**50.** What does the writer say has happened?

- ○ Many picturesque features of English life have vanished.
- ○ Life is forever changing and doubtless this is for the best.
- ○ The present environment is delightful but the past should be recollected.
- ○ The best relics of English life have not vanished.

Did you colour in one of the circles?

# END OF TEST

Well done! You have completed the final Reading Test. It means that you have answered or attempted 200 Reading questions. Now take a long break before you do any more tests.

How did you find these questions? We hope you found them interesting. You will have noticed that we tried to include more difficult questions than normal in these practice tests. We have gone beyond the curriculum in order to challenge you.

Use the diagnostic chart on pages 116–117 to see which level of ability you reached. This is only an estimate. Don't be surprised if you answered some difficult questions correctly or even missed some easier questions.

Please note that multiple interpretations are possible for the levels of difficulty of these tasks. Also, some questions involve skills from different levels. This is only an initial guide to the approximate level of the reading skill assessed. No claim is made that this will be identical to the scores a student will receive in the actual tests, as the assessors will use a complex scoring system to estimate a student's level of ability.

## Instructions

As you check the answer for each question, mark it as correct (✓) or incorrect (✗). Mark any questions that you omitted or left out as incorrect (✗) for the moment.

Then look at how many you answered correctly in each level. You will be able to see what level you are at by finding the point where you started having consistent difficulty with questions at a certain level. For example, if you answer most questions correctly up to the Intermediate level and then get most questions wrong from then onwards, it is likely your ability is at a Intermediate level. You can ask your parents or your teacher to help you do this if it isn't clear to you.

**Am I able to ...**

| | SKILL | ESTIMATED LEVEL | ✓ or ✗ |
|---|---|---|---|
| 1 | Identify a source for a text? | Standard | |
| 2 | Estimate the probability from the details in the text? | Standard | |
| 3 | Define a word in context? | Intermediate | |
| 4 | Find the object of thanks? | Standard | |
| 5 | Check a word that is different in meaning? | Standard | |
| 6 | Attribute an event? | Advanced | |
| 7 | Indicate the purpose behind a text? | Advanced | |
| 8 | Allow for the meaning of a conditional term *if*? | Advanced | |
| 9 | Interpret a common but technical verb? | Intermediate | |
| 10 | Summarise a text? | Standard | |
| 11 | Locate some details from a text? | Standard | |
| 12 | Explain an action? | Intermediate | |
| 13 | Suggest a meaning of a phrase? | Intermediate | |
| 14 | Explain an abbreviation? | Intermediate | |
| 15 | Complete an analogy? | Advanced | |
| 16 | Locate a battle in a historical period? | Intermediate | |
| 17 | Find a person's decision from information in the text? | Intermediate | |
| 18 | Decide on the direction of travel from a map and information? | Standard | |
| 19 | Find a simple fact? | Standard | |
| 20 | Indicate a reason? | Standard | |
| 21 | State an outcome for a character? | Intermediate | |
| 22 | Find a reason for disbelief? | Intermediate | |
| 23 | Infer the character of a person? | Advanced | |
| 24 | Find a clue to the season in a paragraph? | Intermediate | |
| 25 | Estimate the time from the details in the text? | Intermediate | |
| 26 | Find a synonym? | Advanced | |
| 27 | State the name of the author of a text from details provided? | Intermediate | |
| 28 | Find the reason for an outcome? | Intermediate | |
| 29 | Find the reason for a response? | Intermediate | |

| | SKILL | ESTIMATED LEVEL | ✓ or ✗ |
|---|---|---|---|
| 30 | Define an unusual word? | Advanced | |
| 31 | Check the location of a conversation? | Standard | |
| 32 | Identify an action that did not occur in a story? | Standard | |
| 33 | Report the probable situation of a character? | Advanced | |
| 34 | Find a category that is stated? | Standard | |
| 35 | Find a category that is stated? | Standard | |
| 36 | Find an answer from general knowledge? | Intermediate | |
| 37 | Find a word that rhymes? | Advanced | |
| 38 | Match a picture to a category? | Intermediate | |
| 39 | Define a term that is not explicit? | Advanced | |
| 40 | Infer the basis for categorisation? | Advanced | |
| 41 | Select a word meaning? | Advanced | |
| 42 | Set out the scope of a text? | Advanced | |
| 43 | Discern the contributors to a work? | Advanced | |
| 44 | Infer what will not be included? | Intermediate | |
| 45 | Define a word? | Advanced | |
| 46 | Find the application of a Latin expression? | Advanced | |
| 47 | Describe the purpose of the text? | Advanced | |
| 48 | Define a term or expression? | Advanced | |
| 49 | Define an unusual term? | Advanced | |
| 50 | Summarise the writer's point of view? | Advanced | |
| | TOTAL | | |

## An important note about the NAPLAN Online tests

The NAPLAN Online Conventions of Language test will be divided into different sections. Students will only have one opportunity to check their answers at the end of each section before proceeding to the next one. This means that after students have completed a section and moved onto the next they will not be able to check their work again. We have included reminders for students to check their work at specific points in the practice tests from now on so they become familiar with this process.

# CONVENTIONS OF LANGUAGE TEST 1

This is the first Conventions of Language Test. There are 50 questions.

Allow around 45 minutes for this test. Take a short break before the spelling if necessary.

**Colour in the circle(s) with the correct answer.**

1. Which sentence has the correct punctuation?
   - ○ some boys are talkative
   - ○ Some boys are talkative
   - ○ Some boys, are talkative.
   - ○ Some boys are talkative.

2. Which sentence has the correct punctuation?
   - ○ where did they play
   - ○ where did they play.
   - ○ Where did they play?
   - ○ Where did they play!

3. Which sentence has the correct punctuation?
   - ○ We bought coffee, tea, milk and sugar.
   - ○ We bought, coffee tea milk and sugar.
   - ○ We bought, coffee, tea, milk and sugar.
   - ○ We bought coffee, tea, milk, and sugar.

4. Which sentence has the correct punctuation?
   - ○ The greek and italian salads had herbs and spices.
   - ○ The Greek and Italian salads had herbs and spices.
   - ○ The Greek and Italian Salads had herbs and spices.

5. Which sentence has the correct punctuation?
   - ○ Hobart is the Capital of Tasmania and is situated on the Derwent river.
   - ○ Hobart is the capital of tasmania and is situated on the derwent river.
   - ○ Hobart is the Capital of Tasmania and is situated on the Derwent River.
   - ○ Hobart is the capital of Tasmania and is situated on the Derwent River.

**6.** Which sentence has the correct punctuation?

○ "I know Jim would be reliable" said Mr Dixon.

○ "I know Jim would be reliable," said Mr Dixon.

○ "I know Jim would be reliable said Mr Dixon".

○ I know Jim would be reliable, said Mr Dixon.

**7.** Which sentence has the correct punctuation?

○ The Leader of the Opposition who is the Member for Bradford challenged the policy and said, "The Federal Government is too slow."

○ The leader of the opposition, who is the member for Bradford, challenged the policy and said, "The Federal government is too slow."

○ The Leader of the Opposition, who is the Member for Bradford, challenged the policy and said, "The Federal Government is too slow."

○ The leader of the opposition who is the member for Bradford challenged the policy and said "The Federal Government is too slow."

**8.** Which sentence has the correct punctuation?

○ He said what do you mean I won?

○ He said, "What do you mean I won?"

○ He said what do you mean, "I won."

○ He said, "what do you mean I won?"

**9.** Which sentence contains an adjective?

○ The most marvellous thing about miracles is that they occur.

○ A boy stood alone against the outline of the landscape.

○ The clouds in the sky came together to form a shape.

○ Alexander was a hero.

**10.** Which sentence contains an adverb?

○ The eyes on the face of the footballer stood out like those of a goldfish.

○ Did they definitely knock over all the items on the shelf?

○ I waited until I saw two priests walking in the avenue.

○ He produced his identification card and said that he was on official business.

Did you colour in one of the circles?

**11.** In which sentence is the word *clean* used as an adjective?

○ He tries to give the car a clean every Friday afternoon.

○ The nurse will clean the instruments before the operation.

○ The sparkling clean air was refreshing to our lungs.

○ The villain came clean to the police after interrogation.

**12.** Which sentence uses commas in the correct place?

○ Nicholas, who kicked the ball into the neighbour's yard, would now have to go and apologise.

○ Nicholas who kicked the ball, into the neighbour's yard, would now have to go and apologise.

○ Nicholas who kicked the ball into the neighbour's yard, would now have to go and apologise.

○ Nicholas, who kicked the ball, into the neighbour's yard, would now have to go, and apologise.

**13.** Colour in **two** circles to show where the missing speech marks (" and ") should go.

"Josephine, get inside right now, said Granny. You need to start your homework immediately."

**14.** Where should the missing apostrophe ( ' ) go?

Mums job was to read books to the twins while Dad helped James and Charles finish their essays.

**15.** Which of the following correctly completes the sentence?

Where have the boys put ▮▮▮▮▮ coats?

their        they're        there        them
○              ○                 ○                ○

**16.** Which word correctly completes the sentence?

The farmers have ▮▮▮▮ by the south road.

| gone | went | go |
|:---:|:---:|:---:|
| ○ | ○ | ○ |

**17.** Which word correctly completes the sentence?

I thought there ▮▮▮▮ two of you playing table tennis.

| is | was | were | am |
|:---:|:---:|:---:|:---:|
| ○ | ○ | ○ | ○ |

**18.** Which word correctly completes the sentence?

It was their ▮▮▮▮ defeat.

| worse | worst | worser | worsed |
|:---:|:---:|:---:|:---:|
| ○ | ○ | ○ | ○ |

**19.** Which of the following correctly completes the sentence?

I was alone and walked ▮▮▮▮ along the path.

| slow | slowest | slowly | slowed |
|:---:|:---:|:---:|:---:|
| ○ | ○ | ○ | ○ |

**20.** Which word correctly completes the sentence?

Either Anthony or John ▮▮▮▮ taken the last one.

| have | having | has |
|:---:|:---:|:---:|
| ○ | ○ | ○ |

Did you colour in one of the circles?

Here is a passage. There are some words missing. These are shown in a numbered space. Select the correct word for each numbered space.

## Happiness

Some recent findings from research ⬛ 21 happiness include the following:

1. For a person, money does buy a ⬛ 22 amount of happiness. For the typical individual, a doubling of salary makes a lot less ⬛ 23 life events like marriage.

2. Nations in the West do not seem to get ⬛ 24 as they get richer.

3. In comparison women report higher well-being ⬛ 25 men.

Source: Reprinted with permission, David R Francis, *The Happiness of Nations*, www.nber.org/digest/jan06/w11416.html, retrieved December 2009

**21.** ○ on        ○ with        ○ for

**22.** ○ reason      ○ reasoned     ○ reasonable

**23.** ○ difference with    ○ difference to    ○ difference than

**24.** ○ more happier    ○ happier    ○ happiest

**25.** ○ than       ○ for       ○ as

**It would be a good idea to check over your answers to questions 1 to 25 before moving on to the other questions.**

# CONVENTIONS OF LANGUAGE TEST 1

**To the student**

Ask your teacher or parent to read the spelling words for you. The words are listed on page 199. Write the spelling words on the lines below.

✏️ **Test 1 spelling words**

26. _____     34. _____

27. _____     35. _____

28. _____     36. _____

29. _____     37. _____

30. _____     38. _____

31. _____     39. _____

32. _____     40. _____

33. _____

**Read the sentences. The spelling mistake in each sentence is underlined. Write the correct word in the box.**

**41.** It was <u>Saterday</u> today, so we went for a swim

**42.** before <u>brekfast</u>. There were many people

**43.** <u>joging</u> along the shore and the surf looked

**44.** <u>deliteful</u> this morning. The sun rose quickly

**45.** over the horizon, turning it red and <u>yello</u>.

**Read the sentences. Each sentence has one word that is incorrect. Write the correct spelling of the word in the box**

**46.** I wondered wen I should start to contact them.

**47.** Just then I herd the telephone.

**48.** There was going to be a great deel of trouble.

**49.** It was bad news write from the beginning.

**50.** I put down the phone and whiped my tears with a handkerchief.

Write your answers in the boxes.

# END OF TEST

Well done! You have completed the first Conventions of Language Test. You have done quite well if you managed to complete this test. We really mean this as there were many questions to answer.

How did you find these questions? Check to see where you did well and where you had problems. Try to revise the questions that were hard for you.

Use the diagnostic chart on pages 125–126 to see which level of ability you reached. This is only an estimate. Don't be surprised if you answered some difficult questions correctly or even missed some easier questions.

There are now three more tests, each containing 50 questions. They include many of the same types of questions, plus a few new types.

## Instructions

As you check the answer for each question, mark it as correct (✓) or incorrect (✗). Mark any questions that you omitted or left out as incorrect (✗) for the moment.

Then look at how many you answered correctly in each level. You will be able to see what level you are at by finding the point where you started having consistent difficulty with questions at a certain level. For example, if you answer most questions correctly up to the Intermediate level and then get most questions wrong from then onwards, it is likely your ability is at a Intermediate level. You can ask your parents or your teacher to help you do this if it isn't clear to you.

**Am I able to ...**

| | SKILL | ESTIMATED LEVEL | ✓ or ✗ |
|---|---|---|---|
| 1 | Use a capital letter for the start and a full stop for the end of a sentence? | Standard | |
| 2 | Use a capital letter for the start and a question mark for the end of a sentence? | Standard | |
| 3 | Use commas to divide items in a list? | Standard | |
| 4 | Use capital letters for proper nouns? | Standard | |
| 5 | Use capital letters for multiple proper nouns? | Intermediate | |
| 6 | Use commas and speech marks in direct speech? | Advanced | |
| 7 | Use multiple commas and speech marks in direct speech? | Advanced | |
| 8 | Use speech marks for direct speech? | Standard | |
| 9 | Identify an adjective? | Standard | |
| 10 | Identify an adverb? | Standard | |
| 11 | Identify an adjective? | Standard | |
| 12 | Find a pair of commas in a complex sentence? | Advanced | |
| 13 | Use speech marks for direct speech? | Standard | |
| 14 | Use apostrophes for possession? | Intermediate | |
| 15 | Use pronouns for possession? | Standard | |
| 16 | Use the present perfect tense? | Standard | |
| 17 | Use the correct form of common verbs? | Standard | |
| 18 | Use superlative adjectives? | Intermediate | |
| 19 | Use adverbial phrases? | Advanced | |
| 20 | Use the correct form of common verbs? | Intermediate | |
| 21 | Use prepositional phrases? | Intermediate | |
| 22 | Use adjectives correctly? | Intermediate | |
| 23 | Use prepositions for comparison? | Advanced | |
| 24 | Use comparative adjectives? | Advanced | |
| 25 | Use prepositions for comparison? | Advanced | |
| 26 | Spell *argue*? | Intermediate | |
| 27 | Spell *plane*? | Standard | |
| 28 | Spell *trouble*? | Intermediate | |

| | SKILL | ESTIMATED LEVEL | ✓ or ✗ |
|---|---|---|---|
| 29 | Spell *fatigue*? | Advanced | |
| 30 | Spell *sweater*? | Advanced | |
| 31 | Spell *taxied*? | Intermediate | |
| 32 | Spell *beginning*? | Intermediate | |
| 33 | Spell *handkerchief*? | Intermediate | |
| 34 | Spell *calves*? | Standard | |
| 35 | Spell *addresses*? | Standard | |
| 36 | Spell *population*? | Intermediate | |
| 37 | Spell *acquainted*? | Intermediate | |
| 38 | Spell *neighbourhood*? | Intermediate | |
| 39 | Spell *adolescents*? | Advanced | |
| 40 | Spell *circumference*? | Advanced | |
| 41 | Spell *Saturday*? | Intermediate | |
| 42 | Spell *breakfast*? | Standard | |
| 43 | Spell *jogging*? | Standard | |
| 44 | Spell *delightful*? | Intermediate | |
| 45 | Spell *yellow*? | Standard | |
| 46 | Spell *when*? | Standard | |
| 47 | Spell *heard*? | Standard | |
| 48 | Spell *deal*? | Standard | |
| 49 | Spell *right*? | Standard | |
| 50 | Spell *wiped*? | Intermediate | |
| | **TOTAL** | | |

This is the second Conventions of Language Test. There are 50 questions.

Allow around 45 minutes for this test. Take a short break before the spelling if necessary.

**Colour in the circle with the correct answer. Colour in only one circle for each answer.**

1. Which sentence uses commas ( **,** ) correctly?

   ○ The patient rather angry, and impatient, left the surgery.

   ○ The patient, rather angry, and impatient, left the surgery.

   ○ The patient rather angry and impatient, left the surgery.

   ○ The patient, rather angry and impatient, left the surgery.

2. Colour in a circle to show where the missing apostrophe ( **'** ) should go.

   ○　　　　　　○　　　　　　○　　　　　　○

   All of the doctors were preparing for the exams when the fire alarms went off in the registrars office.

3. Where do the **two** missing speech marks ( **"** and **"** ) go?

   ○　○　　　　　　○　○

   His daughter asked, Has the package arrived yet ?

4. Which word correctly completes the sentence?

   He voted for the emissions trading scheme ▮▮▮▮ the fact that it would not be approved in the Senate.

   | despite | although | whereas | even though |
   |---------|----------|---------|-------------|
   | ○ | ○ | ○ | ○ |

5. Which word correctly completes the sentence?

   The Prime Minister had ▮▮▮▮ overseas to visit the other heads of government in Copenhagen.

   | went | gone | goed | going |
   |------|------|------|-------|
   | ○ | ○ | ○ | ○ |

**6.** Which of the following correctly completes the sentence?

There are hopes that the Prime Minister's proposals will be formed ▨▨▨▨ a new carbon plan for the environment.

| into | at | around | in |
|------|----|--------|----|
| ○ | ○ | ○ | ○ |

**7.** Which word correctly completes the sentence?

He asked all members of parliament to be patient ▨▨▨▨ further discussions are underway.

| while | however | during | if |
|-------|---------|--------|----|
| ○ | ○ | ○ | ○ |

**8.** Which sentence contains an adjective?

○ It was a coincidence that Michael married a woman called Michaela.

○ Understanding life should count on what is not expected.

○ To find an answer to a problem he followed what was unlikely.

○ Life is surprising: if you are not open to it, you miss things.

**9.** Which sentence contains an adverb?

○ "Which way did they head?" snapped the police officer.

○ "They boarded a blue bus over there," answered the passer-by. "The one that goes to Maroubra."

○ The officer spoke quickly and ordered his men to follow the bus.

○ He dodged the pedestrians as he followed the villains.

---

**Read the sentences. They have some gaps. Choose the correct word or words to fill each gap. Colour in only one circle for each answer.**

---

**10.** The man and woman ▨▨▨▨ seated on my right.

| was | were | we're | |
|-----|------|-------|----|
| ○ | ○ | ○ | 10 |

**11.** The farmers plough the northern field and then ▨▨▨ come back through the valley.

| they | you | them | these | |
|------|-----|------|-------|----|
| ○ | ○ | ○ | ○ | 11 |

**12.** I thought there were two flights but both have been ▨▨▨▨.

○ cancels
○ cancelling
○ cancel
○ cancelled

| 12 |

**13.** They played three games and this was their [____] victory so far.

| good | better | best | bestest |
|:---:|:---:|:---:|:---:|
| ○ | ○ | ○ | ○ |

13

**14.** Anthony is the [____]. He is 30, John is 25 and Nicholas is 14.

- ○ old
- ○ oldest
- ○ eldest
- ○ elder
- ○ older
- ○ most elder

**15.** Some people say this building is [____] than the church steeple but really they are the same height.

- ○ tallest
- ○ taller
- ○ more tallest
- ○ more taller

**Read the text *That there dog o' mine*. The text has some gaps. Choose the correct word or words to fill the gap. Colour in only one circle for each answer.**

## That there dog o' mine

Macquarie the shearer [__16__] with an accident. To tell the truth, he [__17__] in a drunken row at a wayside shanty, from which he had [__18__] with three fractured ribs, [__19__], and various minor abrasions. His dog, Tally, had been a sober but savage participator [__20__], and had escaped with a broken leg. Macquarie afterwards [__21__] the track ten miles to the Union Town hospital. Lord knows how he did it. He [__22__]. Tally limped behind all the way, on three legs.

The doctors examined the man's injuries [__23__] at his endurance. Even doctors are surprised sometimes—[__24__]. Of course they would take him in, [__25__]. Dogs were not allowed on the premises.

From The Project Gutenberg e-book of *While the Billy Boils* by Henry Lawson

**16.** ○ had met    ○ has met    ○ will meet

**17.** ○ has been    ○ had been    ○ have been

**18.** ○ escaping    ○ escapes    ○ escaped

**19.** ○ a crack head

○ a cracked head

○ a cracking head

**20.** ○ in the drunk row

○ by the drunken row

○ in the drunken row

**21.** ○ shouldered his swag and staggered and struggled along

○ shouldering his swag and staggering and struggled along

○ shouldered his swag or staggered or struggled along

**22.** ○ did exactly knew himself

○ didn't exactly know himself

○ did exactly know himself

**23.** ○ and were surprised

○ and are surprised

○ but were surprised

**24.** ○ though they do always show it

○ though they don't always show it

○ though they didn't always show it

○ though they doesn't always show it

**25.** ○ but they objected for Tally

○ but they objected with Tally

○ but they objected to Tally

Did you colour in one of the circles?

---

**It would be a good idea to check over your answers to questions 1 to 25 before moving on to the other questions.**

---

# CONVENTIONS OF LANGUAGE TEST 2

**To the student**

Ask your teacher or parent to read the spelling words for you. The words are listed on page 200. Write the spelling words on the lines below.

## Test 2 spelling words

26. _____

27. _____

28. _____

29. _____

30. _____

31. _____

32. _____

33. _____

34. _____

35. _____

36. _____

37. _____

38. _____

39. _____

40. _____

**Read the sentences. The spelling mistake in each sentence is underlined. Write the correct spelling of the underlined word in the box.**

## Henry Hudson

41. Henry Hudson was one of the best sea <u>captens</u> in all England.

42. He loved the ocean, and he did not <u>kno</u> the word "fear."

43. In 1607 a company of London <u>merchents</u> sent him to look for a northwest passage to China.

44. If such a passage could be found, the <u>jerney</u> to China would be much shorter.

45. It takes more time to sail around the earth near the <u>equata</u>.

**Read these sentences. Each sentence has one word that is incorrect. Write the correct spelling of the word in the box.**

46. Everyone who had attempted to sail west had reached, insted, that long coast of the New World, through which but one opening had been found.

47. The route through the Strait of Magellan was too long for use in comerse, so traders were trying hard to find a northwest passage.

48. Captain Hudson tried to pass between Greenland and Spitzbergen and sail acros the north pole into the Pacific.

49. Failing in this attempt, he made a second voyege, during which he tried to pass between Spitzbergen and Nova Zembla.

50. This also was unsucesfull and Hudson returned to England but he had been nearer the north pole than any man had ever been before.

Adapted from The Project Gutenberg e-book of *Discoverers and Explorers* by Edward R Shaw

Write your answers in the boxes.

# END OF TEST

**Well done! You have completed the second Conventions of Language Test. We really mean this as there were many questions to answer.**

**How did you find these questions? Check to see where you did well and where you had problems. Try to revise the questions that were hard for you.**

**Use the diagnostic chart on pages 133–134 to see which level of ability you reached. This is only an estimate. Don't be surprised if you answered some difficult questions correctly or even missed some easier questions.**

**There are now two more tests, each containing 50 questions. They include many of the same types of questions, plus a few new types.**

## Instructions

As you check the answer for each question, mark it as correct (✓) or incorrect (✗). Mark any questions that you omitted or left out as incorrect (✗) for the moment.

Then look at how many you answered correctly in each level. You will be able to see what level you are at by finding the point where you started having consistent difficulty with questions at a certain level. For example, if you answer most questions correctly up to the Intermediate level and then get most questions wrong from then onwards, it is likely your ability is at a Intermediate level. You can ask your parents or your teacher to help you do this if it isn't clear to you.

**Am I able to ...**

| | SKILL | ESTIMATED LEVEL | ✓ or ✗ |
|---|---|---|---|
| 1 | Use commas in a complex sentence? | Advanced | |
| 2 | Use apostrophes for possession? | Intermediate | |
| 3 | Use speech marks for direct speech? | Standard | |
| 4 | Use conjunctions to join two clauses? | Intermediate | |
| 5 | Use the past perfect tense? | Standard | |
| 6 | Use prepositional phrases? | Intermediate | |
| 7 | Use conjunctions to join two clauses? | Advanced | |
| 8 | Identify a sentence with an adjective? | Intermediate | |
| 9 | Identify a sentence with an adverb? | Average | |
| 10 | Use a plural verb for two singular nouns? | Intermediate | |
| 11 | Use the third person pronoun? | Standard | |
| 12 | Use the present perfect passive tense? | Intermediate | |
| 13 | Use superlatives? | Intermediate | |
| 14 | Use superlatives? | Intermediate | |
| 15 | Use comparatives? | Intermediate | |
| 16 | Use the past tense? | Intermediate | |
| 17 | Use correct tense? | Intermediate | |
| 18 | Use correct tense? | Intermediate | |
| 19 | Use noun phrases in a list? | Intermediate | |
| 20 | Use adverbial phrases? | Advanced | |
| 21 | Use phrases with conjunctions and the correct tense? | Advanced | |
| 22 | Use complex adverbial phrases? | Advanced | |
| 23 | Use phrases with conjunctions and the past tense? | Advanced | |
| 24 | Use complex phrases? | Advanced | |
| 25 | Use complex phrases? | Advanced | |
| 26 | Spell *knew*? | Standard | |
| 27 | Spell *lavish*? | Standard | |

| | SKILL | ESTIMATED LEVEL | ✓ or ✗ |
|---|---|---|---|
| 28 | Spell *money*? | Standard | |
| 29 | Spell *purpose*? | Intermediate | |
| 30 | Spell *people*? | Intermediate | |
| 31 | Spell *freedom*? | Standard | |
| 32 | Spell *nation*? | Intermediate | |
| 33 | Spell *terrible*? | Intermediate | |
| 34 | Spell *progress*? | Standard | |
| 35 | Spell *history*? | Standard | |
| 36 | Spell *undoubtedly*? | Advanced | |
| 37 | Spell *emancipation*? | Advanced | |
| 38 | Spell *taciturn*? | Advanced | |
| 39 | Spell *anonymous*? | Advanced | |
| 40 | Spell *avaricious*? | Advanced | |
| 41 | Spell *captains*? | Standard | |
| 42 | Spell *know*? | Standard | |
| 43 | Spell *merchants*? | Standard | |
| 44 | Spell *journey*? | Standard | |
| 45 | Spell *equator*? | Standard | |
| 46 | Spell *instead*? | Intermediate | |
| 47 | Spell *commerce*? | Standard | |
| 48 | Spell *across*? | Standard | |
| 49 | Spell *voyage*? | Intermediate | |
| 50 | Spell *unsuccessful*? | Intermediate | |
| | **TOTAL** | | |

This is the third Conventions of Language Test. There are 50 questions.

Allow around 45 minutes for this test.

Take a short break before the spelling if necessary.

---

**Colour in the circle with the correct answer.**

---

**1.** Which sentence uses commas ( **,** ) correctly?

○ As a matter of fact, writing, the most important of all inventions, is quite new.

○ As a matter of fact, writing the most important of all inventions, is quite new.

○ As a matter of fact writing the most important of all inventions, is quite new.

○ As a matter of fact, writing the most important of all inventions is quite new.

**2.** Which sentence uses apostrophes ( **'** ) correctly?

○ The worker's were unable to lift the heavy loads.

○ They asked for assistance from the company's large forklifts.

○ They called for the operator's of the electric cranes in the factory.

**3.** Colour in **two** circles to show where the missing speech marks ( **"** and **"** ) should go.

Go now, Hodja, to your box, she said.

**4.** Where do the **two** missing speech marks ( **"** and **"** ) go?

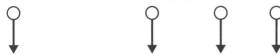

Take down your sign and write instead: 'The wit of woman is twofold the wit of

man,' for I am a woman, and in one day I have fooled two men.

Did you colour in one of the circles?

---

# CONVENTIONS OF LANGUAGE TEST 3

Here is the last verse of a poem by the Australian poet Henry Kendall. It has some gaps. Choose the correct word to fill each gap. Colour in only one circle for each answer.

> **5** I sit, looking back to a childhood
>
> Mixt with the sights and the sounds of the wildwood,
>
> Longing for power and the sweetness **6** fashion
>
> Lyrics with beats like the heart-beats of passion—
>
> Songs interwoven of lights and of **7**
>
> Borrowed from bell-birds in far forest rafters;
>
> So I might **8** in the city and alleys
>
> The beauty and strength of the deep mountain valleys,
>
> Charming to slumber the pain of my losses
>
> **9** glimpses of creeks and a vision of mosses.
>
> From "Bell-Birds", in The Project Gutenberg e-book of *The Poems of Henry Kendall*

**5.** _____ I sit, looking back to a childhood

Mixt with the sights and the sounds of the wildwood,

   ○ Often      ○ However      ○ Rarely      ○ Although

**6.** Longing for power and the sweetness _____ fashion

Lyrics with beats like the heart-beats of passion—

   ○ of      ○ to      ○ for      ○ by

**7.** Songs interwoven of lights and of _____

Borrowed from bell-birds in far forest rafters;

   ○ laughing      ○ laugh      ○ laughters      ○ laughs

**8.** So I might _____ in the city and alleys

The beauty and strength of the deep mountain valleys,

   ○ keeps      ○ keeping      ○ kept      ○ keep

**9.** Charming to slumber the pain of my losses

_____ glimpses of creeks and a vision of mosses.

   ○ for      ○ with      ○ at      ○ of

**Colour in the circle with the correct answer.**

**10.** Which word correctly completes the sentence?

The man and woman [        ] seated on my right.

| is | are | am |
| ○ | ○ | ○ |

**11.** Which of the following correctly completes the sentence?

The audience listened to the lecture and then [        ] to their feet and cheered loudly.

| rise | rose | will rise | are rising | have risen |
| ○ | ○ | ○ | ○ | ○ |

**12.** Which of the following correctly completes the sentence?

The Labor and Liberal parties have [        ] new leaders after caucus meetings earlier today.

| elect | elects | elected | will elect | are electing |
| ○ | ○ | ○ | ○ | ○ |

**13.** Which word or words correctly completes the sentence?

They played all three symphonies this season and this was their [        ] performance by far.

| melodious | more melodious | most melodious |
| ○ | ○ | ○ |

**14.** Which of the following correctly completes the sentence?

Anthony is 30, John is 25 and Nicholas is 14. Nicholas is [        ] than John or Anthony.

| young | younger | youngest | most younger | more younger |
| ○ | ○ | ○ | ○ | ○ |

Did you colour in one of the circles?

Read the text "Shall we gather at the river?" Some words are missing. Choose the correct word or words to fill each gap. Colour in the circle with the correct answer.

## "Shall we gather at the river?"

I never told ____15____ about Peter M'Laughlan. He was a sort of bush missionary up-country and out back in Australia, and before he died he was known from Riverina down south in New South Wales to away up through the Never-Never country in western Queensland.

His past was a mystery, so, of course, there were all sorts of yarns about him. He was ____16____ to be a Scotchman from London, and some ____17____ that he had got into trouble in his young days and had had to clear out of the old country; or, at least, that he had been a ne'e-er-do-well ____18____ sent out to Australia on the remittance system. Some said he'd studied for the law, some said he'd studied for a doctor, while others believed that he was, or had been, an ____19____ minister. I remember one man who swore (when he was drinking) that he had known Peter M'Laughlan as a medical student in a big London hospital, and that he had started ____20____ for himself somewhere near Gray's Inn Road in London. ____21____, as I got to know him he ____22____ me as being a man who had looked into the eyes of so much misery in his life that some of it had got into his own.

From "Shall we gather at the river?" in the Project Gutenberg e-book of *While the Billy Boils* by Henry Lawson

15. ○ you     ○ me     ○ us

16. ○ suppose     ○ supposed     ○ supposing     ○ supposes

17. ○ say     ○ says     ○ said

18. ○ and had been     ○ but had been     ○ but has been     ○ and has been

19. ○ ordain     ○ ordained     ○ ordaining     ○ ordinary

20. ○ by practising     ○ in practise     ○ for practice     ○ in practice

21. ○ Anyway     ○ Unless     ○ At least     ○ On the other hand

22. ○ strikes     ○ struck     ○ striking

# CONVENTIONS OF LANGUAGE TEST 3

Colour in the circle with the correct answer.

**23.** Which sentence contains an adjective?
- ○ It was half-way through the afternoon and he had not stopped for a coffee.
- ○ There was something on that flight of stairs that made him stop and look.
- ○ He looked at the white powder on the landing.
- ○ He tasted it; it was flour.

**24.** Which sentence contains an adverb?
- ○ The teacher told the class they were progressing well.
- ○ The blue bus increased its speed and the passengers were frightened.
- ○ He was interested in the exhibits at the national museum.
- ○ The hungry children felt an increasing desire for something to eat.

**25.** In which sentence is the word *fast* used as a noun?
- ○ Before Easter, some Christians will fast from meat and other foods.
- ○ The police drove as fast as they could to keep up with the car thieves.
- ○ The express train moved along the fast track to avoid the slow freight train.
- ○ Ramadan involves a fast during the daylight hours.

**It would be a good idea to check over your answers to questions 1 to 25 before moving on to the other questions.**

**To the student**

Ask your teacher or parent to read the spelling words for you. The words are listed on page 200. Write the spelling words on the lines below.

### Test 3 spelling words

26. _____      34. _____

27. _____      35. _____

28. _____      36. _____

29. _____      37. _____

30. _____      38. _____

31. _____      39. _____

32. _____      40. _____

33. _____

**Read the sentences. The spelling mistake in each sentence is underlined. Write the correct spelling of the underlined word in the box.**

**41.** It was our <u>intendion</u> to write about birds in captivity.

**42.** In some cases the situation is cruel and <u>pithetic</u>.

**43.** Many <u>spicies</u> are confined in small cages.

**44.** Birds are sometimes kept in <u>inadequite</u> or cruel conditions.

**45.** People have no moral right to deprive an <u>inocent</u> creature of liberty.

Adapted from The Project Gutenberg ebook of *Birds Illustrated by Colour Photography*,
vol II, no. 4, Nature Study Publishing Co., 1897

**Read the sentences. Each sentence has one word that is incorrect. Write the correct spelling of the word in the box.**

**46.** For the first time in my life I was confronted by an example of audable silence.

**47.** When we had climbed the first flight of stairs, I added another discovery to my limited knowledge of natural phemonema— that of tangible darkness.

**48.** A match showed us where the upward road continue.

**49.** We went to the next floor and then to the next and the next until I had lost count and then there came still another floor, and sudenly we had plenty of light.

**50.** This floor was on an even height with the roof of the church, and it was used as a storoom.

From The Project Gutenberg e-book of *The Story of Mankind* by Hendrik van Loon

# END OF TEST

**Well done! You have completed the third Conventions of Language Test.**

**How did you find these questions? Check to see where you did well and where you had problems. Try to revise the questions that were hard for you.**

**Use the diagnostic chart on pages 141–142 to see which level of ability you reached. This is only an estimate. Don't be surprised if you answered some difficult questions correctly or even missed some easier questions.**

**There is now only one more test to complete. It contains 50 questions. They include many of the same types of questions, plus a few new types.**

## Instructions

As you check the answer for each question, mark it as correct (✓) or incorrect (✗). Mark any questions that you omitted or left out as incorrect (✗) for the moment.

Then look at how many you answered correctly in each level. You will be able to see what level you are at by finding the point where you started having consistent difficulty with questions at a certain level. For example, if you answer most questions correctly up to the Intermediate level and then get most questions wrong from then onwards, it is likely your ability is at a Intermediate level. You can ask your parents or your teacher to help you do this if it isn't clear to you.

**Am I able to ...**

| | SKILL | ESTIMATED LEVEL | ✓ or ✗ |
|---|---|---|---|
| 1 | Use commas in a complex sentence? | Advanced | |
| 2 | Use apostrophes for possession? | Intermediate | |
| 3 | Use speech marks for direct speech? | Intermediate | |
| 4 | Use speech marks and single quotation marks? | Advanced | |
| 5 | Use adverbs of frequency? | Intermediate | |
| 6 | Use prepositions with nouns? | Intermediate | |
| 7 | Use rhyming nouns? | Advanced | |
| 8 | Use modal verbs? | Advanced | |
| 9 | Use prepositions with nouns? | Intermediate | |
| 10 | Use agreement in subject and verb? | Standard | |
| 11 | Use the past tense? | Intermediate | |
| 12 | Use the present perfect tense? | Intermediate | |
| 13 | Use superlatives? | Intermediate | |
| 14 | Use comparatives? | Intermediate | |
| 15 | Use personal pronouns? | Intermediate | |
| 16 | Use past tense verbs? | Intermediate | |
| 17 | Use the past tense? | Intermediate | |
| 18 | Use a phrase with conjunctions and verbs? | Advanced | |
| 19 | Complete a complex phrase? | Advanced | |
| 20 | Use prepositions with nouns? | Advanced | |
| 21 | Use adverbs to link sentences? | Advanced | |
| 22 | Use the past tense? | Advanced | |
| 23 | Identify a sentence with an adjective? | Average | |
| 24 | Identify a sentence with an adverb? | Advanced | |
| 25 | Identify a word that is used as a noun? | Intermediate | |
| 26 | Spell *another*? | Standard | |
| 27 | Spell *battles*? | Standard | |
| 28 | Spell *language*? | Intermediate | |

| 29 | Spell *inhabit*? | Standard | |
|----|------------------|----------|--|
| 30 | Spell *divided*? | Standard | |
| 31 | Spell *stationery*? | Intermediate | |
| 32 | Spell *bravery*? | Standard | |
| 33 | Spell *farthest*? | Standard | |
| 34 | Spell *allocate*? | Intermediate | |
| 35 | Spell *frontiers*? | Advanced | |
| 36 | Spell *waging*? | Intermediate | |
| 37 | Spell *scimitar*? | Advanced | |
| 38 | Spell *receipt*? | Advanced | |
| 39 | Spell *civilisation*? | Advanced | |
| 40 | Spell *separate*? | Intermediate | |
| 41 | Spell *intention*? | Intermediate | |
| 42 | Spell *pathetic*? | Standard | |
| 43 | Spell *species*? | Advanced | |
| 44 | Spell *inadequate*? | Advanced | |
| 45 | Spell *innocent*? | Intermediate | |
| 46 | Spell *audible*? | Advanced | |
| 47 | Spell *phenomena*? | Advanced | |
| 48 | Spell *continued*? | Intermediate | |
| 49 | Spell *suddenly*? | Standard | |
| 50 | Spell *storeroom*? | Standard | |
| | **TOTAL** | | |

This is the final Conventions of Language Test. There are 50 questions. Allow around 45 minutes for this test. Take a short break before the spelling if necessary.

**Colour in the circle(s) with the correct answer.**

**1.** Colour in the circle(s) where the missing apostrophe ( ' ) should go. There may be more than one missing apostrophe.

His   Majestys   informers brought him the word that the people rejoiced in the fall of the old

Grand   Vizier, and the appointment of the new one, Doctor Ali Pashas   son.

**Colour in the circle with the correct answer.**

From The Project Gutenberg Australia e-book of *Monsters of Mars* by Edmond Hamilton

**2.** Which sentence has the correct punctuation?

○ That's why I sent for you, Allan, he said quietly. To go to Mars with us to-night!

○ "That's why I sent for you, Allan," he said quietly. "To go to Mars with us to-night!"

○ "That's why I sent for you, Allan," he said quietly. To go to Mars with us to-night!

○ Thats why I sent for you Allan he said quietly. "To go to Mars with us to-night!"

**3.** Which sentence has the correct punctuation?

○ "To Mars!" he repeated. "Have you gone crazy, Milton—or is this some joke you've put up with Lanier and Nelson here?"

○ To Mars! he repeated. Have you gone crazy, Milton—or is this some joke you've put up with Lanier and Nelson here?

○ "To Mars" he repeated. "Have you gone crazy, Milton—or is this some joke you've put up with Lanier and Nelson here"

**4.** Which sentence is correct?

○ Milton shook his head gravely. It is not a joke, Allan Lanier and I are actually going to flash out over the gulf to the planet Mars to-night

○ Milton shook his head gravely. "It is not a joke, Allan". Lanier and I are actually going to flash out over the gulf to the planet Mars to-night.

○ Milton shook his head gravely. "It is not a joke, Allan. Lanier and I are actually going to flash out over the gulf to the planet Mars to-night."

**Read the text. It has some gaps. Choose the correct word or words to fill each gap. Colour in only one circle for each answer.**

Two households, both alike in dignity,

In fair Verona, where we ⬛ 5 our scene,

From ancient grudge break to new mutiny,

Where civil blood ⬛ 6 civil hands unclean.

From forth the fatal loins of these two foes

A ⬛ 7 of star-cross'd lovers take their life;

Whose misadventur'd piteous overthrows

Doth with their death bury their parents' strife.

The fearful passage of their death-mark'd love,

And the continuance of their parents' rage,

Which, but their children's end, naught ⬛ 8 remove,

Is now the two hours' traffic of our stage;

The which if you with patient ears ⬛ 9,

What here shall miss, our toil shall strive to mend.

From *The Tragedy of Romeo and Juliet* by William Shakespeare

**5.** Two households, both alike in dignity,

In fair Verona, where we ⬛ our scene,

○ lay          ○ laid          ○ lie          ○ lays

**6.** From ancient grudge break to new mutiny,

Where civil blood ⬛ civil hands unclean.

○ make          ○ makes          ○ making

**7.** A ▮▮▮▮▮ of star-cross'd lovers take their life;
Whose misadventur'd piteous overthrows
Doth with their death bury their parents' strife.

- ○ pair
- ○ pare
- ○ pear
- ○ par
- ○ peer

**8.** The fearful passage of their death-mark'd love,
And the continuance of their parents' rage,
Which, but their children's end, naught ▮▮▮▮▮ remove,

- ○ could
- ○ has
- ○ is
- ○ can

**9.** Is now the two hours' traffic of our stage;
The which if you with patient ears ▮▮▮▮▮,

What here shall miss, our toil shall strive to mend.

- ○ attending
- ○ attends
- ○ attend
- ○ attended

## Colour in the circle with the correct answer.

**10.** Which word correctly completes the sentence?

The captain and the members of the team ▮▮▮▮▮ three cheers for the other side.

- ○ shouts
- ○ shouting
- ○ shouted

**11.** Which word correctly completes the sentence?

The audience listened to the concert and then rose to their feet and cheered ▮▮▮▮▮.

- ○ loud
- ○ louder
- ○ loudly
- ○ loudest

**12.** Which of the following correctly completes the sentence?

The team played four games at home and this was their ▮▮▮▮▮ victory this season.

- ○ convinced
- ○ more convinced
- ○ most convinced
- ○ most convincing

# CONVENTIONS OF LANGUAGE TEST 4

Read the text. It has some gaps. Choose the correct word or words to fill each gap.
Colour in only one circle for each answer. (Hint: If you aren't sure of the correct word,
try each one of the options to see which one makes sense.)

Rhetoric, also, as well as Grammar, _____ 13 amongst us till a
late period, and with still more difficulty, inasmuch as we find
that, at times, the practice of it _____ 14 . In order to leave no
doubt of this, I will subjoin an ancient decree of the senate, as
well as an edict of the censors:—"In the consulship of Caius
Fannius Strabo, and Marcus Palerius Messala: the praetor
Marcus Pomponius moved the senate, that an act be passed
respecting Philosophers and Rhetoricians. In this matter, they
have decreed as follows: 'It shall be lawful for M. Pomponius,
the praetor, _____ 15 , and make such provisions, as the good
of the Republic, and the duty of his office, require, that no
Philosophers or Rhetoricians _____ 16 at Rome.'"

After some interval, the censor Cnaeus Domitius Aenobarbus and Lucius Licinius Crassus
_____ 17 the following edict upon the same subject: "It is reported to us that certain persons
have instituted a new kind of discipline; that our youth resort to their schools; that they have
assumed the title of Latin Rhetoricians; and that young men waste their time there for whole
days together. Our ancestors have ordained what instruction _____ 18 their children should
receive, and what schools they should attend. These novelties, contrary to the customs and
instructions of our ancestors, we neither approve, _____ 19 to us good. Wherefore it appears
to be our duty that we should notify our judgment both to those who keep such schools, and
those who are in the practice of _____ 20 them, that they meet our disapprobation."

From The Project Gutenberg e-book of *The Lives of the Twelve Caesars* by C Suetonius Tranquillus

13. ○ were not introduced    ○ was not introduced    ○ have not introduced

14. ○ were even prohibited    ○ has even prohibited    ○ was even prohibited

15. ○ has taken such measures    ○ to take such measures
    ○ will take such measures    ○ have taken such measures

16. ○ be suffered    ○ to suffer    ○ will suffer    ○ are suffering

17. ○ issue    ○ issued    ○ will issue    ○ are issuing

18. ○ it has fitted    ○ it fits    ○ it is fitting

19. ○ nor do they appear    ○ nor does they appear
    ○ nor does it appear    ○ nor appear

20. ○ frequently    ○ frequenting    ○ frequented    ○ frequents

**Colour in the circle with the correct answer.**

21. Which sentence contains an adjective?
    - ○ The shop was popular with the customers of the neighbourhood.
    - ○ There was an array of goods on display in the shop.
    - ○ The ticket on the almonds said $1 each but it should have been $16 a kilogram.
    - ○ Someone had played a trick on the owner and swapped the tickets on the items.

22. Which sentence contains an adverb?
    - ○ If you know what someone will steal, get there earlier than the thief.
    - ○ Follow the thief when you do not know what they might steal.
    - ○ There was a connection between that crime and the lack of security.
    - ○ The red-faced man looked at the policeman with an air of embarrassment.

23. In which sentence is the word *square* used as a verb?
    - ○ A square has four equal sides.
    - ○ When you square a number you multiply it by itself.
    - ○ A misfit is described as a square peg in a round hole.
    - ○ His actions were fair and square.

24. Which of the following correctly completes the sentence?

    The old sailor saved the boy ▓▓▓▓▓ was caught by the tide.

    | that | which | what | who |
    |------|-------|------|-----|
    | ○ | ○ | ○ | ○ |

25. In which sentence is the word *right* used as an adverb?
    - ○ We have the right to vote for our politicians.
    - ○ The young student will try to right what is wrong in the community.
    - ○ Make a right turn when you come to the lights.
    - ○ We were told to stand right here.

Did you colour in one of the circles?

**It would be a good idea to check over your answers to questions 1 to 25 before moving on to the other questions.**

**To the student**

Ask your teacher or parent to read the spelling words for you. The words are listed on page 200. Write the spelling words on the lines below.

✏ **Test 4 spelling words**

26. _____

27. _____

28. _____

29. _____

30. _____

31. _____

32. _____

33. _____

34. _____

35. _____

36. _____

37. _____

38. _____

39. _____

40. _____

**Read these sentences. The spelling mistake in each sentence is underlined. Write the correct spelling of the underlined word in the box.**

41. The cyclone struck and events <u>succedded</u> each other.

42. Rainfall is a form of <u>pressipitation</u>.

43. Our system of government in Australia is described as <u>parlamentary</u>.

44. The police <u>persude</u> the getaway car.

45. The government will <u>integrait</u> bus and train services in the city.

# CONVENTIONS OF LANGUAGE TEST 4

Read these verses from a long poem. Each verse has one word that is incorrect. (Hint: Don't worry about the abbreviated words with an apostrophe.) Write the correct spelling of the words in the boxes provided.

**XXVI**

Oh, come with old Khayyam, and leav the Wise
To talk; one thing is certain, that Life flies;
    One thing is certain, and the Rest is Lies;
The Flower that once has blown for ever dies.

46. [ ]

**XXVII**

Myself when young did eagerly frequent
Doctor and Saint, and heard great Argument
    About it and about: but evamore
Came out by the same Door as in I went.

47. [ ]

**XXVIII**

With them the Seed of Wisdom did I sow,
And with my own hand labour'd it to grow:
    And this was all the Harvesst that I reap'd—
"I came like Water, and like Wind I go."

48. [ ]

**XXIX**

Into this Universe, and why not knowing,
Nor whence, like Water willy-nilly flowing:
    And out of it, as Wind along the Waiste,
I know not whither, willy-nilly blowing.

49. [ ]

**XXX**

What, without asking, hither hurried whence?
And, without asking, whither hurried hence!
    Another and another Cup to drown
The Memory of this Impertanence!

50. [ ]

From The Project Gutenberg e-book of *Rubaiyat of Omar Khayyam* by Omar Khayyam

# END OF TEST

Well done! You have completed the final Conventions of Language Test. It means that you have answered 200 Conventions of Language questions.

Our aim has been to include as much demanding material as possible in the practice tests. If you found this difficult at times, it is to be expected. Don't worry.

Use the diagnostic chart on pages 150–151 to see which level of ability you reached. This is only an estimate. Don't be surprised if you answered some difficult questions correctly or even missed some easier questions.

## Instructions

As you check the answer for each question, mark it as correct (✓) or incorrect (✗). Mark any questions that you omitted or left out as incorrect (✗) for the moment.

Then look at how many you answered correctly in each level. You will be able to see what level you are at by finding the point where you started having consistent difficulty with questions at sa ceertain level. For example, if you answer most questions correctly up to the Intermediate level and then get most questions wrong from then onwards, it is likely your ability is at a Intermediate level. You can ask your parents or your teacher to help you do this if it isn't clear to you.

**Am I able to ...**

| | SKILL | ESTIMATED LEVEL | ✓ or ✗ |
|---|---|---|---|
| 1 | Use apostrophes for possession? | Intermediate | |
| 2 | Use speech marks for direct speech? | Advanced | |
| 3 | Use speech marks for direct speech? | Intermediate | |
| 4 | Use speech marks for direct speech? | Intermediate | |
| 5 | Use the present tense and agreement in subject and verb? | Intermediate | |
| 6 | Use agreement in subject and verb? | Advanced | |
| 7 | Use collective nouns? | Advanced | |
| 8 | Use the past tense? | Advanced | |
| 9 | Use the present tense? | Intermediate | |
| 10 | Use the past tense? | Intermediate | |
| 11 | Use adverbs of degree? | Intermediate | |
| 12 | Use a superlative with a participle? | Advanced | |
| 13 | Use a phrase to agree with a complex subject? | Advanced | |
| 14 | Use a phrase to agree with a complex subject? | Advanced | |
| 15 | Use a phrase with an infinitive? | Advanced | |
| 16 | Use a verb phrase? | Advanced | |
| 17 | Use the past tense? | Intermediate | |
| 18 | Use a verb phrase? | Advanced | |
| 19 | Complete a phrase with *neither ... nor ...?* | Advanced | |
| 20 | Use the present participle? | Advanced | |
| 21 | Identify a sentence with an adjective? | Intermediate | |
| 22 | Identify a sentence with an adverb? | Intermediate | |
| 23 | Identify a word that is used as a verb? | Intermediate | |
| 24 | Use relative pronouns? | Advanced | |
| 25 | Identify a word used as an adverb in a sentence? | Intermediate | |
| 26 | Spell *added?* | Standard | |
| 27 | Spell *wrong?* | Standard | |
| 28 | Spell *already?* | Standard | |

| 29 | Spell *remain?* | Standard | |
| 30 | Spell *course?* | Intermediate | |
| 31 | Spell *catastrophes?* | Intermediate | |
| 32 | Spell *companion?* | Intermediate | |
| 33 | Spell *alternative?* | Intermediate | |
| 34 | Spell *certainly?* | Intermediate | |
| 35 | Spell *assured?* | Intermediate | |
| 36 | Spell *perceive?* | Advanced | |
| 37 | Spell *goddess?* | Advanced | |
| 38 | Spell *conceivble?* | Advanced | |
| 39 | Spell *notorious?* | Advanced | |
| 40 | Spell *democracy?* | Advanced | |
| 41 | Spell *succeeded?* | Intermediate | |
| 42 | Spell *precipitation?* | Advanced | |
| 43 | Spell *parliamentary?* | Advanced | |
| 44 | Spell *pursued?* | Intermediate | |
| 45 | Spell *integrate?* | Advanced | |
| 46 | Spell *leave?* | Standard | |
| 47 | Spell *evermore?* | Standard | |
| 48 | Spell *harvest?* | Standard | |
| 49 | Spell *waste?* | Intermediate | |
| 50 | Spell *impertinence?* | Advanced | |
| | **TOTAL** | | |

## About the test

The NAPLAN Writing Test examines a student's ability to write effectively in a specific type of text. Students will come across a number of types of text at school. These can be factual or literary. Although we provide you with some graded sample answers on pages 156–157 and 170–171, we do not provide any others because grading writing is a time-consuming task which can be very subjective. It's more important that you focus on improving the standard of your writing.

Usually there is only one Writing question in the NAPLAN Writing Test. You will be provided with some stimulus material that acts as a prompt to writing: something to read or a picture to look at. Your response will be written on supplied paper.

**Check the Writing section** (www.nap.edu. au/naplan/writing) **of the official NAPLAN website for up-to-date and important information on the Writing Test.** Sample Writing Tests and marking guidelines that outline the criteria markers use when assessing your writing are also provided. Please note that, to date in NAPLAN, the types of texts that students have been tested on have been narrative and persuasive writing.

The Australian Curriculum for English requires students to be taught three main types of texts:

- imaginative writing (including narratives and descriptions)
- informative writing (including procedures and reports)
- persuasive writing (expositions).

Informative writing has not yet been tested by NAPLAN. The best preparation for writing is for students to read a range of texts and to get lots of practice in writing different types of texts.

## Marking the Writing Test

When the markers of the NAPLAN Writing test assess your writing they will mark it according to various criteria. Knowing what they look for will help you understand what to look out for in your own writing. The emphasis is on the quality of expression and what the student has to say. Some features that may be emphasised are:

- the quality of the content
- what the student thinks about the topic
- what feelings are developed
- how it is structured
- whether the writing is organised clearly, using paragraphs and appropriate sequencing
- whether the writing is cohesive
- the quality of the spelling and punctuation/ grammar.

## Advice for parents and teachers

If students aren't sure how to write a persuasive or narrative text then use the practice tests to develop these skills. It may not be easy for them at first. One way to start is to ask them to talk about the topic and to state their views on the subject. Next you could show them how to plan their writing. Then they can start to write.

Give plenty of praise and encouragement. Remember that Year 7 students are still quite young. Emphasise whatever is good and overlook any errors at first. Space out the time between the writing tasks. Do not attempt one immediately after the other as this does not allow time for development. Come back to these errors at a much later stage, perhaps a little before you start the next practice test.

In this book we look at persuasive and narrative writing. We start with writing a persuasive text on the following page.

In this section we start with a sample of a persuasive text. First we give some details about this type of writing, then there is a sample question with answers, and finally there are two practice Writing Tests for persuasive texts.

## What is a persuasive text?

- A persuasive text is designed to convince. It states one side of a case and expresses a point of view. The first step is to decide your opinion: are you for or against?

- You don't need to list reasons for and reasons against. Support your point of view with facts, examples and evidence.

- Persuasive texts can be posters, advertisements, letters, debates or reports.

- Their main purpose is to persuade the reader to see an issue from the author's point of view. The writing aims to persuade the reader to change their mind, and to win the support of the reader on a specific isssue. To do this the author uses persuasive devices.

## Examples of persuasive devices

- Appealing to the reader
  e.g. *The government should protect the rights of citizens to live peacefully and safely in the community. It should increase the police presence in the suburbs and on public transport. This is an opportunity to write to your local Member of Parliament and let them know you are concerned.*

- Posing rhetorical questions
  e.g. *Isn't it true that students are best at what interests them? Why do we then force them to study courses which they don't like? If we really wanted an education system that was best for each person, shouldn't we then harness the value of personal interests as a resource for learning?*

- Reporting statistics
  e.g. *Official statistics indicated that the average age for retirement in Australia is much lower than sixty.*

- Citing facts
  e.g. *The opinion of most experts is that childhood obesity is the major factor in the increased levels of juvenile diabetes in New York.*

- Using persuasive adjectives
  e.g. *valid, official, reasonable, established, necessary, significant, fair, best*

- Using persuasive adverbs
  e.g. *ideally, obviously, possibly, probably, certainly, definitely, ultimately, therefore, accordingly, consequently*

## Structure of a persuasive text

### Introduction

- The first paragraph should be a short paragraph of approximately 3–4 sentences. It introduces the topic and states your opinion. It should include a strong sentence which captures the reader's interest.

### Arguments

- The paragraphs that follow are called the arguments. The word *argument* does not mean 'a dispute'. An argument means showing how you think. It lists the reasons for your opinion; it is the case that you are putting forward, just like a lawyer puts forward a case in court.

- The arguments follow the introduction. Here you should focus on the main points and elaborate on them.

- Use a new paragraph for each new point or idea. Include reasons, evidence and examples to support your opinion. Try to include 3–5 paragraphs with at least three points for each reason. Avoid using paragraphs with one sentence.

# WRITING: PERSUASIVE TEXTS

## Conclusion

- The conclusion is a strong, convincing, ending statement used to repeat your position and summarise all your key points, e.g. *In conclusion, it is evident that ...*

- The conclusion does not contain any new information or points. The conclusion should be about 3–4 sentences in length.

## Hints for writing a persuasive text

- State your arguments or ideas in order, one after the other. They should be logical, i.e. they should make sense. Start with the strongest argument.

- Express your point of view clearly. Use strong, persuasive language. Back up each idea, opinion or argument with evidence

- Use linking words. Linking words are sometimes called connectives. Connectives are words that are used to join ideas. They make the flow between ideas smooth, e.g. *firstly, secondly, thirdly, finally, because, in addition, next, then, when, after, consequently, so, therefore, furthermore, however, even though, for this reason, although, pay attention to, in contrast, another point of view, in spite of this, on the other hand, alternatively, the evidence supports a different point of view.*

- Use strong modal verbs, e.g. *will not, must, should, can, might, could, would*

- Use words that make the reader think. Thinking words can include persuasive statistics, e.g. *95% of children are watching too much television.* They can also include emotional language, e.g. *Many people consider that ...; We must protect ...; Certainly we must try ...; I am absolutely appalled that ...,* or emotional adjectives, e.g. *important, significant, invaluable.*

Thinking words can also include rhetorical questions. A rhetorical question asks the reader a question but does not expect an answer. It is used for its persuasive effect. It makes the reader think and tries to emphasise one likely answer, e.g. *Are we to think that ...?* Don't be afraid to use rhetorical questions.

- Use the present tense to explain ideas or put forward arguments, e.g. *I believe that ...*

- Use the past tense to give examples, e.g. *I have heard that ...; People have tried to ...*

- You should acknowledge your sources when you use information or quote statistics, i.e. give the reader an idea of where the facts were obtained. This makes your argument more believable.

---

On the following page we have provided a Sample Writing question for a persuasive text. In the persuasive text you will be required to:

- express an opinion
- include facts to support your opinion
- make sure that the first sentence of each paragraph is the key to what follows
- write in an easy-to-understand way
- persuade the reader
- use a new paragraph for each new idea.

---

We have also provided three sample answers to the sample question. We have grouped them into three levels of ability, which correspond to the three levels used throughout this book. Please note that these are approximate guidelines only.

# SAMPLE QUESTION: PERSUASIVE WRITING

## Topic: Water is precious and we should protect it.

Today you are going to write an article for a school bulletin or newsletter giving your opinion on whether water is important for our life or something we'll always have plenty of.

Write an answer that shows your opinion and ideas.

- Begin with a clear opening paragraph: tell the reader what you are going to write.
- Then write your opinions.
- Give your reasons: be convincing.
- Explain so that someone else can understand easily.
- At the end give a short summary of your ideas.

Remember to:

- include a headline showing your opinion, i.e. either FOR or AGAINST the topic
- use a by-line (a line under the heading giving the writer's name)
- begin your writing with an introduction stating whether you think water is important for our lives
- give evidence and examples to support your opinion
- finish your writing with a conclusion that summarises your main points
- plan your writing
- use paragraphs
- write in sentences
- check your spelling and punctuation
- write at least two pages.

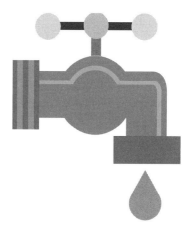

# SAMPLE ANSWERS: PERSUASIVE WRITING

## Water is precious and we should protect it

### STANDARD LEVEL

Water is precious for us because all of the criturs there they would be happy in the water

Water is precious because plants and animals are in the water and the animals eat leaves off the trees and water give them lot's of other things

Firstly all so animals would not been alive if there was no water and water gives us some were to do activitys like fishing

Secondly water is made so animals can live there the plants and the animals would not be there they would be gone and we would not do alot of other fun things.

Don't waste it.

THE END

### INTERMEDIATE LEVEL

I believe that water is extremely precious for life. Water is so precious that it should be protected by law to stop people wasting and polluting what we have left. We need water to drink, to wash our hands, to cook, and many other things. They also have fun activities to do. Without water, the plants would die and people and animals would go thirsty or even die.

Firstly, we need water for our future so we still have animals and food. Plants need water to survive, so the animals have a safe place to live. If animals like cows don't get water to drink, then we don't get beef to eat. If the animals are extincted then the world would be an empty place.

Secondly, we absolutely need water in our homes. Have you ever had the plumber came over and turn off your water? Then you really understand how important water is. We need water for showering, brushing your teeth and going to the toilet, we need water to make a cup of tea or coffee to stay warm, and also for cooking, washing clothes and cleaning.

Finally, water is also important for attractions and activities. We go to the beach for a relaxing swim or fish in the river or go skiing in the mountains.

So, in conclusion, I agree that the importants of water is extremely important because it keeps us nice and clean, it feeds and clothes us, it provides activities to do too. We need to make sure we are not wasting it because, although we can recycle some of it, once it's gone, it's gone forever.

Please note: Spelling, punctuation and grammar errors have been included to replicate the likely response of a Year 7 student.

## ADVANCED LEVEL

# WHY IS WATER SO PRECIOUS?

**By Michael Smith, School reporter**

If you ever whinge about water, just try spending one day without it. It may not occur to you that water is an essential resource for our society. We certainly couldn't do without water.

Firstly, one of the most common uses of water is in our homes. We use water inside the home for bathing and grooming, washing dishes and clothes, cooking and for hygiene. Similarly, we use water outside the home for lawns and gardens, washing cars, fighting fires and filling swimming pools. Plant and animal communities depend on water in much the same way we do: for food, water and shelter. It is important then to protect this precious resource, because we share it with all other living things, past, present, and future.

Secondly, without water we would not live. Did you know that even our bodies are mostly water? I've been told that two-thirds of our bodies are made up of water. Also, we need to drink at least one litre of water everyday. Water cools our bodies and carries nutrients through it. We drink lots of milk, soft drinks and juice everyday and these contain water too. So, as you can see, water is very important for our bodies.

In addition, think about how many everyday things revolve around the use of water somehow. We depend on water for drinking, cleaning, preparing and processing food, growing crops and also for recreation activities like water parks, water skiing and fishing. We use water in emergencies like fire fighting.

Most of these uses are justified, however, we waste an excessive amount of water. Billions of litres of water are used each year for recreational purposes like water parks or swimming pools. One of the ways we can have a great effect on improving our water quality is protecting it from future pollution by changing the ways that we use water. People need to realise that it's the little things that you do in your house, backyard or school that can conserve water and improve its quality. A simple leaky tap, if left unattended, can increase normal household water usage by three times!

Furthermore, we over-use water, thinking it is an endless resource. Some say that water is not important because there is so much of it about, and we can recycle it anyway. In our city, we have never really gone without water, so it is easy to take it for granted.

In conclusion, water needs to be protected because it is such a valuable resource. One thing is certain; there are serious ramifications if it ever ran out. We need to remember how valuable it is. We should find out what needs to be done to help, and do whatever it takes.

Please note: Spelling, punctuation and grammar errors have been included to replicate the likely response of a Year 7 student.

# WRITING TEST 1

In this part you will be doing some writing. Each Writing Test should take you 42 minutes. Write your answer on separate sheets of paper or on a tablet or computer. Use the top part of the first sheet or the persuasive text planning page to plan your ideas.

## Topic: Libraries should be closed since books can now be read on the Internet.

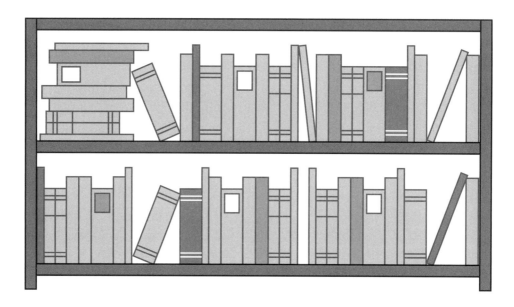

Today you are going to write a persuasive text to convince the reader whether libraries should or should not be closed now that books can be read on the Internet. Provide facts and reasons. Defend your opinion against opposing ideas and prove that your opinion is correct.

Write an answer that shows your opinion and ideas.

- Begin with a clear opening paragraph: tell the reader what you are going to write.
- Then write your opinions.
- Give your reasons: be convincing.
- Explain so that someone else can understand easily.
- At the end give a short summary of your ideas.

Remember to:

- think about your views on the topic
- include a clear opening and concluding statement
- plan your writing, thinking about arguments for your point of view
- use paragraphs
- write in sentences
- check your spelling and punctuation
- write at least two pages.

# WRITING TEST 1

Here is a persuasive text planning page to start you off. Use this page to plan your ideas.

# PERSUASIVE TEXT

### INTRODUCTION/ORIENTATION:
Introduce the topic and state your opinion. What do you think about the issue? Are you for or against?
(3–4 sentences)

## Arguments
Supporting reasons for your opinion (3–5 paragraphs)

| **Argument 1** | Points and examples to back up your reasons |

| **Argument 2** | Points and examples to back up your reasons |

| **Argument 3** | Points and examples to back up your reasons |

## Further arguments and points

### LINKING WORDS

*although ... even though ...
however ... on the other
hand ... at the same time ...*

### MODAL VERBS

*must ... can ... might ...
should ... could ... would*

### PERSUASIVE WORDS

*naturally ... obviously ...
definitely ... probably ... certainly ...
possibly ... always ... it ... unless ...
sometimes ... unlikely ...
hopefully ... perhaps ... absolutely ...*

### THINKING WORDS

*Experts believe that ... It can be
said that ... In my view ...
Another point of view is ... The
evidence supports ... In my
opinion ... Some people feel ...
On the other hand ...
Surely ...*

### CONCLUSION:
Repeat your opinion and summarise the main points of the argument. (3 sentences)

*In conclusion ... Therefore ... I believe that ... It's evident that ... Overall ... Although there are many benefits to/in ...
As a result ... In considering these arguments ...*

Use this chart to evaluate your writing.

| GUIDELINES FOR WRITING A PERSUASIVE TEXT | ✓ or ✗ |
|---|---|
| Have you clearly expressed your point of view on the specific issue? | |
| Have you made at least three points with strong arguments and solid supporting points? | |
| Have you backed up each argument with evidence? | |
| Have you used the simple present tense to give views, e.g. *We must try …*? | |
| Have you used the present perfect tense to give examples, e.g. *I have heard that …, People have tried to …*? | |
| Have you used a variety of correct sentence structures—including simple, compound and complex sentences—to develop arguments? | |
| Have you linked arguments by using a variety of time connectives, e.g. *firstly, secondly, thirdly, finally, because, in addition, next, then, when, after, consequently, so, therefore, furthermore, however, even though, for this reason, although, pay attention to, in contrast, another point of view, in spite of this, on the other hand, alternatively, the evidence supports a different point of view …*? | |
| Have you used clear, descriptive and persuasive words? | |
| Have you used modal verbs/conditionals, e.g. (high) *always, undoubtedly, certainly, absolutely, definitely, obviously, never, must*; (medium) *probably, maybe, apparently, often, can, might, should, could, would, if, unless*; (low) *unlikely, hopefully, perhaps, sometimes, possibly*? | |
| Have you used persuasive devices such as statistics (e.g. *75% of students in my class have a mobile phone and believe that …*), emotive language (e.g. *Many people consider that …, We must protect …, Certainly we must try …, I am absolutely appalled that …, important, significant, invaluable*) and rhetorical questions (e.g. *Are we to think that …?*)? | |
| Have you considered the audience and purpose of the text? | |
| Have you organised your writing into new paragraphs for each separate idea or argument? | |
| Have you used thinking and action verbs to build arguments, e.g. *In my opinion …, Some people feel …, On the other hand …, Probably …, It is certain …, Surely …*? | |
| Have you used a variety of conjunctions, e.g. *when, because, so, if, but, because*? | |
| Have you used reported speech, e.g. *'I've noticed that …', 'I've heard that …'*? | |
| Have you punctuated sentences correctly with capital letters, full stops, commas, exclamation marks and question marks? | |
| Have you used the following correctly most of the time: speech marks, possessive apostrophes, dashes, colons, semicolons and parentheses? | |
| Have you used the correct spelling of common words? | |
| Have you used the correct spelling of unusual or difficult words? | |
| Have you provided an effective and convincing concluding statement that summarises your opinion, introduced by an appropriate phrase, e.g. *Consequently …, Admittedly …, In conclusion …, It's evident that …, Overall …, In considering these arguments …*? | |

# WRITING TEST 2

## Topic: Should we have no-dog zones in our communities?

**NO DOGS ALLOWED**

Today you are going to write a persuasive text that outlines your position on the question of whether we should have no-dog zones in our communities. Support your opinion with facts and reasons.

Write an answer that shows your opinion and ideas.

- Begin with a clear opening paragraph: tell the reader what you are going to write.
- Then write your opinions.
- Give your reasons: be convincing.
- Explain so that someone else can understand easily.
- At the end give a short summary of your ideas.

Remember to:

- think about your views on the topic
- include a clear opening and concluding statement
- plan your writing, thinking about arguments for your point of view
- use paragraphs
- write in sentences
- check your spelling and punctuation
- write at least two pages.

# WRITING TEST 2

Use this persuasive text planning page to plan your ideas.

# PERSUASIVE TEXT

### INTRODUCTION/ORIENTATION:
Introduce the topic and state your opinion. What do you think about the issue? Are you for or against?
(3–4 sentences)

**Arguments**
Supporting reasons for your opinion (3–5 paragraphs)

| **Argument 1** | Points and examples to back up your reasons |
|---|---|

| **Argument 2** | Points and examples to back up your reasons |
|---|---|

| **Argument 3** | Points and examples to back up your reasons |
|---|---|

**Further arguments and points**

### LINKING WORDS
*although ... even though ... however ... on the other hand ... at the same time ...*

### PERSUASIVE WORDS
*naturally ... obviously ... definitely ... probably ... certainly ... possibly ... always ... it ... unless ... sometimes ... unlikely ... hopefully ... perhaps ... absolutely ...*

### THINKING WORDS
*Experts believe that ... It can be said that ... In my view ... Another point of view is ... The evidence supports ... In my opinion ... Some people feel ... On the other hand ... Surely ...*

### MODAL VERBS
*must ... can ... might ... should ... could ... would*

### CONCLUSION:
Repeat your opinion and summarise the main points of the argument. (3 sentences)

*In conclusion ... Therefore ... I believe that ... It's evident that ... Overall ... Although there are many benefits to/in ... As a result ... In considering these arguments ...*

# CHECK YOUR SKILLS: WRITING TEST 2

Use this chart to evaluate your writing.

| GUIDELINES FOR WRITING A PERSUASIVE TEXT | ✓ or ✗ |
|---|---|
| Have you clearly expressed your point of view on the specific issue? | |
| Have you made at least three points with strong arguments and solid supporting points? | |
| Have you backed up each argument with evidence? | |
| Have you used the simple present tense to give views, e.g. *We must try …*? | |
| Have you used the present perfect tense to give examples, e.g. *I have heard that …, People have tried to …*? | |
| Have you used a variety of correct sentence structures—including simple, compound and complex sentences—to develop arguments? | |
| Have you linked arguments by using a variety of time connectives, e.g. *firstly, secondly, thirdly, finally, because, in addition, next, then, when, after, consequently, so, therefore, furthermore, however, even though, for this reason, although, pay attention to, in contrast, another point of view, in spite of this, on the other hand, alternatively, the evidence supports a different point of view …*? | |
| Have you used clear, descriptive and persuasive words? | |
| Have you used modal verbs/conditionals, e.g. (high) *always, undoubtedly, certainly, absolutely, definitely, obviously, never, must*; (medium) *probably, maybe, apparently, often, can, might, should, could, would, if, unless*; (low) *unlikely, hopefully, perhaps, sometimes, possibly*? | |
| Have you used persuasive devices such as statistics (e.g. *75% of students in my class have a mobile phone and believe that …*), emotive language (e.g. *Many people consider that …, We must protect …, Certainly we must try …, I am absolutely appalled that …, important, significant, invaluable*) and rhetorical questions (e.g. *Are we to think that ...?*)? | |
| Have you considered the audience and purpose of the text? | |
| Have you organised your writing into new paragraphs for each separate idea or argument? | |
| Have you used thinking and action verbs to build arguments, e.g. *In my opinion …, Some people feel …, On the other hand …, Probably …, It is certain …, Surely …*? | |
| Have you used a variety of conjunctions, e.g. *when, because, so, if, but, because*? | |
| Have you used reported speech, e.g. *'I've noticed that …', 'I've heard that …'*? | |
| Have you punctuated sentences correctly with capital letters, full stops, commas, exclamation marks and question marks? | |
| Have you used the following correctly most of the time: speech marks, possessive apostrophes, dashes, colons, semicolons and parentheses? | |
| Have you used the correct spelling of common words? | |
| Have you used the correct spelling of unusual or difficult words? | |
| Have you provided an effective and convincing concluding statement that summarises your opinion, introduced by an appropriate phrase, e.g. *Consequently …, Admittedly …, In conclusion …, It's evident that …, Overall …, In considering these arguments …*? | |

# WRITING: NARRATIVE TEXTS

In this section we start with a sample of a narrative text. First we give some details about this type of writing, then there is a sample question with answers, and finally there are two practice Writing Tests for narrative texts.

## Improving your narrative writing

For the NAPLAN Writing Test you might be asked to write a narrative. If you are, try to write in a way that is a true response and that indicates your interests.

Don't just write in a formal and rehearsed manner or by simply repeating something that is known to you. Look at the task and consider the following:

- Does it want me to set out a conversation?
- Does it want me to describe something?
- Does it want me to say how something happened?
- Does it want my point of view?
- Does it want me to write a poem?

When people are doing something that interests them, they achieve at a higher level. Try to include something that interests you in your writing.

Below are some ways to help you improve your writing and make it more interesting to read.

## Tips for writing a narrative

- Always try to make the opening of a narrative interesting or exciting for the reader. Start with dialogue, suspenseful action or description, e.g. *"Where am I?" I yelled, to no one in particular*, or *Smoke started eerily moving throughout the house, creeping under doors, choking me with every movement*.
- Take a look at the beginnings of some of your favourite books to see how the authors started their narratives.

- Try to make the characters in your narrative sound realistic and convincing. Give them appropriate names.
- Remember to describe what the characters look like and how they act and feel, using plenty of adjectives and adverbs, e.g. *relieved*, *grumpy*, *terrified*, *politely*, *mad*, *immature*, *fearlessly*, *angrily*, *daring*, *persuasive*.
- Try to show their personalities in the things they do, say and think. Here are some examples:
  - *talkative*—someone who is friendly and chatty, someone who is inclined to talk a great deal, someone who is not quiet or shy or someone who might interrupt other people
  - *clumsy*—someone awkward, someone without skill or someone who is always breaking things
  - *confident*—someone sure of themselves or someone who is not shy or insecure.

  What type of character in your story (a talkative, clumsy or confident person) would be likely to say the following: *"I was sure I would be able to climb over the wall to escape"*?
- Build descriptions by using alliteration (words starting with the same letter), e.g. *the rising river rushed*; rhyme, e.g. *hustle and bustle*; onomatopoeia (words that sound like the thing they describe), e.g. *crashed and banged*; similes and metaphors.
- Imagine that you are photographing everything you see happening.

# WRITING: NARRATIVE TEXTS

- Expand sentences to explain who, what, how, where, when and why something happened, e.g. *The frightened boy collapsed wearily to the floor, then slowly grabbed the old, wrinkled and itchy blanket and pulled it over his shaking body.*

- Write sentences of different lengths.

- Base your narrative on an unexpected chain of events, a catastrophe or a problem that needs to be solved. Narratives may even consist of more than one problem. They become exciting when things don't go as planned, when an accident has occurred or when someone or something gets lost or stolen. Suspense is also built up by slowly leading up to events. Instead of writing *The house collapsed*, use speech, description and action to build up to the event: *The wind was howling and the sound of thunder became louder and louder. We heard an almighty crash. "What was that?" I asked my brother Michael, with a shaky voice. "Just the wind," he replied, not too confidently. As bits of the ceiling crumbled all around us, I huddled up against Michael. "No, it's not just the wind," I replied, looking at the fearful look on his face. The house started to tremble and things were crashing and banging all around us. We ran, not looking behind us at all as the roof caved in and then everything went black.*

- Include dialogue between descriptions.

- Use questions.

- Start sentences in different ways.

- Think about the final sentence of your narrative. This is just as important as the opening sentence. Remember: this is the last thing that will be read, and this image is the one that will stay with the reader. The ending will need to explain how the problem was solved or the event resolved.

# WRITING: NARRATIVE TEXTS

## Alternative descriptive words

**Make your writing more interesting by using alternatives for these common words.**

**BIG**: large, huge, enormous, gigantic, vast, massive, colossal, immense, bulky, hefty, significant

**GOT/GET**: obtain, acquire, find, get hold of, gain, achieve, take, retrieve, reach, get back, recover, bring

**WENT/GO**: leave, reach, go away, depart, exit, move, quit, scramble, crawl, trudge, tread, trample, skip, march, shuffle, swagger, prance, stride, strut

**GOOD**: decent, enjoyable, superior, fine, excellent, pleasant, lovely, exquisite, brilliant, superb, tremendous

**NICE**: pleasant, good, kind, polite, fine, lovely

**SAW/SEE**: glimpse, notice, spot, witness, observe, watch, view, consider, regard, perceive, detect

**SMALL**: little, minute, short, tiny, miniature, petite, minor, unimportant, microscopic, minuscule, puny

**HAPPY**: content, pleased, glad, joyful, cheerful, in high spirits, ecstatic, delighted, cheery, jovial, satisfied, thrilled

**SAD:** depressed, gloomy, miserable, distressed, dismal, disappointed

**BAD:** awful, terrible, horrific, horrifying, horrendous, evil, naughty, serious, regretful, rotten, appalling, shocking, ghastly, dire, unpleasant, poor, frightening, inexcusable, atrocious, abysmal, sickening, gruesome, unspeakable, outrageous, disgusting, deplorable

**GOING:** leaving, departing, disappearing, separating, exiting

**RUN:** sprint, jog, scuttle, scamper, dart, dash, scurry, rush, hurry, trot

**WALK:** stroll, march, stride, pace, hike, stagger, move, wander, step, tread

| **SAID:** | boasted | exclaimed | mumbled | replied | stammered |
|---|---|---|---|---|---|
| acknowledged | boomed | explained | murmured | requested | stated |
| added | bragged | expressed | nagged | responded | stormed |
| admitted | called | feared | noted | revealed | stuttered |
| advised | claimed | giggled | objected | roared | suggested |
| agreed | commanded | grinned | observed | screamed | taunted |
| alerted | commented | grunted | ordered | screeched | thought |
| announced | complained | indicated | pleaded | shouted | told |
| answered | cried | insisted | pointed out | shrieked | urged |
| argued | decided | instructed | questioned | snapped | uttered |
| asked | declared | laughed | rambled | sneered | wailed |
| babbled | demanded | lied | reassured | sobbed | warned |
| began | denied | mentioned | remarked | spoke | whined |
| blurted | emphasised | moaned | repeated | squealed | whispered |

# WRITING: NARRATIVE TEXTS

## Useful adjectives

**Using a variety of adjectives will add interest to your story.**

### A

able, absolute, active, adorable, adventurous, affectionate, alert, alive, almighty, amazing, amusing, ancient, angelic, angry, annoying, awful, awkward

### B

babyish, bad, bald, bare, beautiful, bending, big, bitter, blunt, boastful, bold, boring, brainless, brainy, brave, brilliant, broken, brutal, busy

### C

careful, caring, cautious, charming, chatty, childlike, chilly, chirpy, choosy, clean, clever, clumsy, cold, colourful, complete, confident, considerate, cool, correct, courageous, crazy, crooked, curious, cute

### D

damaged, dangerous, daring, dazzling, deadly, delicate, delicious, desperate, determined, difficult, dirty, diseased, disgraceful, dishonest, disobedient, dreamy, dried, drowsy, dull, dusty

### E

eager, easy, elderly, elegant, enchanting, energetic, enormous, entertaining, envious, excellent, exciting, experienced, expert, extreme

### F

fabulous, faint, fair, faithful, false, fancy, fashionable, faultless, fearful, fearless, feeble, ferocious, fierce, fiery, fine, firm, fit, flabby, flashy, floppy, fluffy, foggy, foolish, forgetful, fortunate, fragrant, freaky, fresh, friendly, frightening, frightful, frosty, funny, fuzzy

### G

generous, gentle, genuine, ghostly, gifted, glamorous, gloomy, glossy, good, gorgeous, graceful, great, greedy, grubby, grumpy

### H

hairy, handsome, handy, happy, hard, harmless, hazy, healthy, heavenly, heavy, helpful, helpless, heroic, honest, hopeful, hopeless, horrible, horrific, hot, huge, humble, humorous, hungry, hurtful

### I

icy, ignorant, immature, important, incredible, indescribable, inquisitive, invisible, irritable, itchy

### J

jealous, jittery, joyful, juicy, jumpy

### K

keen, kind

### L

large, lazy, light, likeable, little, lively, loaded, lonely, long, loud, lousy, lovely, lucky, luxurious

### M

mad, magical, magnificent, marvellous, massive, masterful, mature, mean, mighty, mindless, miniature, modern, modest, monstrous, muddy, musical, mysterious

### N

nasty, natural, naughty, neat, nervous, new, nice, noisy, nosy, numb, nutritious, nutty

## O

obedient, observant, occasional, odd, old, organised, original, outrageous, outstanding, overgrown

## P

pale, paralysed, peaceful, peculiar, perfect, persistent, persuasive, picky, piercing, pimply, plain, playful, pleasant, pleasing, poisonous, polite, poor, popular, precious, pretty, priceless, prickly, proper, protective, proud, puffy, pushy, puzzling

## Q

quarrelsome, queer, questionable, quick, quiet, quirky

## R

radiant, rare, rattled, raw, reasonable, reckless, refreshing, relaxed, relieved, remarkable, respectable, restless, revolting, rich, rigid, rosy, rotten, round, rowdy, royal, rubbery, rude, rusty

## S

sad, saggy, savage, scary, scheming, scrappy, scrawny, scruffy, scrumptious, secretive, selfish, sensible, serious, shaky, shapeless, shattered, shiny, shocking, short, shy, silent, sincere, skilful, skinny, sleek, sleepy, slimy, slippery, sloppy, slow, small, smart, smelly, smooth, snappy, sneaky, soapy, soft, solid, sorrowful, sour, sparkly, special, speedy, spellbound, spicy, spiky, spoilt, spooky, sporty, spotty, squeaky, stainless, sticky, stranded, strange, streaky, strong, stupid, stylish, sudden, sulky, sunny, super, sweet, swift

## T

talkative, tall, tame, tearful, tedious, tempting, tender, terrible, terrifying, thirsty, thorny, thoughtful, thoughtless, thrilling, ticklish, tidy, timid, tiny, tiresome, traditional, trendy, tricky, troublesome, trusting, truthful, trying

## U

ugly, unexpected, unfair, unfortunate, unkind, unknown, unsteady, unwell, unwilling

## V

vain, valued, venomous, vicious, victorious, vigorous, violent, vulgar

## W

wacky, warm, wasteful, weak, wealthy, weary, weird, well, wet, whimpering, wicked, wide, wiggly, wild, wise, wishful, witty, wobbly, wonderful, woolly, worthy, wrecked, wrinkly, wrongful

## Y

young, youthful

## Z

zany, zealous

**Here is a Sample Writing question for a narrative text.**

## Topic: A brush with disaster

Today you are going to write a narrative or story. The idea for your story is
*A brush with disaster*.

Remember to:

- think about the characters
- make sure there is a complication or problem to be solved
- plan your writing
- use paragraphs
- write in sentences
- check your spelling and punctuation
- write at least two pages.

# SAMPLE ANSWERS: NARRATIVE WRITING

We have provided three sample answers to the sample question. We have grouped them into three levels of ability, which correspond to the levels used throughout this book. Please note that these are approximate guidelines only.

## A brush with disaster

### STANDARD LEVEL

Last year I stayed with my Aunt Anastasia for a week while my parents were overseas. There was lots to do at Aunt Anastasia's and I really liked going to stay with her. One thing I was not allowed to do was go into her attic, but I didn't know why. One day while Aunt Anastasia was destructed I thought I would sneak up to her attic just for a quick peek.

I opened the attic door and nearly chocked on all the stinky dust that blew everywhere. I could hardly see. It was very dark up there and the light didn't work. Suddenly I heard a knock at the front door. I heard a man whispering something to Aunt Anastasia. They both then rushed upstairs. What was I going to do now? I heard him say that a crazy driver drove straight towards him, but he managed to run away and he came straight here. Then the attic door opened and they both came in quickly saying we need to find it now. Aunt Anastasia was angry to see me in the attic and asked me what I was doing there. I didn't like this man so I tried to run downstairs to go and call the police, but the man said he wouldn't let me leave. He looked at Aunt Anastasia and said that I already know too much and I would have to stay in the attic. I was really scared. What would happen next?

### INTERMEDIATE LEVEL

I had lived with Granny for seven years now. In that time I was never allowed to go into her garage, and I really didn't know why. I had always avoided it like a bowl of brussel sprouts until my adventurous friend Anthony decided that we should go and take a look, while Granny was inside preparing dinner.

"Anthony, I don't think it's a good idea. I don't want to get into any trouble." I said to him. "Ah, come on, Leo, what are you, chicken?" he teased me. "I suppose a quick look won't hurt," I mumbled. But I didn't feel good about it. So off we went, out to the dark and creepy garage, slowly hanging onto the wall, taking little steps at a time.

The door was locked. "What do we do now, genius?" I asked Anthony. "Don't worry, I've done this before," he replied.

And so Anthony took a pin out of his jeans pocket and opened the lock. We tiptoed inside and saw a room full of dust and lots of sheets covering furniture and things.

We pulled one of the sheets off and underneath it was a cage. We slowly opened the cage, and a fang-toothed creature popped out! The dog was a pit-bull and looked like a ravenous monster. I could smell meat on its long canines. Saliva was dripping from its chin all over the cage floor. We both screamed, and quickly shut

Please note: Spelling, punctuation and grammar errors have been included to replicate the likely response of a Year 7 student.

the door. It must have been our lucky day. I can't believe we got out of there in one piece. We ran all the way back inside as fast as we could only to meet Granny at the door. She was very angry and said we were lucky the dog hadn't bitten us. I realised that what we did was dangerous and silly, but I was a little bit pleased that we had gotten that close to a scary dog, and lived to tell the tale.

## ADVANCED LEVEL

It was early Saturday afternoon, and outside the wind howled angrily. Thunder roared, and rain had just began to hit the rusty corrugated roof. I was so scared, I began to tremble and wished that Grandma was back from her doctor's appointment. I made sure all the windows and doors were properly shut. Just when I was about to shut the very last window, a lightning bolt struck just in front of me, shattering the window into smithereens.

I must have a guardian angel looking out for me, I thought. I reached down to tidy up the broken glass, when under the desk, a rolled up piece of paper caught my eye. It was wedged between the back of the desk and the drawer. "Hello, what do we have here?" I questioned, in utter wonder. I stuck my hand in to pull it out. Curiously, I unravelled the yellowing piece of paper. It was a map! I turned it around until it was clear; it was an old map of Grandma's house! There was a large red "X" in the right top hand corner. I examined it closely and then realised the "X" was where Grandma's attic was. "What is hidden

here?" I murmured. There was only one way to find out.

The rain had now stopped (but it was still eerily quiet). With my map in hand, I slowly began to rummage through the attic. I crawled behind a bookshelf. Nothing! Dust came flying at me, irritating my eyes and making me sneeze.

I searched and searched, turning over every item. Still nothing! I could not seem to find any hint of a so-called treasure. Looks like this brush with disaster didn't bring me anything positive after all. I was feeling frustrated and thought it may be someone's bad idea of a joke. Should I give up? Just then, I stumbled on a loose floorboard and lifted it up excitedly. Underneath, I could see the corner of a wooden, gold decorated box. Finally, the treasure! I bent down to pull the box up when I heard a loud BANG! Suddenly pieces of wood came flying past me from above. The floor started shaking, furniture came tumbling down with books being hurled at me like cannons. It felt like an earthquake. What had I done? What had I disturbed by removing this box?

Panic overcame me, as I couldn't feel my left leg anymore. All I wanted to do was put the box back before anything else went wrong. I already had one brush with disaster today. I just wanted to scream for help, but then I remembered that Grandma was probably still at the doctor's. I sobbed in desperation, and looked around at the mess surrounding me. I was still somehow grasping the box. How much worse could things get? Hands shaking, I slowly opened it, and then everything went black ...

Please note: Spelling, punctuation and grammar errors have been included to replicate the likely response of a Year 7 student.

# WRITING TEST 3

## Topic: The idea hit me like a tornado

Look at the picture below.

Write about what happened.

Remember to:

- use paragraphs in your writing
- write in sentences
- check your spelling and punctuation
- write at least two pages.

# WRITING TEST 3

Here is a narrative text planning page to start you off. Use this page to plan your ideas.

# NARRATIVE TEXT

**INTRODUCTION/ORIENTATION: introduction of the main characters and setting**

**WHO?**

**WHAT?**

**WHEN?**

**WHERE?**

**COMPLICATION (PROBLEM): what triggered the problem**
(There may be more than one.)

**SEQUENCE OF EVENTS: what happens**

**BEGINNING**

**Connectives:** *First(ly), next, later, after, afterwards, while, as, meanwhile, eventually, when, so, because, soon, consequently, immediately, previously, however, on the other hand, similarly, finally, despite this, otherwise ...*

**MIDDLE**

**END**

**RESOLUTION: how the characters resolved the problem**

**CONCLUSION: the final outcome**
Does it end with a question; a mystery; a statement; or with a coda (a moral or lesson learnt from the experience)?

# CHECK YOUR SKILLS: WRITING TEST 3

Use this chart to evaluate your writing.

| GUIDELINES FOR WRITING A NARRATIVE TEXT | ✓ or ✗ |
|---|---|
| Is there a clear beginning, middle and end? | |
| Is there a clear introduction stating who/what/where/when? | |
| Is the cohesive story organised into paragraphs that focus on one idea or a group of related ideas? | |
| Is there a variety in paragraph length to pace the story? | |
| Have you incorporated a theme into the story? | |
| Does the writing develop a complication: create a problem, or trigger a surprising/unexpected chain of events? | |
| Have you developed characters/setting through description or dialogue? | |
| Have you added expression: feelings, thoughts, actions, what is seen, heard or felt? | |
| Have you made deliberate and appropriate word choices to enhance the mood of the story? | |
| Have you used a variety of correct sentence structures, including simple, compound and complex sentences? | |
| Have you used good adjectives/adverbs to build description and add information to your writing? | |
| Have you used imagery effectively, such as a simile or metaphor, e.g. *The sky lit up like fireworks* ...? | |
| Have you used past/present/future tense accurately? | |
| Have you used pronouns correctly? | |
| Have you used verbs with correct tense and number, e.g. *he is, they are*? | |
| Have you used a variety of time connectives, e.g. *firstly, next, later*? | |
| Have you used a variety of conjunctions, e.g. *when, because, so, if, but, because*? | |
| Have you made an attempt at humour? | |
| Have you punctuated sentences correctly with capital letters, full stops, commas, exclamation marks and question marks? | |
| Have you used the following correctly most of the time: speech marks, possessive apostrophes, dashes, colons, semicolons and parentheses? | |
| Have you used the correct spelling of common words? | |
| Have you used the correct spelling of unusual or difficult words? | |
| Does the writing end in an interesting way? | |

# WRITING TEST 4

## Topic: Putting my foot in my mouth

Look at the picture below.

You 'put your foot in your mouth' when you say something that causes an embarrassing situation, or that makes a person feel embarrassed. Write a narrative about a situation where you have 'put your foot in your mouth'. Talk about what happened and why it was so embarrassing.

Remember to:

- use paragraphs in your writing
- write in sentences
- check your spelling and punctuation
- write at least two pages.

Use this narrative text planning page to plan your ideas.

# NARRATIVE TEXT

**INTRODUCTION/ORIENTATION: introduction of the main characters and setting**

| WHO? | WHAT? | WHEN? | WHERE? |
|---|---|---|---|
| | | | |

**COMPLICATION (PROBLEM): what triggered the problem**
(There may be more than one.)

**SEQUENCE OF EVENTS: what happens**

| BEGINNING | MIDDLE | END |
|---|---|---|
| **Connectives:** *First(ly), next, later, after, afterwards, while, as, meanwhile, eventually, when, so, because, soon, consequently, immediately, previously, however, on the other hand, similarly, finally, despite this, otherwise ...* | | |

**RESOLUTION: how the characters resolved the problem**

**CONCLUSION: the final outcome**
Does it end with a question; a mystery; a statement; or with a coda (a moral or lesson learnt from the experience)?

# CHECK YOUR SKILLS: WRITING TEST 4

Use this chart to evaluate your writing.

| GUIDELINES FOR WRITING A NARRATIVE TEXT | ✓ or ✗ |
|---|---|
| Is there a clear beginning, middle and end? | |
| Is there a clear introduction stating who/what/where/when? | |
| Is the cohesive story organised into paragraphs that focus on one idea or a group of related ideas? | |
| Is there a variety in paragraph length to pace the story? | |
| Have you incorporated a theme into the story? | |
| Does the writing develop a complication: create a problem, or trigger a surprising/unexpected chain of events? | |
| Have you developed characters/setting through description or dialogue? | |
| Have you added expression: feelings, thoughts, actions, what is seen, heard or felt? | |
| Have you made deliberate and appropriate word choices to enhance the mood of the story? | |
| Have you used a variety of correct sentence structures, including simple, compound and complex sentences? | |
| Have you used good adjectives/adverbs to build description and add information to your writing? | |
| Have you used imagery effectively, such as a simile or metaphor, e.g. *The sky lit up like fireworks* ...? | |
| Have you used past/present/future tense accurately? | |
| Have you used pronouns correctly? | |
| Have you used verbs with correct tense and number, e.g. *he is, they are*? | |
| Have you used a variety of time connectives, e.g. *firstly, next, later*? | |
| Have you used a variety of conjunctions, e.g. *when, because, so, if, but, because*? | |
| Have you made an attempt at humour? | |
| Have you punctuated sentences correctly with capital letters, full stops, commas, exclamation marks and question marks? | |
| Have you used the following correctly most of the time: speech marks, possessive apostrophes, dashes, colons, semicolons and parentheses? | |
| Have you used the correct spelling of common words? | |
| Have you used the correct spelling of unusual or difficult words? | |
| Does the writing end in an interesting way? | |

# GLOSSARY OF GRAMMAR AND PUNCTUATION TERMS

## Adjective

An adjective is a word used to describe and give more information about a noun.

Some examples include *multiple* books, *a delicious* cake, *my gorgeous* friend.

## Adjectival clause

An adjectival clause provides further information about the person or thing named. It functions as an adjective, describing a noun and answering the questions What? Who? How many? or Which?

*This is the bike that was given to me by Dad.*

An adjectival clause contains a subject and verb and usually begins with a relative pronoun (*who, whom, whose, which* or *that*).

## Adjectival phrase

An adjectival phrase is a group of words, usually beginning with a preposition or a participle, that acts as an adjective, giving more information about a noun.

*The man in the blue jumper is my uncle.* (preposition)

*The man wearing the blue jumper is my uncle.* (participle)

## Adverb

An adverb is a word used to describe or give more information about a verb, an adjective or another adverb, to tell us how, when or where the action happened. Adverbs often end in *-ly*.

*The flag flapped wildly in the wind.* (how)

*I always brush my teeth in the morning.* (when)

*He slid downwards towards the side of the boat.* (where)

## Adverbial clause

An adverbial clause acts like an adverb. It functions as an adverb, giving more information about the verb, usually telling when, where or how. It indicates manner, place or time, condition, reason, purpose or result.

*Water is important because plant and animal communities depend on water for food, water and shelter.* (reason)

## Adverbial phrase

An adverbial phrase is a group of words, usually beginning with a preposition, that acts as an adverb, giving more information about the time, manner or place of the verb, telling us where, when, how far, how long, with what, with whom, and about what.

*Chloe hit Ava with the old broom.*

## Apostrophe

An apostrophe is a form of punctuation used to show:

1. a contraction (missing letters in a word), e.g. *can't = cannot*
2. possession, e.g. *David's book*, *the boys'* (plural) *mother*

## Brackets ( )

Brackets are a form of punctuation used to include an explanatory word, phrase or sentence.

*He took the book from his friend (Anthony) but never returned it.*

## Capital letter

Capital letters are used at the beginning of sentences, as well as for proper nouns, e.g. the names of people, places, titles, countries and days of the week.

## Colon (:)

A colon is a form of punctuation used to introduce information, such as a list, or further information to explain the sentence.

*The following should be taken on the trip: a warm jacket, socks, jeans, shirts and shoes.*

*The warning read: "Give up now or else!"*

# GLOSSARY OF GRAMMAR AND PUNCTUATION TERMS

## Comma ( , )

A comma is a form of punctuation used to break up the parts of a sentence, or to separate words or phrases in a list.

*The children, who have not completed their homework, will be punished.*

*My brother likes to eat peanuts, steaks, oranges and cherries.*

## Conjunction/connective

A conjunction or connective is a word joining parts of a sentence or whole sentences.

Conjunctions: *and, but, where, wherever, after, since, whenever, before, while, until, as, by, like, as if, though, because, so that, in order to, if, unless, in case, although, despite, whereas, even though*

*My button fell off because it was not sewn on properly.*

Connectives: *in other words, for example, therefore, then, next, previously, finally, firstly, to conclude, in that case, however, despite this, otherwise*

*First we do our homework, and then we go out to play.*

## Dash ( — )

A dash is a form of punctuation used to indicate a break or pause in a sentence.

*Life is like giving a concert while you are learning to play the instrument—now that is really living.*

*We really hoped that he would stay—maybe next time.*

## Exclamation mark ( ! )

An exclamation mark is a form of punctuation used to mark the end of a sentence where strong emotions or reactions are expressed.

*Ouch! I cut my finger.*

*I listened at the door. Nothing!*

## Full stop ( . )

A full stop is a form of punctuation used to indicate the end of a sentence. Full stops are used before the closing of quotation marks.

*David sat under the tree.*

*Nicholas said, "Come with me, James."*

## Imagery

Imagery includes:

**Metaphor** is when one thing is compared to another by referring to it as *being* something else, e.g. *The thief looked at her with a vulture's eye.*

**Simile** is comparing two different things using the words *as* or *like*, e.g. *The hail pelted down like bullets. He was as brave as a lion.*

**Personification** is giving human qualities or characteristics to non-human things, e.g. *Trees were dancing in the wind.*

**Alliteration** is the repetition of consonant sounds at the beginning of successive words for effect, e.g. *The sun sizzled softly on the sand. The rising river rushed.*

**Onomatopoeia** is the formation of words to imitate the sound a certain thing or action might make, e.g. *banged, crashed, hissed, sizzled.*

**Repetition** is repeating words or phrases for effect, e.g. *Indeed there will be time, time to relax, time to enjoy the sun and surf, time to be oneself once more.*

## Modality

Modality is the range of words used to express different degrees of probability, inclination or obligation. Modality can be expressed in a number of ways:

- Verbs: *can, could, should, might, must, will, it seems, it appears*
- Adverbs: *perhaps, possibly, generally, presumably, apparently, sometimes, always, never, undoubtedly, certainly, absolutely, definitely*

# GLOSSARY OF GRAMMAR AND PUNCTUATION TERMS

- Nouns: *possibility, opportunity, necessity*
- Adjectives: *possible, promising, expected, likely, probable.*

## Noun

Nouns are words used to represent a person, place or thing. There are different types of nouns:

**Common nouns** are nouns that represent things in general, e.g. *boy, desk, bike.*

**Proper nouns** take a capital letter. They represent a particular thing, rather than just a general thing. Proper nouns are used to name a place, person, title, day of the week, month and city/country, e.g. *Michaela, November, Monday, Madagascar.*

**Abstract nouns** are things we cannot see but can often feel, e.g. *sadness, honesty, pride, love, hate, issue, advantages.*

**Collective nouns** are nouns that name a group of things, e.g. *herd, litter, team, flock.*

## Preposition

Prepositions are words that connect a noun or pronoun to another word in the sentence. They also indicate time, space, manner or circumstance.

*I am sitting <u>between</u> my brother and sister.*

Some common prepositions are *in, at, on, to, by, into, onto, inside, out, under, below, before, after, from, since, during, until, after, off, above, over, across, among, around, beside, between, down, past, near, through, without.*

## Pronoun

A pronoun is a word that is used in place of a noun. Pronouns refer to something that has already been named, e.g. *My brother is 10 years old. <u>He</u> is taller than me.*

Be careful of repetition and ambiguous use of pronouns: <u>*He went to the shops with <u>his friend</u> and <u>he</u> told <u>him</u> to wait outside.*</u>

The pronouns are *I, you, me, he, she, it, we, they, mine, yours, his, hers, ours, theirs, myself, ourselves, herself, himself, themselves, yourself, this, that, these, those, each, any, some, all, one, who, which, what, whose, whom.*

## Question mark ( ? )

Question marks are needed at the end of any sentence that asks something, e.g. *What did you say?*

If a question is asked in an indirect way it does not have a question mark, e.g. *I asked him what he said.*

## Quotation marks ( " " )

Quotation marks have several uses.

- They are used to show the exact words of the speaker:

  *John said, "I prefer the colour blue."*

  *"What are you doing?" asked Marie.*

  *"I like cats," said Sophia, "but I like dogs too."*

  When there is more than one speaker, a new line should be used when the new person begins to speak:

  *"What should we do now?" asked Ellen.*

  *"I'm not too sure," whispered Jonathan.*

- They are used when writing the names of books and movies.
- They are used when quoting exact words or phrases from a text.

## Semicolon ( ; )

A semicolon is a form of punctuation used to separate clauses. It is stronger than a comma but not as final as a full stop.

*Eighteen people started on the team; only twelve remain.*

*In our class we have people from Melbourne, Victoria; Sydney, New South Wales; and Brisbane, Queensland.*

## Sentence

A sentence is a group of words consisting of one or more clauses. It will begin with a capital letter and end with a full stop, question mark or exclamation mark.

**Simple sentence:** *I caught the bus.*

**Compound sentence:** *I caught the bus and arrived at school on time.*

**Complex sentence:** *Since I managed to get up early, I caught the bus.*

## Tense

Tense is the form of the verb (a doing word) that tells us when something is happening in time—present, past or future.

*I look, I am looking* (present)

*I will look* (future)

*I looked, I was looking* (past)

Auxiliary verbs (e.g. *be*, *have* and *do*) help change the verb to express time, e.g. *I have looked, I have been looking, I had looked, I had been looking, I will have looked, I will have been looking.*

## Verb

A verb is a word that expresses an action, e.g. I <u>ran</u>, he <u>forgot</u>, she <u>went</u>, Mary <u>shouted</u>. It can also express a state, e.g. *the boys <u>are laughing</u>, he <u>is</u> clever, he <u>was</u> all smiles, I <u>know</u> my spelling words.*

**Active verb:** The verb is in the active voice when the subject of the sentence does the action, e.g. <u>*James*</u> *broke the glass.* (*James* is the subject of this sentence.)

**Passive verb:** The passive voice tells you what happens to or what is being done to the subject, e.g. <u>*The glass*</u> *was broken by James.* (Here *the glass* is the subject of the sentence.)

The passive is often used in informative writing, where it is not always necessary to state the doer of an action, or the doer is not known, or it is not relevant.

# Congratulations!

You have now finished all of the practice tests. This was a considerable effort and you deserve a reward for all this hard work! We hope that these tests were of some help to you. We wish you every success in your schooling.

## Reader comments

Thank you for using this guide to the NAPLAN Tests. We hope that you found the practice tests helpful for your students or your child. If you have any comments or questions, we would be pleased to respond. Also let us know if you found any errors or omissions. We benefit from this feedback as it often highlights matters we have overlooked.

## NUMERACY TEST 1
### (pp. 24–31)

1. **8 pictures.** There are 32 squares and each picture covers four squares.

2. **C.** This has only four out of the eight spaces coloured.

3. **B.** This is H-shaped with five blocks. The others are quite different. It may help if you try to draw the shape and then rotate it.

4. **1963 − 1898**

5. **My book and phone together are the same length as my computer.** The computer is 30 cm, the book is 20 cm and the phone is 10 cm. Do you understand how to read the chart?

6. **1 out of 6 chances.** When you spin the arrow it could land anywhere. There are six sections so the chance of landing in one of them is called one-in-six. It is the same when you throw dice. Sometimes it will be a two and sometimes it will not. Overall, we expect that it will be the number that we want about one in every six times.

7. **14**

8. **3:30 pm.** Remember that in a 24-hour clock any time after 12:00 is in the afternoon. So 15:30 would be 3:30 in the afternoon.

9. **720.** The numbers increase by 100. We start with 520 and add 100 to make 620. Then we add 100 to 620 to make 720.

10. **35.** There were 19 tulips and 16 daisies (19 + 16 = 35). Did you write your answer in the box?

11. **15.** The average is the total of all the flowers divided by the number of types of flowers. Here is the number of flowers.

    | 13 |
    |----|
    | 19 |
    | 16 |
    | 12 |

    The total is 60 and there are four different types of flower. That means that the average is 15 (60 ÷ 4 = 15).

12. **9**

13. **\$5.50, \$22.** \$5.50 × 4 = \$22. Each football costs \$5.50, so four footballs will be four times \$5.50. Did you write your answer in the boxes?

14. **\$5 + \$3 + \$16.** You need to round the numbers up or down before adding them to estimate the answer quickly. So \$4.70 becomes roughly \$5 (it is closest to \$5), \$3.20 becomes \$3.00 (it is closest to \$3.00), and \$16.10 becomes \$16 (it is closest to \$16). If the number ends in 50 cents or more, then round it up; otherwise, round it down.

15. **515.** 684 − 169 = 515. Make sure that you know how to do this type of sum.

16. **106.** $5^2$ equals 25 and $9^2$ equals 81, so the total must be 106. Remember to revise all the square numbers from $1^2$ to $16^2$.

17. **12.4.** 5.6 + 6.8 = 12.4

18. **263.** 2104 ÷ 8 = 263.

19. The missing numbers are 7 and 9, and the sum is 274 + 59 = 333.

20. **30 cm.** The wood starts at 25 cm and finishes at 55 cm, making 30 cm. The drawing may not be exact but this is the closest answer.

21. **3.** This question asks you to find the square root of 4 plus 5. First add 4 and 5 to give 9, and the square root of 9 is 3. The square root is the number that when multiplied by itself gives the answer you want. You may not have seen square roots before but you can easily find the answer on most calculators.

22. **(24 + 6) ÷ 3 + 1 = 11.** Two brackets, or parentheses, are needed to make this statement true. This was not an easy question.

23. **50.** Speed is distance divided by time. So if the speed is 150 and the time is 3, then the speed must be 50 because 50 = 150 ÷ 3. The calculation is actually easy but understanding what to do might have been unclear to you.

24. **Monolos Islands.** Did you recognise some of these names? Some were jumbled from names of places in Oceania.

25. **16 cm.** You need to guess the parts that are not indicated. You know that each side is 4 cm so that is a start. You also know that part of the side is 2 cm. This is also 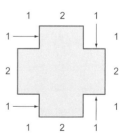 helpful. The best way to proceed is to subtract the 2 cm length from the 4 cm; this leaves 2 cm for the corner areas. It is a little hard to explain in words, so we have also drawn it for you.

# ANSWERS TO NUMERACY TESTS

26. **Each number is made up of the previous two added together.** In the Fibonacci series the two earlier numbers are added together to make the next number. So, $1 + 1 = 2$, $1 + 2 = 3, 2 + 3 = 5, 3 + 5 = 8, 5 + 8 = 13$, $8 + 13 = 21$ and so on.

27. **Take the last digit of the number, then double it and subtract it from the rest of the number to see whether that is divisible by seven.** For instance the number 672 is divisible completely by seven. Take the last digit of the number, which is 2, then double it to give you 4 and then subtract 4 from the rest of the number ($67 - 4 = 63$) to see whether that is divisible by seven (and 63 is completely divisible by 7 to give you 9). That way you know whether a number is divisible by seven.

28. **6.5 kg.** The average weight of a cat is 5 kg ($15 \div 3 = 5$) and the average weight of a dog is 8 kg ($32 \div 4 = 8$). So we can estimate that a cat weighs 5 kg and a dog weighs 8 kg, or 13 kg together. Therefore the average weight of a cat and a dog is 6.5 kg. This is a little tricky.

29. **48 m².** There are 16 striped squares and each square is an area of 3 m², giving you 48 m².

30. **250 grams.** This is one-quarter of a kilogram because $2.25 is one-quarter of $9.

31. **4 cm, 9 cm.** The perimeter is $4 + 4 + 9 + 9 = 26$ and the area is $4 \times 9 = 36$. One way to start is with the area. Find out the factors of 36 (that is, 1 and 36; 2 and 18; 3 and 12; 4 and 9; 6 and 6). Then check whether each of these factors would give a perimeter of 26 cm.

32. **120.** You start with one quarter and you add 60 balls to give you three-quarters. So that means that the 60 balls are half the box (because $\frac{3}{4} - \frac{1}{4} = \frac{1}{2}$) and $\frac{1}{2}$ in this case is equal to 60. Again, it could be a little tricky, or maybe easy if you see the main point straightaway.

33. **200.** It is 1.28 times 200 to give you 256 cm.

34. **123°.** The angles are shown in this diagram. You need to remember that the angles in a triangle add up to 180°.

35. **70.** There is one team leader and seven workers, making eight in a group. That means if you divide 560 by 8 this will give you 70 groups and, therefore, 70 leaders.

36. **15.** There are six entrants in a competition so that means every entrant will play against five others, but this will not mean that there are 30 games. After the first entrant has played five games, the second entrant will only need to play another four people and the third entrant will only need to play three others (because they have played against the first and second entrants already). This is another way to work it out. If there are six entrants (A, B, C, D, E and F), the possible combinations are AB, AC, AD, AE, AF, BC, BD, BE, BF, CD, CE, CF, DE, DF, EF.

37. **35.** We start four levels below ground and can call this –4, and end up on Level 31 so that means we have travelled 35 levels.

38. **135°.** The angle $x$ is a co-interior angle on a parallel line. The outside angle is 45° because these are parallel lines, so the interior angle must be 135° because this makes up a straight line. Our explanation may be too brief, so please ask someone to help you if needed.

39. **4 times.** Each time a liquid is processed its purity increases by one-fifth. So assume we start with zero purity and increase it by one-fifth or 20%; then the second time we have 80% impurity and we increase the purity of that 80% by one-fifth so that it becomes 16% purer (one-fifth of 80% is 16% plus the 20% we started with now gives 36% purity); the third time we start with 64% impure and it becomes one-fifth purer again to make it 12.8% purer (20% plus 16% plus 12.8% is now 48.8% pure); the fourth time the 48.8% becomes 9.76% purer giving us 48.8% plus 9.76% or a total of 58.56% purity, which is more than half. Remember that it is not the quantity of the liquid but the purity that is important.

40. **4 in 16.** There are 16 possible combinations of boys (B) and girls (G). I have listed all the combinations. These are BBBB, BBBG, BBGB, BBGG, BGBB, BGBG, BGGB, BGGG, GBBB, GBBG, GBGB, GBGG, GGBB, GGBG, GGGB, GGGG. The ones that are underlined have exactly three boys and one girl.

**41. 20 minutes.** After 20 minutes the man has walked 2 kilometres and the cyclist has travelled 4 kilometres, which makes up the total of 6 kilometres. Remember that distance is the speed in kilometres per hour multiplied by the time taken. This means that the time is the distance divided by the speed. Ask someone to help you if it isn't clear.

In this case the distance has to be 6 kilometres. So to find the time divide the distance that needs to be travelled (which in this case is 6 kilometres) by the total of the two speeds $(6 + 12)$ and this gives $\frac{1}{3}$ (that is, one-third of an hour).

**42. 14.4**

**43. 15 cm.** The enlargement is twice the size of the original and so the length of $x$ is 15 cm, which is half the enlargement (30 cm).

**44. 21.** The first number is $1 + 2 = 3$, the next number is $1 + 2 + 3 = 6$, the next number is $1 + 2 + 3 + 4 = 10$ and the next is $1 + 2 + 3 + 4 + 5 = 15$. The next number must be $1 + 2 + 3 + 4 + 5 + 6 = 21$. The difference between successive numbers increases by one, so the series is 3, 6, 10, 15 and 21. This is something you might not have been taught in school.

**45. 100.** The series is 0, 1, 9, 36, 100, 225. It actually depends on another series, namely the cubes of 1, 2, 3, 4 and 5 being added to the previous number.

| Cube | $1\,(1^3)$ | $8\,(2^3)$ | $27\,(3^3)$ | $64\,(4^3)$ | $125\,(5^3)$ |
|------|------|------|------|------|------|
| Series | 0 | 1 | 9 | 36 | 100 | 225 |
| | | $(0 + 1)$ | $(1 + 8)$ | $(9 + 27)$ | $(36 + 64)$ | $(100 + 125)$ |

**46. 11.** They are 108, 117, 126, 135, 144, 153, 162, 171, 180, 189, 198. The digits in each of these numbers add up to a number that is divisible by nine. This makes it easy to go through the series because the first number has to be '1', then you try each other number in turn. Start with 1, then 10, 12, 13 and so on, and each time you just add the third number that is needed.

**47. A$90, or $90.** This question is easier than it looks. First find out how much US$70 is in euro. This is 50 euro from the second chart. Then find out how much 50 euro is in Australian dollars and you will see that it is A$90. So US$70 is A$90.

**48. $15 and $9.** This can be a tricky problem. It is very important to work backwards from the fact that both end up with $12. Assume that Player 1 lost the first game and Player 2 lost the second time. You have to think about how much each person has and how much they lose at each step. At each step there has to be $24. Here are the values at each step, working backwards:

| Comments | Player 1 | Player 2 |
|----------|----------|----------|
| Final situation | $12 | $12 |
| Player 2 lost and gave $6 to Player 1; since Player 2 ends up with $12 then he or she must have $18. | $6 | $18 |
| Player 1 lost and Player 2 must have had $9 because this was doubled to $18. This means that Player 1 gave Player 2 $9 and ended up with $6, meaning that Player 1 started with $15. | $15 | $9 |

# NUMERACY TEST 2
## (pp. 35–43)

**1.** The column for Fish should show 800 species.

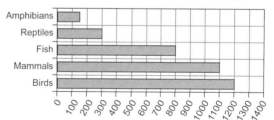

**2. 2.** There were 12 dots and there are 10 remaining, so 2 must be covered. This is the easy way to answer the question. A harder way is to imagine the dots behind the figure.

3. **16.** The grid has 28 squares and there are 12 uncovered which means that 16 must be coloured. This is a little like the previous question.

4. **B.** The others are quite different. It may help if you try to draw the shape and then rotate it.

5. **502 000 – 395 000**

6. **When the forecast is for fine and high cloud the temperature is highest.**

7. **Top.** It is 1 out of 3 chances for the top row. The middle row is 1 out of 4 chances and the bottom row is 1 out of 5 chances. 1 out of 5 is worse than 1 out of 4 and both are worse than 1 out of 3. You have a better chance of picking the glasses, or spectacles, in the top row.

8. **Flip.** The shape has been flipped over.

9. **350.** The numbers increase by 200. Start with 150 and then add 200 to make 350. Then add 200 to 350 to make 550. Or you can work backwards from 550. Did you write your answer in the rectangle?

10. **75.** Looking at the chart you can probably see that it is midway between 50 and 100.

11. **88.** The average is the total divided by the number of people. The total was 440 and there were five people: $440 \div 5 = 88$.

12. **306.** Remember to use your calculator if you cannot work it out.

13. **8.** There were eight years from Pong to Pac-Man ($1980 - 1972 = 8$).

14. **12.** The wood is 60 centimetres. Each piece will be 5 cm, so the sum is $60 \div 5 = 12$.

15. **270.** The answer to the sum is 270 because the $47 is rounded to $50 and four times $50 is $200. The table is $73 and we round this off to $70, making the overall total $270.

16. $\frac{5}{12}$. In this question you have fractions that are thirds and quarters. Change them to twelfths. If $\frac{1}{3}$ come by car, this is $\frac{4}{12}$; $\frac{1}{4}$ come by bus so this is $\frac{3}{12}$. It leaves $\frac{5}{12}$ to walk. Make sure that you know how to do this type of sum.

17. **100 cm.** Starting at the top and working around the figure clockwise, the perimeter is $(30 + 10 + 5 + 10 + 20 + 10 + 5 + 10)$ cm.

18. **105.** There are 300 people and 35% attend football. 35% of 300 is 105 (find 35% of 100 and then multiply that by three).

19. **6.3.** The difference between 8.9 and 3.7 is 5.2. Half of 5.2 is 2.6. Then add that half, that is, 2.6 to 3.7 to give 6.3.

20. **18.** $2556 \div 18 = 142$

21. **44.** The circumference of a circle is found by the formula $C = 2\pi r$ where $C$ is the circumference, $\pi$ (pi) is the number ($\pi = \frac{22}{7}$) and $r$ is the radius. So $C = 2 \times (\frac{22}{7}) \times 7 = 44$. You could use your calculator to get an answer of around 43.98.

22. **140 m.** The shape is 30 m long and 40 m high and so you need to add $30 + 40 + 30 + 40 = 140$.

23. $2\frac{3}{4}$.

24. **60.** This is divisible by three and five.

25. **166.6.** $23.8 \times 7 = 166.6$.

26. **39 cm².** You need to divide the figure into two parts and work out the area of each. To do this you first need to find the parts that are not indicated. It is a little hard to explain in words, so we have also drawn it for you.

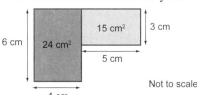

27. **160 km.** You need to count the squares or sections. There are four sections from Giorgis to Limani, one section from Limani to Ro and maybe three sections from Ro to Parasta. This makes eight sections of 20 km each.

28. **two-fifths.** There are 500 mL in the jar and when the object is placed in the jar the water increases to around 700 mL. I hope that you were able to read the levels from the drawing.

29. **36.** The first square number is $2 \times 2$, then $3 \times 3$, $4 \times 4$, $5 \times 5$ and the last one is $6 \times 6$.

30. **3 out of 19.** There are 20 socks. One grey sock is chosen, leaving 19 socks and 3 of the 19 are grey socks.

31. **80 days.** The total size of the job is 600 days ($5 \times 120$). Each day the five experienced workers and the five new workers will do $7\frac{1}{2}$ days' work (5 plus half of 5). Divide 600 by $7\frac{1}{2}$ and this will give you 80 days for the whole job. This is not an easy question.

**14.** Here is a map. It shows three cities. The map is divided into sections.

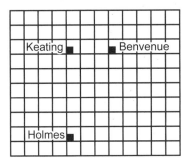

Not to scale

The distance from Keating to Holmes is 1800 km.

How far is it from Keating to Benvenue?

- ○ 300 km
- ○ 600 km
- ○ 900 km
- ○ 1200 km
- ○ 1500 km

**15.** The length of this car from the front to the back is 3.0 m.

The size of the wheel is half a metre (0.5 m).

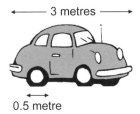

3 metres

0.5 metre

How long is the car compared to its wheel?

- ○ 3 times as long
- ○ 4 times as long
- ○ 5 times as long
- ○ 6 times as long

**16.** In a group of 80 people 40% are doctors. How many people are doctors?

- ○ 30
- ○ 32
- ○ 34
- ○ 36
- ○ 38
- ○ 40

**17.** A plane leaves Perth at 6:40 and arrives at its destination overseas at 18:20 (Perth time). How long was that journey?

| 11:40 | 6:40 | 24:60 | 12:20 |
|:-:|:-:|:-:|:-:|
| ○ | ○ | ○ | ○ |

**18.** Solve:

$$(0.6 \times 5) \div \frac{3}{4} - (0.5 \times 3) = ?$$

| 1.5 | 1.75 | 2.25 | 2.5 |
|:-:|:-:|:-:|:-:|
| ○ | ○ | ○ | ○ |

**19.** This graph shows employment in Australia from 1978 to 2007. It starts at around 6 million and reaches just over 10 million.

Employed – total persons (in thousands)

By which period had employment in Australia increased by 50% from 1978?

- ○ 2000–2001
- ○ 1998–1999
- ○ 1990–1991
- ○ 2004–2005

**20.** Here is a table that shows today's currency values. The currencies are the euro and the Australian dollar.

| Euro | Australian Dollar |
|:-:|:-:|
| €1 | A$1.83 |
| €50 | ? |

What is the value in Australian dollars of €50?

| A$89.50 | A$95.50 | A$91.50 | A$97.50 |
|:-:|:-:|:-:|:-:|
| ○ | ○ | ○ | ○ |

Here are some sample Numeracy: Non-calculator questions. Make sure you read each question carefully so that you know exactly:
- what information is given to you in the question
- what the question is asking you to find.

Then make sure you read each answer option carefully in order to choose the correct answer. Calculators are not allowed in this test. There is no time limit for the sample questions.

To answer these questions, write the answer in the box or colour in the circle with the right answer. Colour in only one circle for each answer.

**21.** Part of this grid is shaded. The grid is made up of squares.

☐ = 1 square

How many square units are shaded? (Hint: Add the half squares.)

   4         6         8        10
   ○         ○         ○        ○

**22.** How many blocks make up this shape? (Note that the pattern in the front is continued.)

   8       12       16       20
   ○       ○       ○       ○

**23.** Here is a pattern of some blocks.

Which one of the four block patterns below is the same as the one above? Is it A, B, C or D?

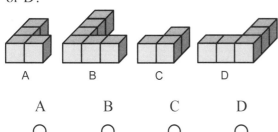

  A        B        C        D
  ○        ○        ○        ○

**24.** There are different types of galaxies. Some, such as our Milky Way, are spiral. Others are irregular spiral, irregular or elliptical. This chart shows the numbers of galaxies in the Local Group (the group that includes the Milky Way).

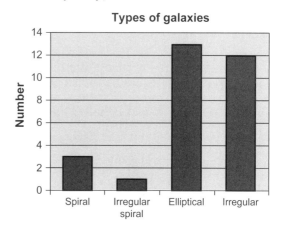

Types of galaxies

Which answer is correct?

○ There are more spiral than irregular spiral galaxies.

○ There are more spiral than elliptical galaxies.

○ There are fewer elliptical than irregular galaxies.

○ There are fewer spiral than irregular spiral galaxies.

**25.** There are some objects in a box.

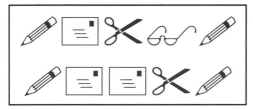

One object is chosen without looking.
What is the chance of choosing a pencil?

- ○ certain
- ○ more than half
- ○ less than half
- ○ impossible

**26.** Two triangular prisms have been joined together.

How many separate faces does the new shape have?

   3        4        6        9

  ○      ○      ○      ○

> Did you colour in one of the circles?

**27.** I folded this pattern in half.

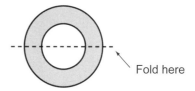

Fold here

Which shape could I see?

  ○       ○       ○       ○

**28.**

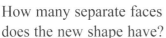

To which letter would the arrow be pointing if it moved two spaces clockwise?

  A       B       D       E

  ○       ○       ○       ○

# END OF TEST

Well done! You have completed the sample questions for Numeracy. Even if you don't practise any others, at least you will have some familiarity with the method used in the NAPLAN Tests.

How did you go with these sample questions? Check to see where you did well and where you had problems. Try to revise the questions that were hard for you.

There are now four more Numeracy Tests to practise, each containing 48 questions. They include many of the same types of questions, plus a few other types.

# ANSWERS TO SAMPLE QUESTIONS—NUMERACY

## Numeracy: Calculator Allowed

1. **180.** The numbers increase by 100. We start with 80 and then add 100 to make 180. Then we add 100 to 180 to make 280. Did you write your answer in the box?

2. **50 grams.** The $\frac{1}{4}$ ounce is 10 grams and the $1\frac{1}{2}$ ounce is 40 grams. Add these together to make 50 grams. We used imperial weights in Australia before changing to the metric system.

3. **$4 × 3 = $12.** The snack packs cost $4. The boy buys three snack packs, so the sum is $4 × 3 = $12. Did you write your answer in the box?

4. **$190 + $120 + $40.** You need to round the numbers up or down before adding them to estimate the answer quickly. So $186 becomes roughly $190 (it is closest to 190), $117 becomes $120 (it is closest to 120), and $41 becomes $40 (it is closest to 40). If the number ends in five or more, round it up; otherwise, round it down.

5. **474.** 763 − 289 = 474. Make sure that you know how to do these types of sums.

6. **6.5.** 2.9 + 3.6 = 6.5

7. **233.** 1631 ÷ 7 = 233

8. **The missing numbers are 7 and 5.** The sum is 379 + 65 = 444.

9. **50 cm.** The wood starts at 10 cm and finishes at 60 cm, and this makes it 50 cm long.

10. **550.** If the speed is 110 and the time is 5, then the distance must be 550 because 110 × 5 = 550. This is actually an easy question but the wording of the problem might have been unclear to you.

11. **1.8.** This number is closest to 1.7.

12. **90.** There are 600 million cubic metres altogether, so 15% for Nigeria is 90. A quick way of working this out is to take 10%, which is 60, and so 5% would be 30. 60 + 30 gives you 90.

13. **15 cm.** The perimeter is 4.5 cm along the bottom, 4.5 cm along the left-hand side, 1.5 cm across the top and 4.5 cm on the right-hand side.

14. **900 km.** You need to count the squares. The six squares from Keating to Holmes equal 1800 km, so each square is 300 km. There are three squares from Keating to Benvenue, and so this distance is 900 km.

15. **6 times**

16. **32.** 40% of 80 = 32. 10% would be 8 people and so 40% would be 4 times 8, equals 32.

17. **11:40.** It takes 11 hours and 40 minutes. You subtract 6:40 from 18:20.

18. **2.5.** This has to be broken down into steps. $(0.6 × 5) = 3$, and then divide this by $\frac{3}{4}$ to give you 4. Then from this subtract the $(0.5 × 3)$, which is equal to 1.5. 4 minus 1.5 equals 2.5.

19. **2000–2001.** In the year 2000 it increased by exactly 50% from 1978. Here is the actual table from which the chart was drawn and the third column shows the percentage increase.

| Month & Year | Persons | % increase |
|---|---|---|
| Aug. 1978 | 5942.1 | 100% |
| Aug. 1979 | 6032.8 | 102% |
| Aug. 1980 | 6220.6 | 105% |
| Aug. 1981 | 6350.0 | 107% |
| Aug. 1982 | 6336.1 | 107% |
| Aug. 1983 | 6220.7 | 105% |
| Aug. 1984 | 6445.9 | 108% |
| Aug. 1985 | 6649.6 | 112% |
| Aug. 1987 | 7073.5 | 119% |
| Aug. 1988 | 7337.3 | 123% |
| Aug. 1989 | 7689.2 | 129% |
| Aug. 1990 | 7795.2 | 131% |
| Aug. 1991 | 7562.7 | 127% |
| Aug. 1992 | 7565.3 | 127% |
| Aug. 1993 | 7607.3 | 128% |
| Aug. 1994 | 7870.2 | 132% |
| Aug. 1995 | 8170.4 | 138% |
| Aug. 1996 | 8254.0 | 139% |
| Aug. 1997 | 8300.6 | 140% |
| Aug. 1998 | 8517.3 | 143% |
| Aug. 1999 | 8640.0 | 145% |
| Aug. 2000 | 8905.9 | 150% |
| Aug. 2001 | 8951.8 | 151% |
| Aug. 2002 | 9120.5 | 153% |
| Aug. 2003 | 9318.0 | 157% |
| Aug. 2004 | 9510.9 | 160% |
| Aug. 2005 | 9815.6 | 165% |
| Aug. 2006 | 10021.6 | 169% |
| Aug. 2007 | 10258.5 | 173% |

20. **A$91.50.** One euro is A$1.83 and so €50 would be 50 times $1.83.

## Numeracy: Non-calculator

**21. 6.** There are four whole squares and four half squares. When you add the four whole plus the four half squares, you get six squares altogether.

**22. 16.** There are four blocks in each section and there are four sections. It may not be easy for you to see because of how it is drawn and you need to visualise or imagine some parts of the diagram.

**23. D.** This pattern is L-shaped with five blocks. The others are quite different. Sometimes you will find these patterns easy to see and sometimes it is a little hard. It may help if you try to draw the shape and then rotate it.

**24. There are more spiral than irregular spiral galaxies.**

**25. Less than half.** There are 10 objects and there are 4 pencils. The chance of choosing a pencil is 4 out of 10. This is less than half.

**26. 6.** Each prism has five faces but when they are joined there are only six faces.

**27. The first answer is correct.** We have tried to show this in the diagram (it is not drawn to scale). When you put both halves together then you get a circle.

**28. E.** After one space the arrow points to D and after another space it points to E.

# SAMPLE QUESTIONS—READING

Here are some sample Reading questions. You will need to look at or read a text. Make sure you read each question carefully so that you know exactly what the question is asking. Then find the relevant section in the text. Finally make sure you read each answer option carefully in order to choose the correct answer. There is no time limit for the sample questions.

To answer these questions, write the answer in the box or colour in the circle with the right answer. Colour in only one circle for each answer.

These questions are meant to be much easier than the questions in the practice tests. If you are already familiar with these type of questions, go straight to the Reading Tests on page 66.

Read *Digital library quick start guide* and answer questions 1 to 5.

## Digital library quick start guide

**Download audio-books and e-books anytime, anywhere.**

The digital library is a new service from our local council library. It is available only to registered borrowers. The digital library download service allows you to browse through a collection of audio-books and e-books.

An audio-book is a digitised version of a recorded reading of a book. The software to download an audio-book is free and easy to use.

The term *e-book* is short for 'electronic book'. It is any publication that can be viewed on a computer monitor. You can browse through the library's collection for e-books online and then download them and read them offline.

A collection of titles is now available to you anytime and anywhere, provided you have computer access. To use this service you will need a computer that is connected to the internet. You will need your library card. The software is available free from the library's own website.

1. What is the main purpose of this text?
   - ○ to sell a new service to borrowers
   - ○ to attract new borrowers to the library
   - ○ to provide new computer software for borrowers
   - ○ to offer a new service to borrowers

2. What is the name of the service described in the text?
   - ○ internet download package
   - ○ digital library download service
   - ○ audio-book digital service
   - ○ e-book library service

3. What is a requirement for the service that is advertised in the text?
   - ○ The service is available to new borrowers.
   - ○ The service is available to anyone with an internet connection.
   - ○ The service is available to registered borrowers.

4. Which product can be read offline?
   - ○ the e-book
   - ○ the audio-book
   - ○ the voice recording
   - ○ the library's collection

**5.** Colour in the circles for the two words that are likely to be the newest words in our language.

- ○ audio-book
- ○ e-book
- ○ download
- ○ software
- ○ internet
- ○ computer
- ○ digital

Read *Celebrate Family History Week* and answer questions 6 to 10.

## Celebrate Family History Week

**Join Peter Tatham from the National Archives for a presentation of how the immigration records in the National Archives can be useful in your family history research.**

Thursday, 3 August 2012
Wellington Library and Community Centre
153–155 Featherston Street, Wellington
2.00 pm – 4.00 pm

Free, but bookings are required on 0496 1880.

Afternoon tea will be served.

**6.** What is the theme of the notice?
- ○ the National Archives
- ○ Wellington Library and Community Centre
- ○ family history
- ○ a presentation

**7.** Who might have a special interest in the topic?
- ○ some children of immigrants
- ○ all historians
- ○ the library

**8.** Find the word that completes the comparison:

Archive is to record as history is to ___?___

- ○ store
- ○ library
- ○ book
- ○ event

**9.** What must be done before attending?
- ○ A booking must be made.
- ○ A family history must be prepared.
- ○ Afternoon tea must be made.

**10.** Which word in the notice means the same as a *talk*?
- ○ record
- ○ presentation
- ○ research
- ○ history
- ○ booking

Did you colour in one of the circles?

**Read *Deposit card* and answer questions 11 to 15.**

## Deposit card

A St James Deposit Only Card gives you true peace of mind. It allows other people to deposit money safely into your account. It is convenient and secure. Money can be deposited through any ATM or branch of St James Bank.

A St James Deposit Only Card is useful for a variety of customers. For example, it is ideal for any company that wants its customers to deposit money into an account, and it is safe for any retailer who wants employees to deposit funds into an account. It may be useful for landlords. They can ask for rent payments to be deposited directly by their tenants. More than one Deposit Only Card can be issued for an account.

All other transactions are barred. This includes withdrawing funds or checking the balance in an account.

**11.** What can we say about a Deposit Only Card?

   ○ A Deposit Only Card allows people to withdraw funds.

   ○ A Deposit Only Card allows people to deposit funds.

   ○ A Deposit Only Card allows people to check account balances.

**12.** Why is a Deposit Only Card useful?

   ○ It can be used for payments.

   ○ It can be used only at a branch.

   ○ It allows someone to make purchases.

**13.** What are *funds*?

   ○ Funds are good times.

   ○ Funds are cheques.

   ○ Funds are deposit slips.

   ○ Funds are money.

**14.** Look at the statement below and decide whether it is correct, partly correct or incorrect.

A Deposit Only Card has limited functions.

   ○ This statement is correct.

   ○ This statement is partly correct.

   ○ This statement is incorrect.

**15.** What is a tenant?

   ○ someone who buys a property

   ○ a landlord

   ○ someone who rents a property

   ○ a real estate agent

**Read *Victor Harbour* and answer questions 16 to 19.**

## Victor Harbour

Source: Ian W Fieggen, www.wikimedia.org
File: 20040610

If you are visiting South Australia, Victor Harbour is a popular holiday and tourist destination on the Fleurieu Peninsula.

It is a little over an hour's drive south from Adelaide and you can also visit the McLaren Vale wine region along the way.

There are many activities to occupy the traveller and much to see. A unique experience when you get to Victor Harbour is to catch the horse-drawn tram across the causeway to Granite Island. This is unforgettable. Hang around until dusk, when you can catch glimpses of the fairy penguins returning to the island.

Its location on the peninsula means that the area is becoming well known as a site for whale watching from mid-winter to the middle of spring. Why not visit the South Australian Whale Centre in Railway Terrace, Victor Harbour? Here you will see interactive displays and you can even undertake a virtual shark dive.

There are many cafes and craft shops for the visitor. These attractions include the Alexandrina Cheese Company in Sneyd Road, Mount Jagged. Here you can sample handmade cheese products. On Saturday mornings Grosvenor Gardens hosts a farmers' market, with fresh fruit and vegetables from the region.

The coastal scenery is beautiful and there are seaside walks, trails and bike paths along the cliffs and shores. Among the nearby seaside villages is Port Elliot. Try some fish and chips at the Flying Fish Cafe, 1 The Foreshore, at Horseshoe Bay, Port Elliot.

You will enjoy Victor Harbour and the surrounding regions.

Adapted from Jane Peach, 'V for Victor', *Qantas Magazine*, November 2009, pp. 65–6

---

**16.** What would you find in Grosvenor Gardens?

- ○ Alexandrina Cheese Company
- ○ Flying Fish Cafe
- ○ South Australian Whale Centre
- ○ the farmers' market

**17.** In what direction is Victor Harbour from Adelaide?

- ○ north
- ○ south
- ○ east
- ○ west

**18.** Where does the horse-drawn tram take the visitor?

- ○ Port Elliot
- ○ McLaren Vale
- ○ Granite Island
- ○ Fleurieu Peninsula

**19.** What is *the virtual shark dive* mentioned in the text?

- ○ a real shark dive
- ○ a real shark dive with experts to help you
- ○ a real shark dive with the protection of a cage
- ○ a simulated shark dive
- ○ an imaginary shark dive
- ○ a video of a real shark dive

**You are about halfway through the sample questions—well done!**

Read *Down the rabbit-hole* and answer questions 20 to 27.

## Down the rabbit-hole

Alice was beginning to get very tired of sitting by her sister on the bank, and of having nothing to do: once or twice she had peeped into the book her sister was reading, but it had no pictures or conversations in it, 'and what is the use of a book,' thought Alice 'without pictures or conversation?'

So she was considering in her own mind (as well as she could, for the hot day made her feel very sleepy and stupid), whether the pleasure of making a daisy-chain would be worth the trouble of getting up and picking the daisies, when suddenly a White Rabbit with pink eyes ran close by her.

There was nothing so VERY remarkable in that; nor did Alice think it so VERY much out of the way to hear the Rabbit say to itself, 'Oh dear! Oh dear! I shall be late!' (when she thought it over afterwards, it occurred to her that she ought to have wondered at this, but at the time it all seemed quite natural); but when the Rabbit actually TOOK A WATCH OUT OF ITS WAISTCOAT-POCKET, and looked at it, and then hurried on, Alice started to her feet, for it flashed across her mind that she had never before seen a rabbit with either a waistcoat-pocket, or a watch to take out of it, and burning with curiosity, she ran across the field after it, and fortunately was just in time to see it pop down a large rabbit-hole under the hedge.

In another moment down went Alice after it, never once considering how in the world she was to get out again.

The rabbit-hole went straight on like a tunnel for some way, and then dipped suddenly down, so suddenly that Alice had not a moment to think about stopping herself before she found herself falling down a very deep well.

From *Alice's Adventures in Wonderland*, by Lewis Carroll, Sam'l Gabriel Sons & Company, New York, 1916

**20.** Who is the main character in this story?
- ○ Alice
- ○ the Rabbit
- ○ Alice's sister

**21.** What type of text is this?
- ○ fiction
- ○ non-fiction
- ○ historical fiction
- ○ science fiction

**22.** How would you describe Alice at the start of this story?
- ○ interested
- ○ excited
- ○ bored
- ○ tired

**23.** What seemed quite natural to Alice at the time?
- ○ that the rabbit-hole went straight on like a tunnel for some way
- ○ that the book had no pictures or conversations in it
- ○ to hear the Rabbit say to itself, 'Oh dear!'
- ○ that the pleasure of making a daisy-chain would be worth the trouble of getting up and picking the daisies

**24.** When did Alice become curious in the first place?

○ when she was sitting by her sister on the bank

○ when she had peeped into the book her sister was reading

○ when she was thinking of whether making a daisy-chain would be worth the trouble of getting up and picking the daisies

○ when the Rabbit actually took a watch out of its pocket

○ when she heard the Rabbit say to itself, 'Oh dear!'

**25.** Why does the word *Rabbit* have a capital letter?

○ It is a proper animal.

○ It is a name.

○ It comes at the start of a sentence.

○ It is a common animal.

**26.** Which word in the text means the same as *opportunely*?

○ fortunately

○ sleepy

○ actually

○ suddenly

**27.** How do we know that Alice was impetuous?

○ Alice was beginning to get very tired of sitting by her sister on the bank.

○ Alice was considering whether the pleasure of making a daisy-chain was worth getting up and picking the daisies.

○ Alice never once considered how she was to get out of the hole again.

○ Alice was burning with curiosity.

---

Read *Uranus and Gaea* and answer questions 28 to 35.

## Uranus and Gaea

The ancient Greeks had several different theories with regard to the origin of the world, but the generally accepted notion was that before this world came into existence, there was in its place a confused mass of shapeless elements called Chaos. These elements, becoming at length consolidated (by what means does not appear), resolved themselves into two widely different substances, the lighter portion of which, soaring on high, formed the sky or firmament, and constituted itself into a vast, overarching vault, which protected the firm and solid mass beneath.

Thus came into being the two first great primeval deities of the Greeks, Uranus and Ge or Gaea.

Uranus, the more refined deity, represented the light and air of heaven, possessing the distinguishing qualities of light, heat, purity, and omnipresence, whilst Gaea, the firm, flat, life-sustaining earth, was worshipped as the great all-nourishing mother. Her many titles refer to her more or less in this character, and she appears to have been universally revered among the Greeks, there being scarcely a city in Greece which did not contain a temple erected in her honour; indeed Gaea was held in such veneration that her name was always invoked whenever the gods took a solemn oath, made an emphatic declaration, or implored assistance.

---

Uranus, the heaven, was believed to have united himself in marriage with Gaea, the earth; and a moment's reflection will show what a truly poetical, and also what a logical idea this was; for, taken in a figurative sense, this union actually does exist. The smiles of heaven produce the flowers of earth, whereas his long-continued frowns exercise so depressing an influence upon his loving partner, that she no longer decks herself in bright and festive robes, but responds with ready sympathy to his melancholy mood.

The first-born child of Uranus and Gaea was Oceanus, the ocean stream, that vast expanse of ever-flowing water which encircled the earth. Here we meet with another logical though fanciful conclusion, which a very slight knowledge of the workings of nature proves to have been just and true. The ocean is formed from the rains which descend from heaven and the streams which flow from earth. By making Oceanus therefore the offspring of Uranus and Gaea, the ancients, if we take this notion in its literal sense, merely assert that the ocean is produced by the combined influence of heaven and earth, whilst at the same time their fervid and poetical imagination led them to see in this, as in all manifestations of the powers of nature, an actual, tangible divinity.

From *Myths and Legends of Ancient Greece and Rome*, by EM Berens, Maynard, Merrill & Co., 1886

**28.** What was the idea of the ancient Greeks about the creation of the world?

- ○ They had a theory that there was Chaos.
- ○ They had a theory that there was Uranus.
- ○ They had a theory that there was Gaea.
- ○ They had a theory that there was Oceanus.

**29.** What did Uranus represent?

- ○ a mass of shapeless elements
- ○ the sky, or firmament
- ○ the firm and solid mass beneath
- ○ the origin of the world

**30.** Which of these is an example of a deity?

- ○ Chaos
- ○ an ancient Greek
- ○ Gaea

**31.** Where would you expect to find a text like this?

- ○ in a book about science
- ○ in a book about history
- ○ in a book about geography
- ○ in a book about myths or legends

**32.** Which word in the third paragraph means nearly the same as *regard*?

- ○ refined
- ○ represented
- ○ omnipresence
- ○ declaration
- ○ veneration

**33.** Which marriage is said actually to exist?

- ○ the marriage of Uranus and Gaea
- ○ the marriage of Uranus and Oceanus
- ○ the marriage of heaven and earth
- ○ the marriage of heaven and the oceans

**34.** Why was the conclusion in the final paragraph described as *logical though fanciful*?

&#9675;  The idea that Uranus and Gaea formed Oceanus was imaginary but made sense.

&#9675;  The imaginary idea that the union of the gods produced the oceans is reflected in reality.

&#9675;  The idea that the union of the gods produced the oceans is imaginary.

&#9675;  The idea that the union of heaven and earth produced the oceans is imaginary.

**35.** What does the author state about the ancient Greeks?

&#9675;  They saw reality in nature.

&#9675;  They related their religious ideas to nature.

&#9675;  They had a poetical view of religion.

&#9675;  They related their religious ideas to imagination.

# END OF TEST

Well done! You have completed the sample questions for Reading. Even if you don't practise any other Reading Tests, at least you will have some familiarity with the method used in the NAPLAN Tests.

How did you go with these sample questions? Check to see where you did well and where you had problems. Try to revise the questions that were hard for you.

There are four more Reading Tests, each containing 50 questions. They are longer and the questions are a little more difficult. We have sorted the questions into levels of difficulty for you.

The spelling, grammar and punctuation questions are in the Conventions of Language sample test. You can do this test now or you can leave it until later. Now take a break before you start any more tests.

1. **to offer a new service to borrowers.** Be careful to read all the text before you start. If you aren't sure of an answer, just guess and come back to it later when you have some time.

2. **digital library download service**

3. **The service is available to registered borrowers.**

4. **the e-book**

5. **audio-book, e-book.** These were the two words that we selected as the newest words in our language. Some other words, such as *download*, *software* and even *internet*, may not appear in some older dictionaries.

6. **family history**

7. **some children of immigrants.** Note that some, but not all, historians may have an interest in the topic.

8. **event.** This is an analogy, which shows the relationship between two words. The analogy is repeated. In the same way that a record makes up an archive, so an event makes up a history.

9. **A booking must be made before attending.**

10. **presentation**

11. **A Deposit Only Card allows people to deposit funds.**

12. **It can be used for payments.**

13. **Funds are money.**

14. **This statement is correct.** It allows deposits but not withdrawals.

15. **someone who rents a property.** The tenant rents the property from a landlord.

16. **farmers' market.** Remember to read the text carefully—the answer is there somewhere.

17. **south**

18. **Granite Island**

19. **a simulated shark dive.** This was a harder question because you need to know the meanings of *simulated* and *virtual*. The answer is not really in the text.

20. **Alice.** This was an easy question.

21. **fiction**

22. **bored.** Later we are told that she was sleepy.

23. **to hear the Rabbit say to itself, 'Oh dear!'**

24. **when the Rabbit actually took a watch out of its pocket**

25. **It is a name.**

26. **fortunately**

27. **Alice never once considered how she was to get out of the hole again.**

28. **They had a theory that there was Chaos.**

29. **the sky, or firmament**

30. **Gaea**

31. **in a book about myths or legends**

32. **veneration**

33. **The marriage of heaven and earth.**

34. **The imaginary idea that the union of the gods produced the oceans is reflected in reality.**

35. **They related their religious ideas to nature.** We thought this was a difficult question. Don't worry if you found it too hard.

# SAMPLE QUESTIONS—CONVENTIONS OF LANGUAGE

This section tests whether you can find spelling, grammar and punctuation errors in a text and whether you can write correctly. Most of the questions are multiple choice. Sometimes you will have to write an answer.

Make sure you read each question carefully and study each answer option in order to choose the correct answer. There is no time limit for the sample questions.

If you are already familiar with these type of questions, go straight to the Conventions of Language Tests on page 118.

---

**Read the following sentence. Correct the punctuation and write the correct sentence on the lines provided. Be careful: There may be more than one mistake.**

1.  in december andrew had an operation to replace a torn knee ligament using screws designed by dr pinkle at the knee research institute of australia

   _____

   _____

---

**Colour in the circle with the correct answer.**

2.  Which sentence has the correct punctuation?

   ○ We can get to Brisbane quicker can't we? If we take the freeway.

   ○ We can get to Brisbane quicker can't we if we take the freeway?

   ○ We can get to Brisbane quicker, can't we? if we take the freeway.

   ○ We can get to Brisbane quicker, can't we, if we take the freeway?

3.  Colour in the circle to show where the question mark ( **?** ) should go.

   "It's nearly the school holidays I hope you will be able to visit us soon When will you

   next be in Perth"

4.  Which word correctly completes the sentence?

   I �       the envelope containing money that I had hidden.

   | found | finded | founded | find |
   |:---:|:---:|:---:|:---:|
   | ○ | ○ | ○ | ○ |

---

**5.** Which sentence is correct?

○ Neither Nick nor Jim likes brussels sprouts.

○ Either Nick nor Jim likes brussels sprouts.

○ Neither Nick and Jim likes brussels sprouts.

○ Neither Nick or Jim likes brussels sprouts.

**6.** Which sentence has the correct punctuation?

○ Chrissy said to meet Amy this afternoon, so we went.

○ Chrissy said "to meet Amy this afternoon, so we went."

○ Chrissy said to "meet Amy this afternoon, so we went."

○ Chrissy said "To meet Amy this afternoon, so we went."

**7.** Which sentence has the correct punctuation?

○ Many companies, make sugar-free soft drinks which contain less sugar but they do not taste quite the same.

○ Many companies, make sugar-free soft drinks, which contain less sugar but they do not taste quite the same.

○ Many companies make sugar-free soft drinks, which contain less sugar, but they do not taste quite the same.

○ Many companies, make sugar-free soft drinks, which contain less sugar, but they do not taste quite the same.

**8.** Read the sentence. Which of the following correctly completes the sentence?

Pedro is the ▓▓▓▓▓ person I have ever met.

| clumsiest | clumsier | most clumsiest | most clumsier |
|:---:|:---:|:---:|:---:|
| ○ | ○ | ○ | ○ |

**9.** Which sentence has the correct punctuation?

○ Yvette said Time for our piano lesson.

○ "Yvette said time for our piano lesson."

○ Yvette said, "time for our piano lesson."

○ Yvette said, "Time for our piano lesson."